P9-BTM-881

FIELD

A PROCESS FOR TEACHING LITERATURE

FIELD: A PROCESS FOR TEACHING LITERATURE

EDWARD R. FAGAN

THE PENNSYLVANIA STATE UNIVERSITY PRESS 1964
UNIVERSITY PARK, PENNSYLVANIA

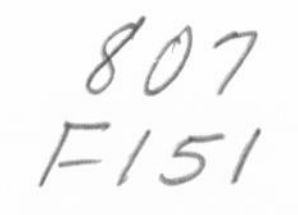

Library of Congress Catalog Card Number: 63-18888

Printed in the United States of America
Designed by Marilyn Shobaken

PREFACE

We teachers of English are accused of being a parochial lot. The accusation is sometimes accurate, particularly where our knowledge of the sciences is concerned. Many of us, I suspect, subscribe to C. P. Snow's description of "the two cultures," one scientific and the other humanistic, separated by a virtually bridgeless chasm of emotion, even of bigotry. Yet we find a psychologist, Jerome Bruner, asking us to reexamine our subject of English in terms of its key structuring ideas. That a reexamination is needed is implicit in Arno Jewett's conclusion after his examination of 285 English syllabi and course outlines in 1960: "The objectives, activities and instructional content . . . have not greatly changed during the past twenty-five years." We cannot plead ignorance of the growing influence of scientific knowledge on the teaching of English. Three decades ago, the Modern Language Association established a "literature and science" group, and ever since then, a burgeoning bibliography of scientific writing that bears directly on the teaching of English has been available to us.

To our students, we are beginning to sound like fossilized pedagogues from the nineteenth century. Fresh from concepts of "sets" and "groups" in mathematics, "half-life" in chemistry, "entropy" and "complementarity" in physics, "homeostasis" in biology, and "metalinguistics" in foreign languages, they must find us quaint to be unaware of the pervasive influences of these scientific concepts and their importance to our own field of literary criticism.

All modern sciences have been deeply influenced by James Clerk Maxwell's field theory; Einstein, Bohr, Lewin, Murphy, Canon, and Wiener all acknowledge debts to Maxwell's genius. This book describes the key scientific concepts based on Maxwell's theory that are shaping the English field and applies these concepts to the process of teaching literature.

After viewing the field theory approach to the teaching of literature, we can more readily understand why colleges and state certification agencies are changing the patterns of their requirements for prospective teachers of English. Whether we practicing English teachers can retool fast enough to keep pace with the advances of science is uncertain, but unless we try, we are in imminent danger of becoming an enclave in the flow of time.

Books are patterns of men's ideas, and I wish to acknowledge my debt to the following persons for their help in the five-year struggle to impose a pattern on the ideas presented in this book:

To Francis Shoemaker, Louis Forsdale, Florence Stratemeyer, and Lennox Grey, of Teachers College, Columbia University, for their patience and encouragement in making critical suggestions on the form of the book.

To James E. Cochrane, Anita E. Dunn, William Kraus, and David Martin, of the Milne School, Albany, New York, for their critical comments and their willingness to assume extra duties while work on the book was in progress.

To my colleagues at the Albany College of Education, State University of New York, and at the Milne School for their suggestions and help on the sections of the book dealing with their specialized fields: Luther Andrews (electromagnetic fields), Anne Oliver (quantum theory), Paul Lemon (biology), Allen Benton (ecology), Morris Eson (psychology), Edwin P. Lawson (psychology), and Donald Allen (chemistry), all of the College of Education, and Randolph Gardner (mathematics), of the Milne School.

EDWARD R. FAGAN

University Park, Pennsylvania
December 2, 1963

CONTENTS

INTRODUCTION

TEACHERS OF ENGLISH speak of various approaches to literature, but the term "approach" does not mean the same thing to all of them. For some, it refers to the *external framework*[1] used in organizing a course in literature: the types approach, the humanities approach, the problem approach, the American, or British, or world literature approach. For others, it refers to the *internal critical method* used in getting at the significance of a given piece of literature: the psychological approach, the biographical approach, the New Criticism approach, or the more recent ecological approach.

The two concepts of approach are not mutually exclusive; the strength of some of the newer courses in American studies, American humanities, and contemporary humanities and of similar broad programs lies in the clarity with which an internal critical method provides criteria for selecting and organizing materials. The mutual reinforcement of external framework and internal method has a long history in many disciplines. The concepts of sets and groups in mathematics, the concept of air mass in meteorology, the concepts of the cell and the DNA molecule in genetics, the concept of holism in cultural anthropology, and the concept of homeostasis in biology all embody the principle of mutuality—a working together of internal method and external structure to present a total image of the unique behavior properties of a given phenomenon. Disciplines currently exploring this principle acknowledge a debt to physicist James Clerk Maxwell's field theory.

The importance of Maxwell's theory for the study of literature has to be considered in relation to one of the major crises in contemporary culture: the proliferation of knowledge beyond the present capacity or skill of the human mind to organize and use it. In 1959, for instance, some 30,000 articles on aspects of chemistry were published; in the decade of 1948-1958, approximately 250,000 articles appeared on psychology.[2] Comparable evidences that the crisis exists in the field of English are the virtual explosion of new knowledge in linguistics, the expanding inquiry into the relation of the symbolic process to personal maturation, and the "communication revolution" in instruments for transmission, storage, and recovery of information. Some scholars have responded to the crisis by advocating a return to traditional contexts for study and teaching—[3]in the English curriculum to the important but by no means wholly sufficient "writing component" and "literature component."[4] Other scholars seek more inclusive curricular patterns of content and context.[5]

The necessity for new patterns in the English curriculum becomes apparent with the realization that a single modern novel may require the reader to deal with concepts from psychology, sociology, physics, mathematics, foreign languages, geography, philosophy, aesthetics, music, and ecology as well as from areas commonly within the range of literary scholarship: folklore and mythology, poetry, world literature, journalism, communication, and linguistics. Add to such concepts literary influences of other writers—from Dante to T. S. Eliot—and a notion of the background required by the English teacher to perform his tasks can be gained. (Literature of the past has increasingly come to require a similarly wide background, as scholarship utilizing concepts from the sciences has added facet after facet to classic works. Shakespeare may not have consciously built an Oedipus complex into the character of Hamlet, but the teacher must understand that interpretation as part of his preparation for teaching.)

When Lawrence Durrell claims that he built *The Alexandria Quartet* on Einstein's principle of relativity, the teacher must be able to discuss relativity intelligently when his students, fresh from their revised science curricula, bring it up in class. The frequent appearance of such new concepts in modern literature demands that the teacher have not only a grounding in science but a new process for teaching the literature itself. *The Fall* or *The Stranger* cannot be taught in the same way *A Tale of Two Cities* is; the often-simple antithesis of "good" and "bad" found in much Victorian literature has given way in the modern novel to a complex moral relativity. The philosophical, psychological, theological, ethical, epistimological, and teleological dimensions of man in contemporary society that are revealed in modern literature require a new scholarly-critical method for exploring it. Literature that reflects wide ranges of knowledge is part of contemporary culture; it is symbolic of the problem of the proliferation of knowledge that confronts society.

In developing structure-method approaches to handle geometric increases in knowledge, many disciplines are making fruitful adaptations of field theory and its modern extensions. Education, for example, is moving to incorporate such new organizations into its curricular patterns. As Jerome S. Bruner points out:

> The problem is twofold: first, how to have the basic subjects rewritten and their teaching materials revamped in such a way that pervading and powerful ideas and attitudes relating to them are given a central role; second, how to match the levels of these materials to the capacities of students of different abilities at different grades in school.[6]

"Revamping materials so that powerful ideas are given a central role" is the structure aspect and "matching the levels of materials to student capacities" is the method aspect of the structure-method approach. Bruner's ideas on the need for coupling structure and method into a unified field of experience to make any approach to knowledge effective have appeared in the literature of many disciplines for at least twenty years;[7] their widespread influence today is due to the current receptivity in America to ideas for improving education.[8]

The coupling or, more accurately, the fusing of structure and method in the various disciplines has long been suggested by such physicists as Niels Bohr, Albert Einstein, Norbert Wiener, Leopold Infeld, and others as a better solution to the problem of the proliferation of knowledge than the intensifying of old procedures.

Such a solution is needed in the teaching of literature, not to make the process more "scientific," but to make the private, professional, and social worlds of the teacher naturally reinforcing.

Field theory as a structure-method approach to many disciplines is still evolving, but its influence is reflected in many of the broadened undergraduate courses. Sometimes the term "field theory" itself is used, as in psychology and education, but more often the concept is embodied in a specialized vocabulary, such as that of "groups" or "sets" in mathematics, both terms implying a reciprocal relationship between structure and method that is characteristic of field theory as a concept. Out of these wide uses of field theory in the sciences has come the problem for this book: the extent to which a concept as yet limited to explicit phrasing in the sciences may be useful for working in the humanities.

Before considering this problem in detail, it seems appropriate to state the reasons for the choice of the three sciences—physics, psychology, and biology—on which the discussion of field theory is based and to review briefly the progress in the application of the theory in education and English.

Physics is the discipline in which field theory emerged. Understandings of its adaptations in other sciences have to be predicated on descriptions of it in its unique setting of physics, particularly in light of recent amplifications of the original theory. For example, a statement on the nature of field made by Freeman J. Dyson, professor of mathematics at the Institute for Advanced Study at Princeton University, implies underlying principles that could have application in the study of literature:

> Again in the broadest sense one may say that the fundamental idea of quantum mechanics is merely the extension to matter of the two-layered view of nature already inherent in Maxwell's treatment of electricity and magnetism. Quantum mechanics ultimately makes no distinction between matter and electricity. The two-layered view of nature thus becomes consistent and universal.[9]

In psychology, Kurt Koffka, particularly in his *Principles of Gestalt Psychology,* paid explicit attention to the contextual field of perception as early as 1935. The concept of field has continued as a generative force in several phases of psychological theory and experimentation; Köhler's attention to dynamic intuition, Lewin's dynamic theory of personality, Hartmann's adaptations of the concept to learning and curriculum design, Gardner Murphy's biosocial and interpersonal theories of personality, and more recent experiments in perception in laboratories at Dartmouth, Princeton, Ohio State, and Iowa utilize the field as a basis for the understanding of human behavior. Principles derived from descriptions of field theory in psychology may also apply to the study of literature, since literary interpretation frequently involves individual perception or, as described in psychology's unique vocabulary, field-ground relationships.

Field theory in biology takes the form of a structure, ecology, and a process, homeostasis. Ecology, defined as the interrelationships between organisms and their environment,[10] used to be a series of courses dealing primarily with the study of flora and fauna. Today, ecology is the study of all organisms, including bacteria, fungi, and other microorganisms, as well as all plants and animals including man himself.[11] This modern definition of ecology implies urgent considerations for interrelationships—a criterion of Maxwell's field theory.

Homeostasis, the tendency for organ systems to sustain balances (for example, the physiochemical process that drives an organism to eat when it is hungry, thereby reducing the tensions produced by hunger pangs and returning the organism to a relatively quiet state), had been used to describe balancing mechanisms such as hunger drives prior to 1939.[12] By 1955, homeostasis had come to represent a process for expressing balancing phenomena between organisms and their total biological environment, had become, in fact, a field theory method for studying human biological behavior.[13] The ecological structure and the homeostasis method have now become integral parts of biology's unique concern with life space, a field theory approach that also suggests principles that may be applied to the study of literature.

Education as a social science has, through many spokesmen, shown a concern for the implications of field theory in learning. George Hartmann, an educational psychologist from the University of Chicago, predicted in 1942 that such implications would be a major concern of all disciplines in the 1950's. Hartmann's predictions have been borne out in the writings of spokesmen from the sciences and from other disciplines, particularly education and philosophy. Significantly, almost all of the scientists, educators, and philosophers presently concerned with field theory are teachers who have explored the relationships of their ideas to structure and process in education. In education itself, Florence Stratemeyer, of Columbia University, has evolved a structure-process program of teacher education that embodies the principles of field theory as described by scientists and philosophers.

English has shared in the tendency to search out significant contexts for the teaching of its values and content. In 1936, the National Council of Teachers of English (NCTE) sponsored the publication of Ruth Mary Weeks's influential *A Correlated Curriculum*, a study that leaned clearly toward a field approach to secondary-school English. Similarly, Walter V. Kaulfer's and Holland D. Roberts' *A Cultural Basis for the Language Arts* (1937) provided the seed for the later language-culture-area studies. The spectacular introduction of sixty humanities programs into colleges between 1933 and 1940, as reported by Patricia Beesley in *The Revival of the Humanities in American Education* (1940), brought a synthesizing, field approach to learning to college-level study. Another phase of English teaching that demonstrates a clear involvement with field theory is communication, drawing as it does on the disciplines of psychology, anthropology, sociology, and political science, as well as on linguistics and literature.

The American Studies Association, founded in 1951, has a dedicated interest in research and teaching that crosses traditional department lines. The Association's interdisciplinary membership—librarians, museum directors, and government officials, as well as scholars from American literature, American history, sociology, anthropology, and similar disciplines—and its recognition of the common aspects of scholarly endeavor suggest the existence of a field—American life and culture—that can be explored through field theory processes.

In the study of literature, individual scholars have moved toward field approaches, from the local color concept of American culture, through a genuine regionalism, to the concerns of Lennox Grey and others with ecology.[14] Grey's ecological approach seeks to employ field-ground concepts and other elements from the ecologists' scientific approach to the study of phenomena to focus methods for the study of literature. Grey's more recent concern with "audience" as part of a "field" of literary evaluation is providing a creative methodology for literary exploration.[15]

ONE

FIELD THEORY IN THREE SCIENCES

THE FIELD THEORY concept is characterized by two mutually supporting elements: a stress on interrelationships and a characteristic method of analyzing phenomena. Neither of these is strange to teachers of English, many of whom are familiar with the relational methods of Taine, supported and extended in comparative, historical, cultural, and other similar approaches to literature.

In attempting to recognize a characteristic method of analysis as part of the field theory concept, however, it is easy to become confused, because the method varies from discipline to discipline. Such variations prompted Good and Scates to recommend that field theory be used only in the discipline of its origin, physics.[1] It might seem then that to apply the field theory concept beyond the field of physics is simply to introduce a new term, not a new concept, into a discipline to describe relationships that already exist. The terms "transactionalism" in education and "generalized behavior" in psychology, for example, explain adequately (according to Good and Scates) the conceptual notion of the interdependence of organism and environment, without requiring the addition of "field theory" to the specialized vocabularies of education and psychology.[2]

At the same time, psychologists Gardner Murphy and Donald Olding Hebb maintain that the uniqueness of the root concepts of field theory justifies a field theory approach to their own discipline, although field-like concepts already exist in specialized aspects of it. Recent advances in knowledge have often resulted from team approaches or pooled specializations, both of which are implied in a field theory approach to knowledge. Institutions such as the Institute for Advanced Study at Princeton University and the Center for Advanced Study in the Behavioral Sciences at Stanford University are specifically designed to facilitate exchange of ideas among specialists from diverse fields.

From these institutions and from similar team efforts have come new vectors on methods for studying man's interaction with his environment. Consider the promise of integrative aspects in the descriptive titles of such books as Oliver Reiser's *The Integration of Human Knowledge,* Lincoln Barnett's *The Universe and Dr. Einstein,* Roy Grinker's *Toward a Unified Theory of Human Behavior,* and Lynn White's *Frontiers of Knowledge in the Study of Man.* Other books that deal with the need for an integrated approach to knowledge, such as William Barrett's *Irrational Man,* Kenneth Boulding's *The Image,* and the numerous editions of *Zen Buddhism,* do not by their titles reflect concerns for integration, but their authors clearly state such concerns and, implicitly, use a field approach in the development of their integrative theses. With these signs of the pervasive influence of field theory, there is still need to define it more explicitly.

Maxwell himself had some difficulty in formulating his theory because, as Freeman Dyson has pointed out, Maxwell had to describe a new concept "by struggling with old ideas, and the old ideas remain in the language of his thinking a long time afterwards."[3] Michael Pupin described in his autobiographical *From Immigrant to Inventor* the trouble he had in finding someone who could explain the "language" of Maxwell's equations. English teachers share Pupin's problem in understanding field theory, but in the descriptive statement that follows they will be spared the difficult "language" of equations in which many of them are not yet literate.

PHYSICS

This discussion of field theory is based on ideas gleaned from a century of research in physics. Justice to all of the scientists and all of the reports cannot be done in a brief space; only the highlights of the development of field theory can be scanned—from James Clerk Maxwell's discovery of the concept to Niels Bohr's current applications of it in quantum mechanics. In spite of this limitation, the important change in field theory from a static to a dynamic concept should become clear, as should the reasons for the evolutionary nature of the change.

James Clerk Maxwell presented his ideas on field theory in a series of papers on electricity and magnetism read before the Royal Society during roughly the period from 1860 to 1868. In 1864, for instance, he stated:

> The theory I propose therefore may be called a theory of the *Electromagnetic Field*, because it has to do with the space in the neighborhood of the electric or magnetic bodies, and it may be called a *Dynamical Theory* because it assumes that in that space there is matter in motion, by which the observed electromagnetic phenomena are produced.[4]

> It appears therefore that certain phenomena in electricity and magnetism lead to the same conclusion as those of optics, namely, that there is an aethereal medium pervading all bodies, and modified only in degree by their presences; that the parts of this medium are capable of being set in motion by electric currents and magnets; that this motion is communicated from one part of the medium to another by forces arising from the connexions of those parts; that under the action of these forces there is a certain yielding depending on the elasticity of these connexions; and that therefore energy in two different forms may exist in the medium, the one form being the actual energy of motion of its parts, and the other being the potential energy stored up in the connexions, in virtue of their elasticity.[5]

> Thus, then, we are lead to the conception of a complicated mechanism capable of a vast variety of motion, but at the same time so connected that the motion of one part depends, according to definite relations, on the motion of other parts, these motions being communicated by forces arising from the relative displacement of the connected parts, in virtue of their elasticity. Such a mechanism must be subject to the general laws of Dynamics, and we ought to be able to work out all the consequences of its motion, provided we know the form of the relation between the motions of the parts.[6]

> In order to bring these results within the power of symbolical calculation, I then express them in the form of General Equations of the Electromagnetic Field . . . there are twenty of the equations in all, involving twenty variable quantities.[7]

The key concepts of Maxwell's theory are contained in the phrases "the space in the neighborhood of electric and magnetic bodies," "an aethereal medium pervading all bodies," "motion is communicated from connexions of parts," "energy in two different forms may exist in the medium," and "the motion of one part depends, according to definite relations, on the motions of other parts." Also significant is that "twenty variable quantities" are necessary to explain these relationships in equations. Such concepts appear not only in physics, but in other sciences and in the broad areas of scholarship associated with English as well.

The contemporary significance of Maxwell's field concept has been explained by Albert Einstein through historical perspectives on space:

> This space was conceived [by Newton] as absolute in another sense also; its inertia-determining effect was conceived as autonomous, i.e., not to be influenced by any physical circumstance whatever: it affected masses but nothing affected it.
>
> And yet in the minds of physicists space remained until the most recent times simply the passive container of all events, playing no part in physical happenings itself.
>
> Thought only began to take a new turn with the wave theory of light and the theory of the electro-magnetic field of Faraday and Clerk Maxwell. . . . The picture was then as follows: space is filled by the ether, in which the material corpuscles or atoms of ponderable matter swim; the atomic structure of the latter had been securely established by the turn of the century.
>
> Since the reciprocal action of bodies was supposed to be accomplished through fields, there had also to be a gravitational field in the ether whose field law had, however, assumed no clear form at that time.
>
> Then came H. A. Lorentz's great discovery—today the discovery may be expressed as follows:—Physical space and the ether are only different terms for the same thing; fields are physical conditions of space.[8]

> But the idea that there were two structures in space independent of each other, the metric-gravitational and the electromagnetic, was intolerable to the theoretical spirit. . . .
>
> The "unitary field theory," which represents itself as a mathematically independent extension of the general theory of relativity attempts to fulfill this last postulate of field theory.[9]

Einstein, in addition to interpreting Maxwell's field theory, added his own "generalized theory of relativity,"[10] with its implicit observer viewpoint, to descriptions of field theory. Einstein's classic description of an observer on a ship and an observer on the shore gauging the speed of a ball rolling down the deck of the ship was given a more contemporary interpretation by Barnett.[11] Barnett, to illustrate the scientific correctness of differing reports of a phenomenon by observers at different viewing points, described the following situation: Two observers, one at the top of the Empire State Building, the other at the bottom, are watching the paths taken by marbles dumped onto an inclined plane tilted toward the base of the building. The paths these marbles take are, according to the observer at the base of the building, determined by various tarred ridges on the inclined plane. Rolling downhill under gravitational force, the marbles, according to the observer at the base, naturally follow the contours of the raised tar, some marbles going straight down the incline, others deviating at tangents caused by variations in the tarred ridges. The observer at the top cannot see the tarred ridges from his viewing position. Hence, he ascribes the unusual movements of the marbles to some "mysterious" force. Scientifically, both observers' descriptions of the marbles' behavior can be accurate, relative to their different viewing positions.

Barnett's illustration of the observer viewpoint serves equally well as a simplified illustration of Niels Bohr's principle of complementarity. On its broadest level, this principle proposes that the behavior of microscopic phenomena is the same as the behavior of macroscopic phenomena when total fields or "universals" are involved. The possibility of applying Bohr's complementarity to problems in biology and psychology was discussed as early as 1957. Following an address by Bohr, the editor of the *Bulletin of the American Academy of Arts and Sciences* noted:

> This led him [Bohr] to the elucidation of the view that in the

> description of atomic phenomena a unique separation of subject and object is no longer possible, and finally to a review of his principle of complementarity.... The other participants in the discussion followed up this theme by elaborating on relevant points of interest such as the importance and difficulty of isolating parts of experience for accurate observation, the nature of physical explanation and the difficulty of staying strictly logical in this business, and the role of complementarity in providing a more profound understanding of problems in biology and psychology.[12]

Bohr's point that subject and object are no longer separable in the description of atomic phenomena seems representative of views held by many scientists in other specialized disciplines. Moreover, the recognition by the other scientists in the discussion cited of "the role of complementarity in providing a more profound understanding" of other disciplines indicates the kind of generalizing that has occurred since Maxwell introduced field theory into scientific literature. Today's scientists, however, have tended to shift their concern from Maxwell's theories as such to the implications of his discoveries for a new concept of the structure of nature. Dyson has described this shift:

> The features of the theory which seem most significant to us now are not those which seemed particularly important to Maxwell. In the broadest sense one may say that the basic idea of the theory is that nature has a double-layered structure. In the lower layer there exist electric and magnetic fields, which satisfy simple wave-equations and travel freely through space in the form of light or radio waves. In the upper layer there are material objects, energies and forces. Only the upper layer is directly accessible to our observation. A lower-layer object such as an electric field can only be observed by looking at the energies and forces which it produces in the upper layer. And these energies and forces are always proportional to the square of the field-strength.[13]

Lower-layer objects can be observed through the X-ray and bubble chamber processes, and in quantum mechanics such processes are used to observe atomic fields.[14]

Niels Bohr has had great influence in the development of quantum mechanics and its theoretical ramifications as extensions of field theory. Although Bohr is often regarded as "the father of the quantum theory,"[15] quantum mechanics, as Dyson has said:

> . . . is merely the extension to matter of the two-layered view of nature already inherent in Maxwell's treatment of electricity and magnetism. Quantum mechanics ultimately makes no distinction between matter and electricity. The two-layered view of nature thus becomes consistent and universal.[16]

Basic to the development of field theory is this last statement, which implies "oneness," a "universal" in the treatment of matter and electricity. "Sameness" may be read into some physicists' use of "universal" and "oneness" as concepts in quantum mechanics. Other physicists, among them Einstein, might insist on the individuality of each atom or part of an atom.[17] The important point is that the "oneness" of Bohr's studies deals with a structure within which individual differences are myriad.

Bohr's implicit application of principles of physics to biology and psychology is reflected by the mathematician-physicist Norbert Wiener. The hyphen is necessary in describing Wiener's specialties because he, like other leaders in the development of knowledge,[18] is recognized as a scholar in two fields. His work with electrical fields demands a physics background, and he uses mathematics in designing computer systems. Wiener has combined the two fields into a new field that he calls cybernetics. Cybernetics, according to Wiener,[19] means "steersman," though Wiener has suggested that "governor" might be a better modern interpretation in the sense that governors operate to control behavior, particularly of machines, through feedback messages.

Understanding Wiener's contribution to field theory requires some knowledge of three of his basic cybernetic concepts: *entropy, feedback,* and *communication.*

The concept of entropy, particularly in its implications in statistical probability as developed by the American mathematician Gibbs, is the basis of Wiener's cybernetics. Wiener has described Gibbs's contribution to cybernetics and extended it in his own discussion of the relation of entropy to biological disorganization:

> His [Gibbs's] central notion concerned the extent to which answers that we may give to questions about one set of

> worlds are probable among a larger set of worlds. Beyond this, Gibbs had a theory that this probability tended naturally to increase as the universe grows older. The measure of this probability is called entropy, and the characteristic tendency of entropy is to increase.
>
> As entropy increases, the universe, and all closed systems in the universe, tend naturally to deteriorate and lose their distinctiveness, to move from the least to the most probable state, from a state of organization and differentiation in which distinctions and forms exist, to a state of chaos and sameness. In Gibbs's universe order is least probable, chaos most probable. But while the universe as a whole, if indeed there is a whole universe, tends to run down, there are local enclaves whose direction seems opposed to that of the universe at large and in which there is a limited and temporary tendency for organization to increase. Life finds its home in some of these enclaves. It is with this point of view at its core that the new science of Cybernetics began its development.
>
> There are those who are skeptical as to the precise identity between entropy and biological disorganization. It will be necessary for me to evaluate these criticisms sooner or later, but for the present I must assume that the differences lie, not in the fundamental nature of these quantities, but in the systems in which they are observed. It is too much to expect a final, clear-cut definition of entropy on which all writers will agree in any less than the closed, isolated system.[20]

Wiener has admitted that the picture of the universe as "deteriorating" is pessimistic, but he has pointed out that such a view is based on geological time and that there are always enclaves operating in opposition to deterioration; one of these is mankind. Mankind must, however, be aware of the entropic process. Awareness, in turn, is dependent upon a second key concept in cybernetics, *feedback*.

Feedback is defined by Wiener as the "control of a machine on the basis of its *actual* performance rather than its *expected* performance."[21] Such control is based on "memory," which in the cybernetic system of computation mechanics is defined as a "message" stored on cards, tapes, or drums. The process of producing "memory" is called "taping."[22] An effective feedback system allows the machine to correct errors that it may make because of environmental conditions. An antimissile missile, for example, mounted on a tracking platform capable of a 360-degree rotation may, in Alaska, be slowed down in its tracking by frozen grease on the rotating mechanism. Data fed to the mechanism may order the platform to a 90-degree azimuth, but frozen grease may cause it to stop at a 75-degree azimuth. To correct the error caused by the frozen grease, a feedback mechanism relying on memory is necessary, and most tracking devices subject to environmental hazards (extreme cold, sand) have such a mechanism that "understands" environmental errors and corrects them when actual performance does not coincide with expected performance.

Wiener's third concept—*communication*—differs in meaning from the popular term and has sub-concepts ("message," "control," "mood," "order") important for understanding it as a base for a field theory:

> In giving the definition of Cybernetics in the original book, I classed communication and control together. Why did I do this? When I communicate with another person, I impart a message to him, and when he communicates back with me he returns a related message which contains information primarily accessible to him and not to me. When I control the actions of another person, I communicate a message to him, and although this message is in the imperative mood, the technique of communication does not differ from that of a message of fact. Furthermore, if my control is to be effective I must take cognizance of any messages from him which may indicate that the order is understood and has been obeyed.
>
> It is the thesis of this book that society can only be understood through a study of the messages and the communication facilities which belong to it; and that in the future development of these messages and communication facilities, messages between man and machines, between machines and man, and between machine and machine, are destined to play an ever-increasing part.[23]

As sketchy as the foregoing descriptions of field theory are, they suggest that from Maxwell's equations on electromagnetism to Bohr's complementarity, physicists are agreed on the importance of field as a necessary concept for understanding phenomena in physics. Some physicists believe that the field as a concept can be usefully applied in disciplines other than physics. Bohr, for example, has suggested complementarity (an extension of field concepts) might be useful in psychology and biology. Before exploring the uses of field theory in these disciplines, it may be helpful to restate the basic principles of field theory in physics.

Maxwell's findings suggest that where multiple forces are operating, adequate descriptions of the observed forces demand consideration of them as a whole. Exploration of a single force within a field of forces without careful control jeopardizes the accuracy and usefulness of the exploration. Bohr's theory of complementarity supports Maxwell's implication of the necessity for field perspectives, except that Bohr uses quantum mechanics for his inferences and goes one step beyond Maxwell by treating the field as a universe rather than a two-layered structure.

Einstein has suggested that the observer is important in the study of fields, and Wiener that the accuracy of the observer is affected by the amount of feedback he gets from his observations. Generally, the higher the frequency of such feedback, the higher the potential for accurate understanding. Too much feedback can, however, cause distortion. *Control* of input and output tends to correct feedback, as in microphones.

PSYCHOLOGY

Research has shown that at any given time in culture the several areas of inquiry move more or less uniformly in developing new and analogous concepts. Such is the case in the relation of psychology and physics; the emergence of field theory in the two has been almost simultaneous. Psychology, like physics, owes a debt to many scientists for the development of a field theory of human behavior. As in the discussion of physics, the description of the evolution of field theory in psychology will be confined to those developments that seem to have implications for a field theory approach to literature and to programs for prospective teachers of English.

Psychology, the scientific study of human behavior, introduces a complicating factor in the description of field theory—the human being. As complex as the phenomena studied by physicists are, they seem infinitely more stable (at least to the extent that controls can be applied to the forces under observation) than the human being. When psychologists attempt to study concept-formation, intelligence, and other similar abstractions, by means of self-contained reference frames, the findings are applicable only to the specialized frame of reference used.[24]

The hypothesis of gestalt psychology,[25] with its connotation in English of "pattern" or "configuration," assumes, according to Koffka [26] and Köhler,[27] that the behavior of an individual at a given time is a function of multiple forces. Multiple forces in the gestalt hypothesis are both internal (individually different) and external (environmental and subject to cultural codes). Time and space tend to modify the individual's behavior, so these two factors must also be taken into consideration in a gestalt study.[28] Human beings constantly attempt to "see" the world in completed patterns, "wholes." Field-ground relations are means humans use to achieve an end called "closure," which brings them satisfaction with the perception of a "whole." Differences between "seeing" and "observing" are, according to contemporary perceptionists, functions of the "observer viewpoint" phenomenon previously noted. An individual's background and bias influence the kind of sense he makes of objects in his field of vision. For example, one possible effect of individual background and bias might be illustrated by Barnett's observers at the bottom and top of the Empire State Building. Even though the observer at the base of the building "sees" that the tarred ridges influence the paths of the marbles, he may, because of his individual background, perceive the tarred ridges as "natural" and not "observe" their influence on the marbles' paths. Likewise, the observer at the top of the building buffeted by high winds may, because of these winds, ascribe the movements of the marbles to a strong wind at the base of the building. Commenting on time-influenced sense impressions and their relationship to a definition of perception, Howard Bartley, a psychologist specializing in the study of perception, has written:

> Perception is the over-all activity of the organism that immediately follows or accompanies energistic impingements upon the sense organs. The sensory apparatus mediates between the more internal ongoing activities of the organism and the events outside it. Mediation is a forerunner of utilization.

> Taken together, these consist in (1) the detection of impinging external energies, be they mechanical, chemical, photic, thermal, or otherwise; (2) transforming the quantitative relations of these energies into a set of quantity relations expressive of the organism (groupings of nerve impulses); and (3) relating the specific impingement patterns to "traces" of previous ones in terms of a code or system peculiar to the organism as a species and the particular organism receiving the impingement. The organism is not a simple mirror of externality, but rather a builder of a world of its own out of the nonexperienceable reality that the physicist calls energy.
>
> Perception does not copy anything. Perceived objects are not existent entities in the outside world that have the visual, tactual, thermal, and solid characteristics which we experience in them. Hence, in studying perception, we are studying what it is that the organism experiences; not what the physical world contains, or is made up of.[29]

Part of what "the organism experiences" is related to its emotions at the time of the experience. Constituents of these emotions and their relationship to perception have been suggested by Lewin:

> We have seen that intellectual processes, which can be viewed as one type of productive activity of the individual, depend upon his emotional state, that is, the tension, the degree of differentiation, the size, and fluidity of the life space as a whole. It is a corollary of the relation between cognitive structure and perception that perception, too, is dependent on the needs and emotions of the individual.[30]

Lewin has also directed attention to the relationship between perception and closure. Perceptions, frequently formed in group situations, tend to fuse intellectual and emotional responses into a single impression. That an individual's feelings can distort or color his intellectual achievements has been demonstrated by research on perception.[31] What determines an individual's emotional field has been partially suggested by Lewin:

> Obviously, forces governing this type of learning are related to the total area of factors which determine motivation and personality development. We have mentioned here but a few—the basic laws of needs and satiation, goal structures, the aspiration, and the problem of group belongingness.[32]

Educational psychologists have long recognized the "laws" mentioned by Lewin, and they are not the only ones that apply to the learning situation.[33] The concept of group dynamics,[34] another result of Lewin's explorations of field theory in psychology, fused two separate aspects of psychology—physiological psychology and social psychology. As a concept and a process used in group therapy (psychodrama and sociodrama), group dynamics focuses on patterns of interaction between an individual and a group, noting the changes the individual makes in group structure and the changes the group makes on the individual. Lewin's views on field theory led to much research on other psychological aspects of group dynamics, for example, "holistic" and "operational" concepts of human behavior.

Some of the phenomena observed by perceptionists and gestaltists have been reinforced by the findings of physiological psychologists like M. A. Winger, D. O. Hebb,[35] and others using the electroencephalograph (EEG) to detect and record brain waves. Hebb, an experimental psychologist who deals with "objective" research, has directed his efforts since the early 1930's to the study of motivation in learning, which he describes as "energizing of behavior and especially the sources of energy in a particular set of responses that keep them temporarily dominant over others and account for continuity and direction of behavior."[36] Research in physiological psychology has led to the "drives" theory of motivation, which roughly parallels Freud's concept of the "id" in psycholanalytic theory.[37] Hebb and Freud both arrived at the common need for "field" as a necessary frame of reference in describing human behavior.

Hebb's theory of the "arousal" and "vigilance" functions in learning is basic to the implications of his research for field theory. His formulation of the theory evolved from his studies of two types of brain waves that supposedly exist in all normal humans. Measurements of these brain waves on the EEG indicated the existence of at least two different kinds of electrical discharge by brain cells. The first of these electrical discharges, registering one millisecond on EEG charts, Hebb called the "spike" potential. The second discharge, measuring fifteen to thirty milliseconds, Hebb called the "dendritic" potential. Translating these electrical discharges into effects on learning in animals, Hebb called the spike potential the "cue" function and the dendritic potential the "vigilance" function. The cue function guides behavior, but without a prior vigilance function the cue function rarely operates.[38] Hebb has distinguished between two "modes of thought":

> (1) *discovery* or invention, the attaining of new ideas, and (2) *verification*, the process of testing, clarifying and systematizing them. When an apparent absence of logical thought is observed in a competent problem-solver, it is mostly in mode (1), not (2). With this distinction, the aimless or futile moves of the baffled problem-solver become more intelligible. When the thinker is completely stuck, having tried everything he can think of, logic is of little use. What can he resort to? One possibility is to leave the problem entirely, hoping that his thought will be running in different channels when he comes back to it—this in fact is a recommended procedure, which often works;—or he may continue to react almost at random to the different elements of the situation, manipulate it this way and that hoping that sensory feedback from one of his moves will give him an idea. In such a process—which also results frequently in success—logic plays no recognizable role.[39]

Frustration at a mild level stimulates or arouses the sensory cortex, and from this arousal comes the "new perception" of ideas, which is a recombination achieved by sensory input and the immediately preceding central processes. Without the "arousal," according to Hebb, the new idea, a result of the "spike" potential that fits his description of the "cue" function, would tend not to occur. In some ways, Hebb's theories on motivation and learning are akin to Maxwell's two-layered view of the electromagnetic field, in which the upper layer is shaped by the lower layer of forces. In Hebb's theory, the dendritic or arousal function is shaped by the spiking or cue function.

Jean Piaget, like Hebb, has explored field theory relationships and the effects of fluctuating boundaries on human behavior, particularly in children, but unlike Hebb and other field-oriented psychologists he has been directly influenced by field concepts from mathematics and physics. In *Logic and Psychology*, Piaget described his fascination with the interrelationships of structures and techniques in examining neurological phenomena. As sources for his discovery of these interrelationships, he credited Boolean algebra and modern theories of sets and groups,[40] useful tools for extending field theory in advanced physics. One result of Piaget's application of mathematical techniques to structured phenomena in the sciences was his development of a systematic theory of structures in which different levels of intellectual development may be identified. Basic to Piaget's rationale is the symbol as a constant in human behavior. Symbols tend to move from the concrete to the abstract as man moves through time and grows older. Symbols also abbreviate structure, which makes possible a recalling, first of the structure, then of its details.

Piaget indicated kinds of "operations" that can be expected of individuals at various age levels up to the late teens. Describing the field tendencies of older adolescent "operations," Piaget stated:

> Operational mechanisms, however, have a psychological existence, and are made up of *structured wholes,* the elements of which are connected in the form of a cyclical system irreducible to a linear deduction.... we have here something that resembles more a system involving biological organization than a linear sequence of demonstrations.[41]

In his studies, Piaget utilized terms and concepts not only from mathematics and, as above, biology, but from physics and cybernetics as well:

> This [highest level of operation] is therefore the final form of equilibrium of regulations, and bears some resemblance to the way in which *feed-back* (regulation) operates in a servo-mechanism as long as there is disequilibrium, and as soon as equilibrium is reached, takes on the form of a group.[42]

Piaget's statement on "equilibrium" and "disequilibrium" implies a truism in learning: that overstructured, prescribed learning experiences tend to produce a "group" much like a "servo-mechanism." Stated another way: The student needs to question, to feed back, to be somewhat discomfited before learning can begin. Piaget's speculations about a "general theory of structures" have interrelational, cross-disciplinary implications: "The use of the logical calculus in the description of neural networks on the one hand, and in cybernetic models on the other, shows that such a programme is not out of the question."[43]

Gardner Murphy seems to have gone beyond Piaget's "general theory of structures" in performing a Hegelian-like synthesis of the results of exploration of field theory in psychology, but he also fuses major concepts from physics and biology in his themes on creative human nature. Just as Niels Bohr has updated and unified Maxwell's concepts in physics, so Murphy has updated Lewin's field theory concept in psychology, which characterized psychological behavior fields as static.[44]

Murphy's research studies were largely responsible for psychology's shift away from Lewin's static concept. Many psychologists now believe that:

> . . . to limit investigation to the observation of action alone would be to ignore the paramount fact that the actor is constantly registering in awareness what is happening to him and that this alters his subsequent acts.[45]

Einstein's theory of relativity and Wiener's feedback principle are both implicit in the above statement of psychology's concern with field concepts of human behavior. Murphy has drawn together the concepts of Einstein, Wiener, and others and explored their implications for learning.

One of the chief characteristics of Murphy's approach to field theory in psychology is his belief in the dynamism, in the constant change in human behavior. Describing some of the sources of this belief, Murphy wrote in 1953:

> Here and there, as in the writing of James Harvey Robinson, George Rusk, Gordon Allport, and now S. E. Asch, there has been a glimpse of a third concept (of the field of life-space) which I believe is nearer to the truth: a conception of man's endless becoming.[46]

The "becoming" posited by Murphy in this statement appeared in his earlier work describing the constant flux of being in terms of biological and physical concepts as a base for the "endless becoming of man." As early as 1947, Murphy demonstrated the implications of the organism-environment field:

> Such a view, if we wish, may be called a *field* view, if we

> note that fields studied by biology are in a state of perpetual *redefinition.*
>
> No single word is likely to serve perfectly for this conception. The word "field" will perhaps serve if we expressly state that it is used as it is in physics; an electromagnetic field, for example, permits no strict demarcation of a boundary and may change continually as a result of varying currents.[47]

In his extensions of field theory through life space to the specification for a "science of human potentialities," Murphy wrote that:

> The first fundamental conception is that of the life space, the experienced totality of the individual, comprising a fluid yet dissoluble unity between the experiencing self and the experienced world without, and comprising not only the clearly conscious but likewise the half-conscious and unconscious dispositions and attitudes which color and give meaning to all that is experienced.[48]

Spelling out the specifications for human potentialities, Murphy continued:

> In the specification of a field science of human potentialities, the first step, I suggest, is quantitative, the second qualitative; the third relates to the addition of new elements, and the fourth is configurational.[49]

The condensed details in each of these four steps, chronologically presented, are:

> Quantitative:
>
> The art of measurements changes with time. Changes in art forms . . . the love of visual representation, the capacity to see richly and subtly, came first, and then came the skills born of the passion to convey what had been felt. . . . Rembrandt did more than add range; he added depth perception. . . . I would suggest there is much more than the logical fulfillment of a trend once set going by a genius; there is the development of a transmissible quality of new experience, which is then further enriched as it is further transmitted.
>
> Qualitative:
>
> In our fascination with a purely quantitative approach to the process of learning, we have given singularly little attention

> to the need to observe, describe, and understand the qualitative changes of the person into something rich and strange. But we can open wide this area of research if we wish.
>
> New Elements:
>
> The third aspect of new experience relates to the discovery of new elements of experience. Man is not absolutely, only relatively free. But in the same sense in which Mother Nature is creative, the mind of man is creative, namely, in the discovery of the qualitatively new.
>
> Configurational:
>
> Our fourth principle is the configurational: it relates to the combination or reorganization into new forms. . . . I might remind you here of the brilliant passages in which McDougall sketched out his hypothesis as to the qualities derived from the compounding of the affective life.[50]

Murphy, with a particular reference to what he called "creative human nature," dealt with the way innovation comes from an individual's organizing meaningful fields within the fields of the contemporary culture, i.e., structuring a book or other created thing to constitute its own self-contained field:

> Because man has this rich potentiality for sensory, motor, intellectual experience and has to combine all this in fresh acts of cultural creativeness, he is doing nothing more than realizing these potentialities when he writes *Macbeth* or flies a plane at Kitty Hawk. . . . The biocultural reality keeps rolling up on itself. As James Harvey Robinson said, we can invent more and more mind as we go along, "now that we have the trick."[51]

But the creative thing that contains its own field always has its central meaning in the cultural field it symbolizes. To the extent that the individual can interpret the symbols in his field, e.g., mathematics or literature, and can experience them as a force that changes his perceptions, his potentiality for life space and self-structure is increased. That dynamism and novelty are central to this extrapolation of Murphy's idea is implicit in his own phrasing of it:

> Such an approach would mean not simply the fulfillment of the known biological nature of man, nor the elaboration of

> the known potentialities of culture, but a constant probing of new *emergent* qualities and forms of experience given by a system of relationships that can today hardly be glimpsed; a leaping into existence of new realms of experience; not an extrapolation of the present, but new in kind.[52]

BIOLOGY

In physics, the concept of field is used to understand nature. In psychology, it operates to describe the way in which man restructures his field of observation to give meaning to life. Biology is concerned with yet another aspect of field—the participation of the organism in its field. For man, such participation means a conscious transaction through which he restructures himself-in-his-field, which in turn alters field—and so on.

Indications of the gyroscopic nature of the human organism in its environment appeared as early as 1878 in the writings of Claude Bernard, a French physiologist. Bernard's theory dealt with the circulating liquids of the body, which he claimed gave the organism adjustable stability against environmental forces. Bernard's expression for this stabilizing phenomena was *milieu intérieur*.[53] Many physicians and physiologists have extended Bernard's theories, and today a contemporary physiologist, Walter B. Cannon, acknowledges Bernard's theories as the base for "homeostasis," his modern extension of *milieu intérieur*.

According to Rapoport,[54] Hippocrates called attention to the homeostatic principle in noting that whenever an organism is disturbed from its normal state it tends to return to it, provided the disturbance is not too great. Bernard suggested in *Leçons sur les Phénomènes de la Vie Commune aux Animaux et aux Végétaux* that the plasma of the blood operates as a buffer for the organism against violent external changes it experiences. Descartes' idea of the body as "mechanism" with some regulating principle similar to a thermostat was another of the forerunners of the modern concept of homeostasis.

Cannon is often acknowledged[55] as the man who first gave the name homeostasis to the balancing mechanism operating in living organisms. Cannon's definition of homeostasis was narrowly confined to the tendency for oxygen concentration of the blood to be constant, and various other concentrations to remain constant.[56] From Cannon's narrow use of the concept in 1939 to Grinker's interdisciplinary use of it in 1956, homeostasis has become a focal point for research in wide areas of biology, particularly in genetics.[57] In *Toward a Unified Theory of Human Behavior,* Grinker stated:

> Homeostasis became an attractive unifying principle, and it is alluded to often in future discussions. Homeostasis is used, not only as a narrow concept alluding to stability of the internal milieu of the living organism but as a principle encompassing growth, evolution, social organization, increasing complexity of organization, increasing range of control, and similar uses.[58]

The broad applications of homeostasis that Grinker mentioned pose a problem for developing the concept within the reference frame of this book. Dempsey hinted at the problem in pointing out that "homeostasis is a generalization applicable to the field of sociology as well as physiology."[59] More than to Dempsey's sociology, homeostasis is applicable to mathematics, physics, psychology, and such coordinate areas as biology and ecology. One generalization about homeostasis seems to be that no matter what discipline uses the concept, some kind of balancing phenomenon is involved. Usually the discussions of balance focus more on the internal than the external structure of phenomena examined. In mathematics, for example, Rapoport has referred to the schema of the neuronal network of the organism as a form of mathematical homeostasis.[60]

Balances between an organism's inner and outer forces can be achieved in many ways. Depending on the discipline using homeostasis as a tool, balances are allegedly achieved by physiochemistry (cytology), sensory cue perceptions (psychology), messages (cybernetics), or genetic components (genetics). Although research on homeostasis tends to reflect the specialized character of the discipline conducting the research, most studies suggest that the findings should be interpreted with reference to the larger life-space field.

Bernard, in 1878, was also concerned with life space. Perhaps typically for him, he had to define life and then qualify his definition:

> If I had to define life in a single phrase, I should clearly express my thought by throwing into relief the one characteristic which, in my opinion, sharply differentiates biological science. I should say: life is creation. When a chicken develops in an egg, the formation of the animal body as a grouping of chemical elements is not what essentially distinguishes the vital force. This grouping takes place only according to laws which govern the chemico-physical properties of matter; but the guiding idea of the vital evolution is essentially of the domain of life and belongs neither to chemistry nor to physics nor to anything else. In every living germ is a creative idea which develops and exhibits itself through organization. As long as a living being persists, it remains under the influence of this same creative vital force, and death comes when it can no longer express itself.[61]

The "creativity" aspects of Bernard's idea—that "in every living germ is a creative idea"—prompted George Wald,[62] a contemporary biologist, to identify as innovators in biology men such as Goethe, Pasteur, Darwin, Hegel, Spinoza, and others. The exploration by these men and their colleagues of the "creative" aspects of human life suggests that much more than classification, taxonomy, and vivesection is involved in biology.

Microscopically at least, the life-space field (as already noted with Bernard's "creative germ") has always been considered to contain the homeostatic principle—at least to the extent that adjustment to change was in a sense built into microscopic generators of life. Moving from the cell in 1925[63] and 1929[64] as the source of the uniqueness of each human being, Sinnott by 1950 had come, along with his colleagues, to see the gene as the seminal source of this uniqueness. Sinnott described genetic adaptability as follows:

> Recent studies ... have strengthened the view that control of heredity is vested primarily in the genes, which are discrete, self-reproducing parts of a cellular organization.... The problem of self-reproduction of the gene is perhaps the most fundamental one of all for it is the property of self-reproduction which enables the gene to maintain its basic

integrity, upon which the continuity of life depends, and still to vary its effects, permitting change and adaptation, which constitute the process of evolution.[65]

Just as static fields were suspect in psychology and physics, so the idea of a discrete gene unaffected by its surroundings became the source of recent biological research leading to an interrelational theory about genetic fields:

> This view [the discreteness of genes] was brought into question by the discovery of so-called position effects, which show that the function of a gene in development depends not only upon the intrinsic properties of that gene alone but also upon what genes lie next to it in the chromosome.[66]

Sinnott, summarizing his ideas about the unique perception of each organism in its "field" of culture with differing curiosity and imaginative sympathy, used the interrelationship aspects common to the uses of field theory in all disciplines in writing:

> The gene ... may be regarded as a unit of structure and a unit of function as well, responsible for originating the synthetic activities of the cell which result in growth and differentiation in higher forms. It has come to occupy also a key position in evolution, not only because, by gaining the ability to duplicate itself and to mutate, it provided an essential early step in the origin of living matter, but because the permanent evolutionary changes in those living organisms which have been carefully studied appear to rest ultimately on particular kinds and distributions of genes.[67]

Since 1950 newer advances in microbiology have revealed elements smaller than the gene that still retain the principles Sinnott noted in connection with genes—interrelationship of structure and function, unique creativity, and dynamic change and adjustment in fields of flux. George Beadle, J. D. Watson, and F. H. C. Crick are recent American geneticists who have developed the theory of deoxyribonucleic acid (DNA),[68] and many other biologists, physicians, and geneticists contributed research that led to the isolation of DNA; such multiple contributions are, as in other sciences, typical of modern team research.

According to science editor William Laurence, "DNA is a chemical that determines heredity in all living things from bacteria to man—and even in viruses, on the borderline between living and non-living."[69] The DNA double helix molecule might be called the string that holds life together and like the cell goes through mitotic-like division in an orderly and almost infinite variety of ways.[70] All of the field properties and homeostatic potentials identified with earlier and larger units of life, e.g., cells, nuclei, and genes, are also present in the infinitely smaller DNA molecule. Such a finding was implicit in Bohr's theory of complementarity of the early 1950's.

Kenneth Boulding, a biologically-oriented economist, has interpreted biological principles and projected possible next steps toward "wholeness" as implied by them.[71] In his projections Boulding, like Bohr in physics and Murphy in psychology, has drawn together principles and research findings from wide sources. Boulding's qualifications for venturing into psychology come from a year spent at the Center for Advanced Study in the Behavioral Sciences at Stanford University, where he had occasion to explore many of his interpretations and theories with leading scientists from many disciplines, especially biology and genetics.

Illustrative of Boulding's views on homeostatic principles and biosphere, broadly interpreted, is his hypothesis of the "image." Boulding describes the image as a process that:

> . . . emphasizes communication and feedback as the great sources for orderly and organized growth; thus linking hands with both cybernetics and semantics. Most of all, perhaps, it brings the actor into the act; it looks beyond mechanism without falling into vitalism.[72]

Boulding's definition suggests his synthesis of principles from many fields. The word "image" occurs in much of the literature of the sciences and humanities today, and where it is used, it seems to imply the homeostatic principle. Agar, in his studies of the homologous organization in mammals, for example, used the word "image" to describe the balance that remains after four-fifths of the cortex in an animal's brain has been removed.[73] Agar suggested that the remaining one-fifth of the animal's brain somehow retained a built-in image that permeated the animal's entire body allowing it to continue to function as a rat, guinea pig, etc.

The development of homeostasis as a current tool for research in the sciences seems to have paralleled field theory development in physics and psychology. Early research on homeostasis, as the previous discussion shows, dealt with inner-versus-outer forces, individual-versus-group processes. Recent research (Rapoport, Dempsey, Boulding, Agar) has tended to combine the two forces into one universe, much as Bohr's work did with Maxwell's two-layered view of electromagnetic fields. That the image is a field and that the image-field is a homeostatic process was advanced by Boulding:

> I have suggested that one of the basic theorems of the theory of the image is that it is the image which in fact determines what might be called the current behavior of any organism or organization. The image acts as a field. The behavior consists in gravitating toward the most highly valued part of the field.[74]

Boulding pointed out that the consequences of the behavior are not necessarily in conformity with the image that produced them. Feedback may modify or destroy the perceived image; in such cases the organism may modify the image or cling to it in spite of the feedback. Such nonconformity in spite of feedback reflects Wiener's and Freud's descriptions of "irrational field elements." Boulding's description of feedback also sustains actor-participation as a modification of the act as noted by Lewin, Einstein, Bohr, and others.

All process tends to operate within some structure, and Boulding suggests a structure growing out of field theory techniques:

> It may be, nevertheless, that we are in the midst, or perhaps only at the beginning, of a profound reorganization of the departmental structure of knowledge and of academic life. The old departmental boundaries are crumbling in all directions in the physical as well as in the social sciences. There is something abroad which might be called an interdisciplinary movement. It is reflected at one level in the interest in general education. It is reflected at another level in the development of cross-disciplinary institutes, for instance, institutes of industrial relations, institutes of international relations, area studies, and so on. It is reflected at another level

> in the development of small groups of interested people pursuing the objective of integration of knowledge. The *Encyclopaedia of Unified Science* centering at Chicago, the Institute of Management Science centering at Pittsburgh, the Social Relations Department at Harvard, and the Society for the Advancement of General Systems Theory now in the process of organization are all perhaps straws in the wind. It may be, however, that what we are witnessing is not so much the unification of knowledge as its restructuring. This restructuring is being forced on us by the very growth of knowledge itself.[75]

On the basis of the foregoing statements by selected biologists and one interpreter of biological principles, some support for a field theory approach to literature can be drawn. Bernard's focus on the *milieu intérieur* acting as a stabilizer against exterior shocks implies the typical two-layered view of phenomena noted in the discussion of Maxwell's theories in physics and Lewin's views of psychology. In the traditional perceptions of literature, it might be said that the "work of art" on the one hand and the audience or readers of it on the other represent a two-layered view of the "field" of literature. Just as homeostasis and positioning as biological concepts made untenable (for accurate description) the narrower *milieu intérieur* and "discreetness of genes," so, too, a "field" theory of literature implies that (aside from intellectually prescribed criteria) a "work of art" occurs in the reader's mind only to the extent that a fusion or unity occurs between the ideas of the author and those of the reader.

TWO

EXTENSIONS OF FIELD CONCEPTS IN EDUCATION

THREE SCIENCES—physics, psychology, biology—do not represent all subjects categorized as "the sciences." Nevertheless, they represent in terms of this book a cross-section of scientific thought on the concept of field theory. Such concepts as groups and sets in mathematics,[1] probability in statistics,[2] holism in sociology,[3] half-life in chemistry,[4] and air mass in meteorology[5] all represent field approaches to the study of the behavior of matter, organic and inorganic, and each of them retains general characteristics and principles associated with field theory in physics, psychology, and biology. This similarity in approach to field theory in the various sciences can be seen in Table A.

The quoted or paraphrased statements in Table A also indicate that a largely common vocabulary exists in the sciences to describe concepts associated with field theory. In their often-parallel explorations of field theory and its uses, other disciplines have likewise developed a more or less common vocabulary. A partial list of characteristics of field theory common to many disciplines includes:

1. Parallel historical development from at least a two-layered view of phenomena to a single-field view—a single universe of interdependent, constantly shifting constellations.
2. Similar concepts such as feedback, input, output, balance, actor-involvement, relativity, perception, and totality.

TABLE A

Field Theory Concepts in Three Sciences

PHYSICS	PSYCHOLOGY	BIOLOGY
MAXWELL: We are led to the conception of a complicated mechanism connected so that the motion of one part depends according to definite relations on the motion of other parts.	*KÖHLER-KOFFKA:* Gestalt: pattern configuration. Behavior of an individual at any given time is a function of multiple forces.	*BERNARD:* Life is creation. *Milieu intérieur:* an organism's adjustable stability against environmental forces.
EINSTEIN: Idea of two structures in space independent of each other is intolerable. The unitary field theory, an extension of the general relativity theory, attempts to fulfill this last postulate of field theory. Descriptions of scientific phenomena must recognize importance of observer viewpoint.	*LEWIN:* Intellectual processes of the individual depend on his emotional state, i.e., tension, degree of differentiation, size and fluidity of the life space as a whole.	*CLEMENTS:* Biosphere: an organism's interaction with all aspects of life, i.e., the area between atmosphere and geosphere.
BOHR: In the description of scientific phenomena a unique separation of subject and object is no longer possible. Complementarity: universal viewpoint. Behavior of microscopic and macroscopic phenomena the same.	*BARTLEY:* The organism is not a simple mirror of externality but rather a builder of a world of its own out of the nonexperienceable reality that the physicist calls energy.	*CANNON:* Homeostasis: oxygen concentration in the blood tends to remain constant (1939). Rapoport/Grinker: Homeostasis: principle encompassing growth, evolution, social organization, tending to increase range of control (1955).
WIENER: I class communication and control together. Society can only be understood through a study of the messages and the communication facilities which belong to it.	*HEBB:* The cue function guides behavior but without a prior vigilance function, the cue function rarely operates.	*SINNOTT:* The gene is a unit of structure and function that contains within it the ability to shape to some extent its growth in terms of biological environment.
	PIAGET: Operational mechanisms have a psychological existence and are made up of structured wholes.	*BOULDING:* The image acts as a field. Behavior gravitates toward parts of a given field.
	MURPHY: The field of life space is nearer the truth: a concept of man's endless becoming. Such a view may be called field, if we note that fields studied by biology are in a state of perpetual redefinition.	

> 3. Common principles such as the need for flexibility and regulation, the recognition of entropic forces and their effect on observed phenomena, the recognition of the value of interdisciplinary approaches to research on matter, organic and inorganic.

Other common characteristics will be developed in the discussion of field theory in English.

The development of field theory in education reflects the development in other disciplines in various ways. George Hartmann, educational psychologist, noted as early as 1942 the growing influence of field theory. His extrapolations into educational consequences led to a dramatic forecast:

> Field theory in its original and most universal meaning refers not primarily to a special system of psychology, but to a comprehensive world view that is essentially a physical philosophy of nature.... Field theory in one form or another is being understood and applied by an increasing number of individuals, and, if current trends continue, by 1950 it may well be a major reference center and professional guide for a clear majority of folks in the academic and teaching worlds.[6]

Hartmann's prediction has been borne out, and since many of the contributors to field theory have been teachers, it is not surprising that some of them have explored ways that the theory might affect education. Maxwell, Einstein, and Bohr, while seldom explicit on educational concepts, shared a belief that "interrelationships," "wholes," "unification," and "observer viewpoints" are all necessary to complete understanding of observed phenomena. These concepts seem to have worked into educational administration, as can be seen in a statement by Thomas Hamilton, former president of the State University of New York:

> A major and too infrequently noted weakness in our education is its segmentation—segmentation which manifests itself horizontally by the unnatural splitting of knowledge into smaller and smaller compartments, and vertically by an insistence that the domains of elementary, secondary, and higher education have boundaries as inviolate as those of sovereign states. Yet nothing could be more false or better designed to weaken the total impact of the educational enter-

> prise. . . . Truly, let an elementary school any place be wounded and some place, some time, a college will bleed.[7]

Wiener's views on education are explicit, though focused on his specialization, communication. Using the rationale that man differs from animal because of his power of speech, Wiener has held that message analysis is one key to *understanding* civilization. Teaching is, according to Wiener, a complicated exchange of messages.

The importance of Wiener's concept of communication for a field theory approach to literature and for the education of prospective English teachers is that the structure and process of an educational system must provide for message exchange. Wiener's truism is not new to people in education,[8] yet the prevalence of closed systems of required courses, the provision for only one-way communication in lectures in some literature courses, the selection of course content on entropic clichés such as "classics, great books, significant literature," may still be found in some college programs.

Wiener and Einstein have suggested that the observer is important in the study of fields and that the accuracy of the observer is affected by the amount of feedback he gets from his observations. Thus, programs for prospective English teachers and programs for the study of literature need to provide students with opportunities for "feedback" of their observations. Ideally, such feedback will allow the college to qualify observations that may be in error. Generally, the higher the frequency of such feedback, the higher the potential for accurate understanding of necessary concepts in both college programs and programs for the study of literature. Too much feedback can, however, cause distortion. Just as the microphone squeals and cuts off the speaker when excess feedback is present, so excessive feedback in programs of English education and college programs for educating prospective English teachers can destroy the "messages" of each program. Control of input and output is a necessary process in teacher education, even as control of input and output tends to correct feedback in microphones.

Psychologists, particularly in the area of learning, have also explored direct implications of field theory for teaching. From the "patterns" and "configurations" of the gestaltists through Lewin's concern for the "fluidity of life space" to Murphy's psychological concern for man's perpetual becoming through creative action, literature in education shows a reflection of psychological research findings. Clarence Faust, president of the Fund for the Advancement of Education, described the American ideal as:

> . . . the development of each individual's capacity to think for himself. We are convinced that every individual is entitled to discover or rediscover the truth for himself and that only as he makes the effort to do so can he really grasp it, truly understand it, and make it a part of himself.[9]

Faust's statement of field theory's "constant discovery or rediscovery" principle is related to Ashley Montagu's concern for the "field of experience" in education:

> By "a soundly based system of education" I mean one that is based on the findings of the anthropological and behavioral sciences concerning the nature of human nature, and the functioning of that human nature in the context of human society.[10]

Akin to Montagu's description of education but focusing more directly on teachers is Arthur Jersild's dictum concerning attitude-formation, with its implication of teacher-effect on students:

> Just as it is within an inter-personal setting that one acquires most of the attitudes involved in one's view of oneself, so it is likely that only in an inter-personal setting can a person be helped to come to grips with some of the meanings of these attitudes.[11]

Awareness of these interpersonal patterns is implicit in Murphy's description of the "good" teacher in light of his own "life-space" and "endless becoming" principles from field theory:

> Good teachers seem to me to be concerned very little with fitting a child into a socially specified pattern; they seem . . . to be ever on the watch for the free movement of the spirit, the reaching out, the yen for new experience. . . . Those who conceive of education in terms of systematic mastery of all that one culture has achieved, as for example in the incorporation within oneself of the 100 great books, or the great cen-

> tral ideas of western civilization seem to me to be missing something fundamental . . . the heart as I see it is the demand of a person for life; the enrichment of what he already is.[12]

While the above statement contains abstractions that might be difficult to describe, e.g., "life" and "free movement of spirit," and although it may be in conflict with Murphy's other remarks on the role of time in structuring intellectual experience, it does dramatize attitudes that affect learning. Such an examination of emotions as Murphy suggests must be made with field concepts in mind—interrelationships and fluctuating boundaries.

English education, through the broadfield of communication, has long been concerned with the role of attitude in relationship to learning. Shoemaker's view of good teaching is derived from the educational implications of field theory. He sees, for instance, a movement:

> From predominant grouping of social studies and language arts in various kinds of core organizations, toward recognition of the need for a communication core, in which students may learn language and other art skills and attitudes appropriate for handling the major aspects of experience in both discursive and non-discursive modes.[13]

Shoemaker's "communication core" resembles Sinnott's biological "nucleus" in that both concepts deal with change, adaptation, and learning as unique to individuals and as a sum of constant environmental stimuli. Clements, Cannon, Rapoport, and Grinker, biologists all, are concerned as a matter of degree with field relationships. "Organism to environment," "mutual modification," "process-structural interrelationships to project total images in arrested time"—these are overarching concerns of modern biologists. One key to the organism's changes is the principle of feedback, which, depending on the individual and his perception, is a matter of degree. Feedback may modify or destroy the perceived image; in such cases the organism may modify the image or cling to it in spite of the feedback. Such nonconformity in spite of feedback reflects Wiener's and Freud's description of "irrational field elements." Boulding's description of feedback also sustains the actor-participation as modification of the act noted by Lewin, Einstein, Bohr, and others.

The foregoing generalizations about field theory and "image" in biology are also present in Boulding's description of field-like approaches to education. Concerning teaching Boulding has written:

> The accumulation of knowledge is not merely the difference between messages taken in and messages given out. It is not like a reservoir; it is rather an organization which grows through an active internal organizing principle much as the gene is a principle or entity organizing the growth of bodily structures. The gene, even in the physico-chemical sense may be thought of as an inward teacher imposing its own form and "will" on the less formed matter around it. In the growth of images, also, we may suppose similar models. Knowledge grows also because of inward teachers as well as outward messages. As every good teacher knows, the business of teaching is not that of penetrating the student's defenses with the violence or loudness of the teacher's messages. It is, rather, that of co-operating with the student's own inward teacher whereby the student's image may grow in conformity with that of his outward teacher. The existence of public knowledge depends, therefore, on certain basic similarities among men.[14]

Educators, particularly those concerned with preservice programs for prospective teachers, have long been aware of the truth of Boulding's statement. Field theory implications for teacher education—curricular designs, individual programming, planned articulation of structure and content—were discussed in an advisory committee report of the American Association of Colleges for Teacher Education (AACTE) entitled *Teacher Education for a Free People* (1956). Field theory principles seemed most apparent in Professor Florence Stratemeyer's article, "Relating the Several Parts of the Teacher-Education Program."[15] The "Parts" mentioned in the title referred to other articles in the book dealing with general education, specialization, and similar areas in the total college program for educating teachers. These articles used findings from psychobiological research as a basic framework of principles on which programs of teacher education might be built.[16] In relating the parts of teacher-education programs in the article, Professor Stratemeyer recognized institutional diversity—liberal arts colleges, colleges of education, universities with affiliated schools of education—and the effect of unique institutional structures on undergraduate programs. Consequently, she outlined tentative programs for prospective teachers within different institutional structures and, in even more detail, described these programs as though majors in particular academic fields were to follow them.[17]

That Professor Stratemeyer's descriptions and model of preservice programs for prospective teachers are based on elements of field theory can be seen in the following summary:

1. The programs are based on the total college life of the students. Out-of-class and summer experiences are an integral and planned part of the prospective teachers' programs.

2. The programs acknowledge and attempt to incorporate the unique interests of each student as an individual, recognizing and guiding the changes that students experience in four or five years of college life.

3. The programs urge the need for integrating experiences; structures are provided in which separate parts can be put together by the student in special seminars, through a faculty adviser assigned to the student for his total undergraduate program, and by special curricular integrative experiences.

4. The programs provide for flexibility and feedback at all stages of the preservice teachers' experiences. Such provision tends to deal with "irrational" elements that may come up during the course of the students' program.

5. The programs are structured on taxonomic objectives that, in turn, are derived from research in biology, psychology, sociology, education, and other disciplines that supply principles for optimum learning and application.

6. The programs recognize learning as primarily an individual, independent, self-motivated process for each student. Mere memorization of atomistic "facts," in Stratemeyer's schema, is implicitly suspect.

7. The programs focus on the "well-rounded" individual; depth and breadth are equally important but individually determined.

8. The programs imply that preservice education of teachers is time-bound. The increase in man's knowledge, particularly in the last twenty years, suggests that minimal prin-

ciples needed by prospective teachers demand a five-year program to accomplish the depth and breadth characteristic of a field theory approach to programs for teacher education.

Thus far, the evolution of scientific thinking on field theory in physics, psychology, and biology has been briefly explored, and some implications field theory has for education have been suggested. Common to these three disciplines has been the gradual emergence of a view of field as a dynamic concept rather than a static one. Looking ahead to implications and applications of this emerging principle of a dynamic field for the "field" of English, "complementarity" might be mentioned briefly as an illustration. An indirect way of making concrete application of complementarity to art's concern for abstractionism and literature's concern for the enigmas of James Joyce's *Ulysses* and *Finnegans Wake* is to cite Dyson's prediction for extending complementarity in the next decade:

> When the great innovation appears, it will almost certainly be in a muddled, incomplete and confusing form. To the discoverer himself, it will be only half understood; to everybody else it will be a mystery. For any speculation which does not at first glance look crazy, there is no hope.[18]

To those who are unaware of the "explosions" of knowledge that have taken place in the "field" of English since the 1920's, Dyson's "crazy" may apply to much of the rest of this book. Yet the studies of the National Council of Teachers of English and the developments in language arts, humanities, language-culture-area studies, communication, and literary criticism are such that they should be explored to see to what degree, without using the term "field theory," they yet exemplify the concept.

THREE

THE BROADENED CURRICULAR FIELD OF ENGLISH

Descriptions of field theory in physics, psychology, and biology have revealed that the field concept is characterized by such processes and ideas as "feedback," "observer participation," and "interrelationship" that constitute the functioning of design or pattern —with their attendant impressions of "oneness" and "wholeness."

Within the concepts of "oneness" and "wholeness" is the "method" of field theory, which is artificially separated for discussion as an entity apart from "design" or "pattern." Common to field theory no matter what the "field" is the so-called "positional effect." Positional effect is characterized by fluctuating dynamisms imposed by field content, by time, and by space. Consequently, to speak of a "method" of field theory is to introduce the field theory notion of observer viewpoint. Given a "field" in any discipline, "method" of analysis depends on the purpose, the interest, the skill, and the background of the analyzer. The method for describing an electromagnetic field in physics, for example, depends on the observer's purpose of analysis—what aspect of the field interests him. If the observer is trained in electronics, he may view the field from that perspective, if in magnetism, from that viewpoint, if in atomic physics, from that aspect. In each case the initial focus on the field resides within the individual observer and tends to limit his outlook and determine his analytical method. Even if a team attempts to cover all aspects of a "field" at a prearranged time, the order of sharing their findings through a discussion tends to reshape the perceived field because language is unilateral and the time and the priority given to the first observer's report will tend to affect perception of the report given by the last observer. Time-prescribed language limitations seriously hamper consideration of "method" as separate from "structure" in discussions of field theory. Recognizing the limiting factors imposed by language in the description of field theory, the attempt shall still be made in the following pages to describe the "field of English" through a combined "structure" and "method" field approach.

Many teachers commonly refer to their working "in the field of English," meaning by this a possibly simple geographic notion of boundary in the division of labor in the curriculum. But closer examination of the various areas of special inquiry in "English" reveals some close resemblances to the concept of field as observed in the sciences—taking into consideration the integral relationship of language and its environing culture, the newer ideas of aesthetic experience that provide a philosophic center for the arts in the term "humanities," and the mutually supporting and clarifying contributions of anthropology, psychology, and other social sciences (in method and material) to the understanding of communication and human community.

In using modern communication as a center for English "field" exploration, one must recognize that he may be dealing with an anachronism. Albert Kitzhaber's *Themes, Theories, and Therapy: The Teaching of Writing in College* (1963) claims that courses labeled "Communication" have seriously declined in recent years in college English programs. Oblique support for Kitzhaber's claim can be seen in the growing popularity of the recommendation of the College Entrance Examination Board (CEEB) and the Commission on English that English teachers concentrate on "language, literature, and composition" as major focuses for their discipline. The Commission seems to think that such a cutting back to manageable centers for teaching English is necessary if teachers are to survive the onslaught of new topics such as psycholinguistics and symbolic logic that are daily added to the discipline of English. In effect, what the Commission seems to have done is enunciate a new "trivium"; the old "grammar, rhetoric, and logic" has become the new "language, literature, and composition." The popularity of the new "trivium" is evident from the number of new studies under the aegis of "Project English" that focus on one or all of the "trivia." Use of the word "trivia" is not meant to demean the Commission's approach to English; rather it is meant to show that, historically considered, today's meaning for "trivial" ("petty" or "banal") derived from the medieval pedantry that occurred when the trivium was taught. While it is true that narrowing English to a new "trivium" will provide the specialization and manageability desired by the Commission, the question should be raised: How realistic is this retreat from the vast fund of information about language that is being provided by communication research? Before attempting to answer this question, it is important to examine more closely the extent to which the field concept has informed contemporary scholarship in English, in the language arts, the humanities, language-culture-area studies, and communication arts and skills and then the extent to which the term "field theory" might with value be consciously extended to critical approaches to literature as one of the needed rapprochements between the arts and the sciences. First, however, it is necessary to examine elements of field theory currently at work in English scholarship and see to what extent they may provide a base for extension into literary criticism. A quick chronological overview of their development follows, beginning with language arts and moving through humanities, language-culture-area-studies, and communication.

LANGUAGE ARTS

"English" is relatively new in the school curriculum. It dates from approximately the turn of this century as a unifying term for the study in high schools and colleges of the literature of England and the art of rhetoric. In the relatively stable culture of the first two decades, there was little pressure to expand these offerings, despite the concern of men like Professor Allan Abbott of Teachers College, working through the U. S. Office of Education, for more inclusive concepts of "communication."

World War I led to a dramatic shift in American culture that was reflected in the teaching of English. To the literature of England, schools all across the country added chronological studies in American literature and world literature, suggestive of the country's new-found role in world history. But the war and these additions to the English curriculum did not have the deeply moving effect of the depression of the 1930's. Then for the first time American culture generally took account of its internal relatedness and its motivating values. In English this new awareness gave rise to two new terms for expanded patterns of study: language arts and humanities. Both have continued as descriptive of the enlarged responsibilities of "English," language arts referring primarily to teaching in the elementary and secondary school, humanities primarily in the colleges and universities, although the late 1950's have seen the extension of this latter term into secondary school planning.

During the depression years, California's fertile valleys attracted great numbers of both migrant workers from Spanish-speaking communities south of the Rio Grande and dispossessed farmers from the Middle South. These "cultures in conflict" created pressures to find an educational channel for harmonizing frictions in attitudes and ways of life that led to the General Education Board's grant in support of what became known as the Stanford Language Arts Investigation, under the direction of Walter V. Kaulfers, Grayson N. Kefauver, and Holland D. Roberts. Comparable experimental work was going forward simultaneously at Ohio State University and in both the Lincoln School and New College of Teachers College, Columbia University, but the dramatic setting in California gave to the Stanford project a special interest. The publication of *A Cultural Basis for the Language Arts* (1937) by Kaulfers and Roberts provided a new perspective for joining the efforts of teachers of English and teachers of foreign languages. Despite previous separations the Stanford project provided an integrative center for an inclusive "field" in:

The development of an active interest in language as man's

> most significant social invention and most indispensable instrument of thought, through learning activities contributive to an understanding and appreciation of the subtle role of language in the daily life of individuals, communities, states, and nations.[1]

The community of interest between teachers of English and of foreign languages lay in a three-fold view of language "as a code whose symbolism is to be mastered . . . as an art with a history, a terminology, and a psychology of its own . . . [and] as a treasury of human thought and experience."[2] From this rich conception of language, study in both English and foreign languages proceeded through supportive use of other art mediums as they symbolized human cultures—music, painting, architecture, drama, and even culturally determined symbolic behavior. As Kaulfers and Roberts saw the possibilities:

> When language is taught from the beginning as a means of communication, with due regard for the essential worthwhileness of the content expressed, the possibilities for integration, not only with English, but also with the social studies, the arts, and the sciences, become infinite.[3]

The authors enumerated reading of varied kinds of printed material, writing, speaking, and dramatizing as explicit avenues to the realization of the overall design.

From the perspective of twenty-five years it is instructive to see how many of these exciting ideas of the 1930's have continued to mature, nurtured by new research in anthropology, psychology, linguistics, and communication theory. But it is also instructive to observe that many of them have matured separately rather than within an embracing context. The "field" element essential to continued unified development was apparently lacking—a clear statement of descriptive method and its relation to teaching method in language and literature study.

Simultaneously with the Stanford investigation, the National Council of Teachers of English, through its Curriculum Commission, was studying some of the integrative characteristics that have been identified with field theory in the sciences. Francis Shoemaker, studying evidences of a modern aesthetic as base for the growth of humanities, summarized the integrative import of the Commission's early publications:

> The attempt to establish a broad "frame of reference" was noteworthy both in the representativeness of the commission, and in the breadth of the idea in the reports; various effects will be seen in the statements of values attainable in or through literature and the arts as set up by these committees. *The Teaching of College English* is primarily concerned with the values of language. *An Experience Curriculum* seems in various ways to be moving toward an aesthetic experience concept. *A Correlated Curriculum* in its major design seems to imply the evolving culture concept which interweaves with a psychological-anthropological aesthetic.[4]

Shoemaker's statement that "various effects will be seen" was somewhat prophetic in that modern concerns for the structure of English programs both at the high school and college levels demonstrate broader perspectives. Factors other than the three Commission reports (culminating in Alfred Korzybski's *Science and Sanity,* 1933, C. C. Fries's *American English Grammar,* 1940, and S. I. Hayakawa's popularization of Korzybski in *Language in Action,* 1941, and *Language in Thought and Action,* 1949) undoubtedly influenced the change. But the concern for "language" noted in *The Teaching of College English*[5] certainly gave some impetus to the concern for semantics, linguistics, and criticism. Similarly, *An Experience Curriculum,*[6] with its attendant "aesthetic experience" concept, supported ideas of regionalism and ecology as important to programs for the study of English. *A Correlated Curriculum,*[7] with its intimations of a "psychological-anthropological aesthetic," supported ideas for "core" programs and the broadening of English perspectives to include fields such as communication in English programs.

The decade between 1936 and 1946 saw the embryonic forces for integrated approaches multiply in such NCTE publications as *Elementary English, The English Journal,* and *College English.*[8] In 1945, the NCTE appointed a Commission on the English Curriculum:

> To study the place of the language arts in life today, to examine the needs and methods of learning for children and

> youth, and to prepare a series of volumes on the English curriculum based on sound democratic principles and the most adequate research concerning how powers in the language arts can best be developed.[9]

In 1952, the Commission published the first of an anticipated five-volume series under a title, *The English Language Arts,* that indicated a significant bridging of concepts. Identifiable specialization was represented in such titles as *The Language Arts in the Elementary School* (Vol. II), *The English Language Arts in the Secondary School* (Vol. III), and *The Education of Teachers of English for American Schools and Colleges* (Vol. V).

As the title *The English Language Arts* suggested, the inclusive language "field" of *A Cultural Basis for the Language Arts* was narrowed to English. At the same time a psychological dimension was added—attention to the relation of language to developmental stages of child growth. Many of the Commission's publications have provided suggestions and clarifications for the administrative relationship of the skills of reading, writing, speaking, and listening, with examples of successful teaching procedures at varying grade levels to realize "aesthetic values, moral perceptions, personality development."

These skills the Commission hoped would "aid in understanding varied cultures, meet individual needs, interests and abilities" and, ideally, should be "related to an integrated language arts program."[10] Relationships of literature to an integrated language arts program were, in 1952, most apparent in elementary and secondary schools.[11] More recently, in 1960, this judgment was amended by the director of the Curriculum Commission, Dora V. Smith, who expressed the belief that literature was more neglected in the elementary school than at any other level. At the college level, the Commission was concerned with the kinds of literature courses generally offered—[12]"American, chronological or historical survey, contemporary, individual author, thematic, type"—and raised questions about the values of certain of these courses for students of literature.[13]

It was not until 1958 that the National Council turned explicit attention from organizational patterns to scholarly method in relation to critical method in literature. The Council's publication, *Contemporary Literary Scholarship,* edited by Lewis Leary, professor of English at Columbia University, presented a series of articles by American scholar-critics that described approaches to literary types and periods and reflected a deep interest in the relationship of literature and culture. Among them, representing some newer perceptions of literary scholarship, were Lennox Grey's article "Literary Audience" and Patrick Hazard's "The Public Arts and the Private Sensibility." Grey's well-documented thesis held that literary audience is a force that determines literary form at any given time and that relatively little attention has been paid to audience in modern scholarship. Understanding the interrelationships between the audience and the literary artists demands a scholarly-critical method that, according to Grey, is just now beginning to evolve. Hazard's thesis is that the popular arts are a potentially new form of literature that demand examination by scholarly-critical methods before their popularity and enigmatic contents come to control private sensibilities. Both articles deal with growing mass media problems in a "film-oriented" culture—a culture that is tending to influence, as an audience, literary structures and methods through montage techniques similar to the simultaneity of film.

The Grey and Hazard chapters from *Contemporary Literary Scholarship* represent one important concern for "fieldness"—important because they represent "a different drummer." More vocal and perhaps more representative of NCTE's concerns in 1963 have been the recommendations of the CEEB and the Commission on English and the views of the Basis Issues in the Teaching of English[14] group. Members of the Basic Issues group (1959) represented the American Studies Association, College English Association, Modern Language Association, and National Council of Teachers of English. Consonant with the Commission on English, the Basic Issues group agreed that restructuring and narrowing were necessary to deal with "basic issues" in the teaching of English. Some of the issues identified by the group included:

> 3. Should certain literary works be required at each of the various levels in a basic program?
>
> 6. At what level is coverage of the field important?

15. Could national standards for student writing at the various levels be established, and what would be their value?

Eclectic as these three illustrations of the many issues raised by the Basic Issues group are, they suggest the tone and focus of the group toward English-teaching. Many English teachers at all levels are seeking answers to questions raised by the group. But about half of the "issues" listed in question form need to be rephrased before a testable hypothesis can be found. In Question 3, what is a "basic program"; in Question 6, what is meant by "coverage"; in Question 15, what kind of "student writing"? Recognizing the intent of the Basic Issues group to establish manageable boundaries for English, such abstractions as "coverage of the field" are still open to question for at least two reasons: First, the group made virtually no attempt to define "coverage." Is it a student's knowledge of content, his behavior change, or his 95 per cent score on an examination? Second, the group seems to have suggested a reversion to arbitrary authority, implying that there are those who can with validity (statistical definition) define "coverage" so that a common application will produce the desired English skill in a relatively uniform way. Until these points are resolved, the basic issues should be recognized as "issues" and not (as some English teachers are wont to interpret them) as rubrics.

In *Contemporary Literary Scholarship* and the first three volumes of the Council's language arts series, it is suggested that:

1. Taxonomy as a basis for literature programs will continue to evolve on some variation of an integrated approach.

2. The process used for studying literature as an integrated whole (characteristic of elementary and secondary schools) will become an increasing part of college programs.

3. Courses in literature based on undeniable research findings in developmental and thematic reading will tend to allow more individual student choices of literature read within a prescribed English department structure.

4. Specialization where it is retained in English programs will tend to be balanced by seminars specially designed to guide course work in literature.

The need for an evolution of structure and process in English is implicit in the findings of a recent Council survey on the teaching of English: Arno Jewett, after surveying 285 state and local English syllabuses in 45 states, the District of Columbia, and the Canal Zone, concluded that "the objectives, activities, and instructional content in areas of written composition, oral communication, and grammar and usage have not greatly changed during the past twenty-five years."[15]

HUMANITIES

Education responded vigorously to the changing values of American culture after World War I and during the depression of the 1930's. All the cultural excesses described in Allen's *Only Yesterday,* plus disillusionment with the narrow specialization and the "elective system," turned colleges toward the administratively economical design of general education; required "broadfield" courses in the major areas of human inquiry replaced unpatterned electives. Concern for intercommunication of specialists made the values and methods of the natural and biological sciences the basis of one broadfield, concern for cultural processes and evolution made the methods and values of social science the basis for a second, and concern for the human values underlying dignity, self-respect, and self-knowledge drew equal attention to the relations of the arts in American culture and the study of them in courses and programs in humanities.

From an initial course in Western civilization given by John Erskine for American doughboys quartered in Paris in 1921 and two comparable courses begun later in 1929 at the University of Chicago and Stephens College, humanities courses and programs came into being in sixty American colleges and universities before the opening of World War II. This was as dramatic a cultural event in its own way as was the conflict of cultures in the California valleys. And again the General Education Board provided research funds, this time for the Cooperative Seminar in the Humanities under the direction of Lennox Grey at Teachers College, Columbia University.

The first definitive study of the program was made by Patricia Beesley in *The Revival of the Humanities in American Education* (1940). This book dealt with the historic sources and lines of development of humanities studies in departments of English and comparative literature and also suggested profitable lines of research into the cultural forces that had led so dramatically to the sudden drawing together of coordinated studies in literature, painting, music, dance, architecture, philosophy, history, and, in some instances, religion.

The second of the studies in the Cooperative Seminar was Francis Shoemaker's *Aesthetic Experience and the Humanities* (1943). In this study, Shoemaker found in modern psychology and anthropology an emerging concept of aesthetic experience in which man's most imperious drive toward order and orderliness is satisfied in every aspect of human life, science, politics, education, and religion—as well as in the cumulative creative experience in any of the arts. Quoting John Steinbeck, Shoemaker showed that "the impulse that drives a man to poetry will send another man to the tide pools and force him to report on what he finds there."[16]

Aware of the cultural field from which literature and the other arts grow and in which they have their meaning, Shoemaker turned to modern anthropology:

> Modern anthropology is concerned with language as the reservoir of human experience and with the arts generally as symbols of culture effecting the integration of self in the community through patterned representation of human values. From these sources have grown expanding ideas of aesthetic experience in the arts as the creative-critical process originating in the artist's interaction with his environment—and ending in the observer's reflective commitment upon the presentation of values in the work of art.[17]

The central value in the aesthetic process is the development of self. In literature the manner of handling language is directly related to the quality of self-realization achieved:

> Loss of adequate use of a common language by any large proportion of a social group, or restriction of otherwise freely undertaken artistic formulations in literature, leads logically

either to chaos or authoritarianism in which individuality in any generous sense is unrealized.[18]

From this central value and the body of literature that comprises the literary component in the humanities, Shoemaker moved to consider the scholarly methods that ultimately define the nature of the field. His findings relative to schools of philosophy underlying the humanities are not of concern here, but it is informative to note the manner in which he relates organizational design and critical procedure—which is pertinent to a concern for field theory and literature:

> Between the external frame of many modern Humanities courses and the St. John's Great Books course there is often no great difference; but between the modern analogical logic and feeling for design implied in modern ideas of aesthetic experience and medieval syllogistic logic and dialectic of St. John's there is a profound difference.[19]

Shoemaker explored all aspects of the humanities and their particular effects on world literature and aesthetics. From this exploration, and based on principles derived from aesthetics and humanities, Shoemaker made a depth study of *Hamlet* as symbol of a cultural epoch and example of man's search for self. Out of these scholarly explorations and explications, Shoemaker drew conclusions that can serve as a working base for the rest of this section on field-like ideas in the humanities:

> What conclusions may we draw from this evidence? We may look for increasingly conscious concern for the unity which aesthetic values are providing in the teaching of Humanities and World Literature courses—first a clear unity for all the arts as symbols of culture expressing through the several media contemporaneous attitudes toward life, and second an increasingly clear focus upon the individually-experienced human values and, in further research and philosophically-planned experimentation, relativistic critical disciplines for developing them. It seems likely that in the next few years many courses will call for critical value judgments of a few selected works of art entire in their quest for the artist's resolution of the cultural concerns of his epoch.[20]

Shoemaker's prediction of unity for all the arts as symbols of culture has been dramatically fulfilled, but his conception of the unique role of each art form was altered by his later contact with Susanne K. Langer, whose *Philosophy in a New Key* (1942) and *Feeling and Form* (1953) opened up still closer consideration of the common aesthetic base for the sciences and the arts.

The "field" then, explored broadly by Beesley and described in depth by Shoemaker, with his initial concern for the integral relationship of philosophy-material-method, maintains considerable dynamism today. In 1949, Earl McGrath, then U. S. Commissioner of Education, edited *The Humanities in General Education,* an overview of philosophies at work in courses in colleges and universities across the country. More recently, some of the urgency of Shoemaker's concern for man's search for design was reflected in the reference to "English and the Humanities," for both high school and college study, in the NCTE pamphlet, *The National Interest and the Teaching of English* (1961). By late 1962, however, the major influences of the Council's recommendations about the humanities were more apparent in high school programs than in those of the colleges. Ingrid Strom reported in 1963 that a study by Joseph Mersand "cited eight types of evidence to support his conclusion that in the 26,000 secondary schools of the United States there appears to be an improvement in the status of the humanities."[21]

The foregoing field-like ideas from the humanities are simply illustrative of structural concerns for unity, but, more importantly, through Shoemaker's aesthetic they also provide an illustration of a method whereby the unified outlook may be obtained. Frequent crossings of disciplines for illustrations, for examples, and for concepts are similar to procedures noted in connection with field theory in the first chapter of this book. That humanities courses have become increasingly important as part of the general curricular patterns in the nation's secondary schools (noted by Mersand) suggests that the focus on "wholeness" in humanities courses is being recognized as a balance to specialization.

LANGUAGE-CULTURE-AREA STUDIES

Language-culture-area studies may seem something of a literary echo of Kaulfers' and Roberts' *A Cultural Basis for the Language*

Arts. And indeed the relationship is close. As has been said, the language arts studies of the California valleys were turned to explication and harmonization of the aspects of great national cultures that had come into conflict in local communities in the United States. "San Francisco has been disposed to make the most of the rich social heritage brought to it in the customs, interests, and traditions of the large population of foreign descent that composes its citizenry."[22] In New Orleans, Charleston, Milwaukee, Montreal, and Quebec as well, Kaulfers and Roberts pointed out, "an appreciation of language, and of the culture of which it forms an integral and often basic part, has educational significance for all interested youth."[23]

The roots of the language arts concept were well planted when the gathering clouds of World War II turned attention to propaganda analysis and the monitoring of allied and enemy broadcasts with particular reference to their predictive value for enemy military intentions. When the country was finally plunged into the war—in Europe, Africa, Southeast Asia, and the Pacific—language was suddenly recognized as a key weapon. The whole accumulated pattern of foreign language learning, with its attention to reading and writing, was drastically altered in the Armed Services Training Program development of aural-oral language-learning. Equally dramatic was the shift to the realization that survival for even the most perfect speaker of a foreign language might well depend on his broad knowledge of the cultural context of the language—its country's history, philosophy, religion, mores, customs, and the like. This was the "culture area," the field and ground for contemporary study of language.

The newly realized survival value of language placed a high premium on its study and teaching. Descriptive linguistics, already a growing "field" in itself, was drawn on fully for studies in structure and meaning, with "context" as a central concept, whether in the minimal sense of the sentence context for designation of meanings for individual words or in the maximum context of the culture as simultaneously determined by and determining both lexical and structural meanings of linguistic communication.

The language-culture-area studies showed all the characteristics of working field theory: a philosophic center in the relation of language to individual and cultural growth, a clearly related body of cultural materials, and the scholarly methods of anthropology and ecology to provide for their coordinated study and inquiry. The table below suggests the range of disciplines involved in language-culture-area studies:

Linguistics	Psycholinguistics	Semantics	Metalinguistics
Relationships of English and foreign languages	Behavior elicited by language	Meanings in context	Patterns of thinking as determined by language

Early research studies in linguistics appeared at the turn of the present century,[24] although linguistic-like attempts to study language had of course been made before.[25] "Appropriateness" or "usage" in language is perhaps the most ancient of the categories of language study and because of its relationship to status and class values tends to remain a concern among some educated people. Semantics, a prewar development, has had a meteoric rise in importance in research studies on language. World War II was a catalyst for communications research and led to major studies on the psycholinguistic and metalinguistic aspects of language. Representative of the thinking behind the language-culture-area studies movement is Roger Brown's comment on the separate areas of concern, language and culture, as they clashed in descriptions of language:

> The doctrines of linguistic relativity and determinism would seem to be embarrassed by the imperfect geographic correspondence of culture areas and language areas. One would suppose that the cognitive categories are caused by the structure of the language and culture areas ought to coincide. There is, of course, some correspondence between the two but it is far from perfect. The Finnish people who are generally well assimilated to European culture speak a Finno-Ugric tongue unrelated to most other European languages. The Hopi and Hopi-Tewan share a general Puebloan culture but speak very different languages. . . . Culture is not exhaustively defined by shared cognitive categories and language is not exhaustively defined by the features likely to be most directly related to cognition; consequently, criteria are available for the definition of culture areas and language areas that will result in imperfect correspondence of the two.[26]

The metalinguistic problem posed by Brown was described by Harry Hoijer in terms of a hypothesis made by Edward Sapir and Benjamin Lee Whorf. The hypothesis is that the languages of different societies do not make the same sense of the same reality. Commenting on the hypothesis Hoijer has written:

> The speaker in any language is seldom aware that, when he expresses what to him is universal logic, he may simply be marching in step with the grammar of his culture. His language inevitably limits and colors his meaning, binding him even when he thinks himself most free.[27]

From thinking such as this, language-culture-area study, an interdisciplinary approach to language, evolved.

LINGUISTICS, PSYCHOLINGUISTICS, AND SEMANTICS

Linguistics, defined as "the study of language,"[28] and psycholinguistics, defined as "the study of linguistic units for their psychological relevance,"[29] suggest field theory approaches to English and, implicitly, to the study of literature. Linguistics seems to have had signal effects on the teaching of English, particularly on the teaching of grammar. Texts such as H. Sweet's *The Practical Study of Language* (1899), Otto Jespersen's *Language: Its Nature, Development, and Origin* (1922) and *The Philosophy of Grammar* (1924), Charles C. Fries's *American English Grammar* (1940), and J. Sturtevant's *Introduction to Linguistic Science* (1947) are examples of texts used in the study of linguistics; applications of linguistic concepts for preservice teachers of English are made in Margaret M. Bryant's *Modern English and Its Heritage* (1962), and direct use of linguistic concepts for the teaching of high school English can be found in parts of G. W. Stone's *Issues, Problems and Approaches in the Teaching of English* (1961),[30] Robert Pooley's *Teaching English Grammar* (1958), Paul Roberts' *Patterns of English* (1956) and *English Sentences* (1961), and Robert Anderson's and Thurston Womack's revised edition of *Processes in Writing*.[31]

All of these texts raise questions implicitly and explicitly about the value of studying language according to obsolete Latin nomenclature. Before considering the implications of linguistics for a field theory approach to literature, it is necessary to describe the linguistic frame of reference in the study of language. According to Joseph Greenberg:

> Linguistic science has as its traditional subject matter the signal systems as such. Its orientation tends to be social rather than individual, since the use of speech communication presupposes a group of intercommunicating people, a speech community.[32]

"Dialect," "regionalism," "ecology," "accuracy," and "system" are direct ramifications of linguistics in a field theory approach to the study of literature. "Realism" is a classification frequently ascribed to some literary works.[33] Without attention to the linguistics of Greenberg's "speech community" in the setting of a piece of literature, important aspects of the piece of literature may be overlooked.

Psycholinguistics, going one step beyond linguistics, asks: What psychological relevance exists in the fact that a given speech community interprets its signal system in a manner different from that of a neighboring community? Psychologists were prompted to raise this question on the basis of the same scientific concerns for field theory noted in the first chapter of this book. John Gardner, commenting on this question, has written:

> The revolution in modern physics has forced us to re-examine fundamental assumptions both in science and in our everyday thinking. No man can predict the ultimate consequences of this re-examination, but nothing seems more certain than that it will lead to a more intensive study of the psychology of perception and the psychology of language. For one of the most significant yields of the recent developments in physics has been a renewed awareness of the role of the observer.[34]

Gardner has shown that the "role of the observer" as a concept is not new, but that out of the studies of its use, particularly in communication, a whole new series of concepts were derived that interested psychologists, philosophers, mathematicians, and physical scientists in possibilities for further research. Unless English teachers are Gardner's "philosophers," he has overlooked them as being concerned with language; nor is Gardner the only linguistically oriented scientist to omit the English field from discussions of linguistic science. Granting that the goals and reference frame for linguistics differ from those of the "grammar" (writing, reading) sections of the English language arts, Gardner and others may be operating on a concept of language arts much like that of Mowrer,[35] who used five double-column pages to analyze, from a psycholinguistic viewpoint, the sentence, "Tom is thief." Much more than the "traditional" Latin nomenclature and diagraming were involved in Mowrer's analysis. Psychological, linguistic, symbolic, historical, and sociological factors (to mention a few) were all brought to bear on that "simple" sentence as an example of psycholinguistic communication. Time factors may prohibit such analysis in secondary school classrooms, or even in college courses in linguistics and related areas for prospective English teachers, but such time limitations raise again the question: What shall be the minimal concepts required for the accomplishment of English goals in modern education? Related to this question raised by linguistics is another: What taxonomic structure shall be used to establish goals for preservice teachers of English?

Integration of specialized contents seems to be one implicit answer, for Gardner, in describing the reasons for symposia on psycholinguistics, has pointed out:

> The descriptive linguists discussing phonemes, the communications engineers discussing binary digits, and the psychologists discussing linguistic responses seemed most of the time to be engaged in wholly separate conversations. Here and there one could find individuals whose training was sufficiently broad to participate in all three conversations, but the overlap was tenuous.[36]

In a sense, psycholinguistics became a field-like discipline because psychologists, communication engineers, and specialists in linguistics discovered that they were dealing with a common field, language. While each specialization, because of its narrowness, could contribute new information to its separate discipline, advances in a cognitive theory of language were recognized as needing an integrated approach.[37] Other specializations were seen to influence findings derived from psycholinguistics, for example, semantics.[38] A consideration of semantics, defined as "the study of techniques by which to accomplish purposes through the use of words,"[39] is crucial to a description of a field theory approach to literature.[40]

Using a psycholinguistic frame of reference, Sebeok[41] has analyzed whole texts of folklore on the basis of discourse analysis. Going beyond Mowrer's single-sentence analysis, he has hinted that prospective teachers of English might profit from some analysis of literature within a linguistic-psycholinguistic frame of reference—a frame of reference suggesting a field theory approach to literature.

Semantics has many definitions and somewhat specialized applications.[42] The focus on semantics here will be on those aspects that serve as coordinating "fields" for the study of language. Acknowledging the pervasive influence of men such as Alfred Korzybski (theory of general semantics) and Anatol Rapoport (mathematician-biologist) on the language–human relations factors in semantics, it is more important here to concentrate on anthropological linguists such as Edward Sapir, Benjamin Lee Whorf, and Bronislaw Malinowski who have provided coordinating fields for the study of language. Clyde Kluckhohn, from cultural anthropology, and Charles Ogden and I. A. Richards, from language-teaching, have also contributed to the semantic background for language-culture-area studies.

According to Robert Moore,[43] four to five centuries of background for semantics as a field may be found in the writings of John Locke, Jeremy Bentham, Samuel Taylor Coleridge, Richard Chenevix Trench (Archbishop Trench), Michel Bréal, C. K. Ogden, I. A. Richards, and Alfred Korzybski. The time span and social change represented by the writings of the above-named men has made for different "approaches" to the study of semantics. Yet they and their contemporaries had a common concern for the importance of word meanings, and they sought some tool or structure beyond the "grammar" books to make people aware of language and its pervasive influence in all human endeavors.

Michel Bréal's *Essai de Sémantique* (1897) is regarded by semantic scholars as the beginning of modern "scientific" semantics. Following Bréal's work, V. Welby's "significs" (1911) dealt with semantic topics without actually using the word "semantics." Welby urged that linguistic expression and interpretation be applied to all forms of human energy.[44] In 1923, Charles Ogden and Ivor A. Richards published *The Meaning of Meaning* and provided structures that are still current in the study of language. Moore has described the contribution of the book to semantics:

> They [Ogden and Richards] consider the power of words, definitions, metaphor, multiplicity of language functions, multiple meanings, etc. The purposes of the authors seem to be (1) to explain what "meaning" is, (2) to explain how meanings are conveyed, and (3) to outline methods of conveying meanings more accurately.[45]

It is the "method" aspect of the Ogden-Richards approach to semantics that has direct bearing on a field approach to literature.

Ogden and Richards refined their methods in later separate works. Ogden's *Basic English* and *Bentham's Theory of Fictions* along with Richards' *Philosophy of Rhetoric, Interpretation in Teaching*, and *How to Read a Page* were examples of such refinements. Richards' books for the study of foreign languages employed methods partially based on his semantic theories. Later sections of this chapter will deal with the Ogden-Richards methodology in more detail in connection with communication and literary criticism.

Language-culture-area studies recognize that proficiency with words alone is not sufficient to classify someone as "understanding" a foreign language. Semantic aspects of this truism pivot on the understanding of the words in the context of cultural values. Historical background for this coordinating "field" technique of language study has been summarized by Solon T. Kimball:

> The need to learn and record native languages posed a practical problem for anthropologists which they had to surmount in order to study the culture of native peoples. Boas and his student Sapir are recognized for their accomplishments in this early period. Subsequent scholars have refined and advanced the techniques until today linguistic analysis is on a scientific basis.
>
> The concern with language as a function of culture is a second major area. Its genesis may be correlated with the rise

in emphasis upon functional analysis as a method of cultural interpretation. Relationships were sought between the structure and meaning of language and other aspects of cultural behavior. Some of the descriptions of kinship systems illustrated vividly the interconnections. But understanding was also sought of the relation of languages to modes of action, systems of logic, values, and world view. Malinowski, Whorf, and Hoijer are representative of interest in this area. Their analyses have shown the relationships between language structure and thought processes and ultimately the connection with cultural forms.[46]

Sapir, exploring the linguistic aspects of cultural reality in the 1933 edition of the *Encyclopaedia of the Social Sciences,* wrote:

> Human beings do not live in the objective world alone, nor alone in the world of social activity as ordinarily understood, but are very much at the mercy of the particular language which has become the medium of expression for their society. It is quite an illusion to imagine that one adjusts to reality essentially without the use of language and that language is merely an incidental means of solving specific problems of communication or reflection. The fact of the matter is that the "real world" is to a large extent unconsciously built upon the language habits of the group. . . . We see and hear and otherwise experience very largely as we do because the language habits of our community predispose certain choices of interpretation.[47]

Kluckhohn, furthering his 1949 explorations in the necessity for studying culture-language as a whole, made the following observation in 1956:

> It seems likely that language both determines and is determined by the rest of culture. And there is small case for the view that reality itself is relative; rather, different languages tend "to punctuate and categorize reality in special ways." Yet we will do well to remember that language, in the cross-cultural as well as in other senses, is fetter to thought as well as its key. As Edward Sapir remarked, "To pass from one language to another is psychologically parallel to passing from one geometrical frame of reference to another."[48]

Kluckhohn's observation was not new; Shoemaker in 1943, discussing "anthropology and language," pointed out that Malinowski, George Herzog, Sapir, Margaret Mead, and others were focusing their research on the ways language circumscribed customs and behavior in primitive societies.[49] More recently the so-called Whorfian hypothesis, postulated on the basis of Benjamin L. Whorf's work with the Hopi Indians, has become the focal point for exploring language-teaching as well as one basis for metalinguistics. According to Robert Redfield and Milton Singer, the simplified Whorfian hypothesis holds that "the very categories of the language predisposed Hopi to think about the nature of the universe in ways different from the ways consistent with speaking English or Russian."[50]

Harry Hoijer, reporting on the background for a conference to explore the ramifications of the Whorfian hypothesis, gave the following historical sketch:

> The Conference which is reported was proposed originally by Robert Redfield.... It was Redfield's idea to bring together a small group of scholars, representative of linguistics, anthropology, psychology, philosophy, and other disciplines, who shared an interest in the problem of meaning and the relationship of language to other aspects of culture, and to have them discuss their own and others' efforts in this area of research. After some oral and written discussion of this project, Redfield and I drew up a preliminary statement of the objectives of such a conference, which may be summarized as follows.
>
> 1. To define, as clearly as possible, the problems raised by the attempt to interrelate language and other aspects of culture, particularly in reference to the hypothesis suggested in Benjamin L. Whorf's *Collected Papers on Metalinguistics* (Washington, D. C., 1952).
>
> 2. To review what has been done, and is being done, in the study and analysis of these problems.
>
> 3. To examine and discuss plans for future research, wherever possible in terms of particular projects and personnel, that may contribute to the solution of ethnolinguistic problems.
>
> 4. To provide, if possible, for the integration of the research of the scholars, whatever their academic discipline, who are working in the area.[51]

The full impact of linguistic research and hypotheses such as Whorf's on the teaching of languages is still being measured, but as a basis for language-culture-area studies the impact of these linguistic theories can be seen in publications such as UNESCO's *The Teaching of Modern Languages,* Henri Peyre's *The Need for Language Study in America Today,* and Roger Brown's *Words and Things.* These books have in common the language-culture-area "field" approach to the study of all languages.

Stuart Chase, a semanticist, has given an example of the cultural influence of language on "reality" and has expanded the implications of the Whorfian hypothesis in terms of metalinguistics:

> Thinking follows the tracks laid down in one's own language; these tracks will converge in certain phases of "reality," and completely bypass phases which may be explored in other languages. In English, for instance, we say, "look at that wave." But a wave in nature never occurs as a single phenomenon. In the Hopi language they say, "look at that slosh." The Hopi word, whose nearest equivalent in English is "slosh," gives a closer fit to the actual physics of wave motion, connoting movement in a mass. (This is only one of several tough matters in physics where Hopi does better than English.)
>
> Perhaps the majority of linguists today, though they are not prepared to follow Whorf all the way, do recognize the vital part which language plays in thought and culture. The study of *metalinguistics,* as they call it, is thus described by Trager and Smith: "Not only does it deal with *what* people talk about and *why,* but also considers *how* they use the linguistic system, and how they react to its use. This leads further to the consideration of how the linguistic system affects behavior, both conscious and unconscious, and the world-view, of the speaker. . . ." Contrasted with microlinguistics, which takes a long time to reach a unit as large as the sentence, the meta- or super-linguistics considers the "organization of sentences into discourse, and the relation of the discourse to the rest of the culture."[52]

The "relation of discourse to the rest of the culture" aspect of metalinguistics and language-culture-area studies suggests exciting developments in language.

The title of a recently founded publication, the *Journal of Verbal Learning and Verbal Behavior*, reveals the nexi between language and the behavior it triggers in the speaker and his audience. According to its statement of purpose, the *Journal* is "devoted to the study of human learning, psycholinguistics and other disciplines with emphasis on experimental and empirical studies." Articles published in the *Journal* might come under the general heading of metalinguistics, except that the category is too broad for accuracy. The experiments with language carried on by John Carroll and his colleagues at Harvard are typical of the *Journal's* content. In the July, 1962, issue, for example, Carroll and others reported their explorations of subject-response to a free-association test and concluded among other things that:

> A large component of what is referred to as commonality of response to the K-R stimulus list [a specified list of words used in other free-association experiments] is based upon responses to a relatively small subset of stimuli which can be identified behaviorally and which here are called opposite evoking stimuli (OES).[53]

Although this finding may mean little out of context, it has at least two implications for English-teaching: First, in support of the Whorfian hypothesis, it implies that linguistic boundaries are apparent even in the same language and that different behaviors are related to such boundaries, and second, it indicates that the mind uses an abbreviating process for memory based on a "key" symbol that, in turn, triggers a constellation of associations under proper stimulation. To discover such keys in the classroom would increase students' efficiency with language, and it is this abbreviating phenomenon of language that brings the novel into focus as symbol of culture.

COMMUNICATION

In times of crisis, man turns to reexamine the language in which he preserves and defines his values. As has been seen, this was true after World War I, during the depression of the 1930's, and after World War II. But American culture has been shifting gradually from dependence on the word alone to increasing use of and dependence on symbols of many kinds and for many purposes. Shoemaker, summarizing and extending Lynn White's extensive descriptions of shift from word to symbol in *Frontiers of Knowledge in the Study of Man,* has written:

> What are these changes of canon? One is the Canon of the Occident—being supplanted by the new *Canon of the Globe;* a second is the Canon of Logic and Language—being supplanted by the *Canon of the Symbol;* a third is the Canon of Rationality—being supplanted by the *Canon of the Unconscious;* the fourth is the Canon of Values, which is undergoing redefinition as the older hierarchy of values is being replaced with newer conceptions of *Spectrums of Values.*[54]

Susanne K. Langer made clear this shift to symbols in her attention to discursive and nondiscursive symbols[55] in *Philosophy in a New Key* in 1942. Lennox Grey also made it clear with his demonstration of the variety of research areas then contributing to understanding of the symbol—psychology, anthropology, political science, folklore, and others in his full-page chart in *What Communication Means Today.*[56]

Grey's insights, drawn almost two decades ago, are only now beginning to be explored in depth. Explaining why English teachers should be aware of the communication arts, Grey has written:

> English today is not a subject, as popular legend has sometimes had it, which any intelligent well-read person can teach skillfully simply because he had read, written, spoken and listened to English all his life, any more than a lifelong cook can forthwith teach the chemistry of foods—though it is a tremendous advantage to start with wide reading and good cooking. The teaching of English as a communication art calls for increasing breadth—which means *specialization in interrelationships*—and also calls for increasing expertness in different media and skills.[57]

In the article in which this statement appeared, Grey used a chart introducing the concept of "symbolic spectrum" to indicate the range of interrelationships involved in the application of communication ideas.

Using that chart, reproduced in Table B, students and teachers, Grey pointed out, can "consider the range from strictly denotative intent of scientific language through the connotative reaches of literary language."[58] Grey's scale serves as a formulation of literary criticism that provides an assortment of communication "tools" for evaluating literature.

TABLE B

← Symbolic Spectrum →

Arbitrary designation of symbolic scope or value	(s)	(s+)	(sy)	(sy+)	(SY)
Idiomatic designation	("mere sign")	("sign plus")	("simple symbol")	("symbol plus")	("Capital Symbol")
Example	a river	the river	Mississippi (Wabash)	Ol' Man River	River of Life
Context	(line on a map, denoting a river course)	(denoting the river near home, with some associations)	(symbolizing some epic or folk associations inescapable unless specifically restricted)	(literary personification)	(cosmic metaphor)

Science ←——Language of——→ Art

Contributors to the further development of the field of communication include Marshall McLuhan, who broadened it to include the newer electronic media, and Susanne Langer, whose *Feeling and Form* was made educationally and "communicationally" pertinent by Shoemaker. Discussion of the key concepts of these contributors to Grey's teaching prognosis of communication for teachers of English is central to a field theory approach to literature.

Marshall McLuhan, a teacher at the University of Toronto, in discussing historical aspects of mass media presented a problem readily recognizable from the earlier discussions in this book of quantum theory:

> What I am suggesting is that it is somewhat unrealistic to offer any merely external history of the media of communication, since their history in shaping the inner life of man and

> society has been and is today inseparable from their outer action. Moreover, today the boundaries between inner and outer effects of the media are confused.[59]

Discussing the impact of "form" on the individual, McLuhan presented a key concept of mass media, "simultaneity." Novels are one form of mass media, and the "simultaneity" concept is central to a field theory approach to them.

> An arch, a wall, a tower is as much a form of mass communication as is the press or Rockefeller Plaza. These shapes express a huge preference, an enormous bias in the patterns of our awareness as much as does a new rhythm in poetry or music. And the very pre-existence of such biases in our culture naturally acts to channel all existing experience. Of this fact we are inevitably aware today when the instantaneity of global communication with all previous cultures makes us sensitive to the patterns and bias of our own. To live in an age when global intercommunication is the very format of the most popular press and magazines is to experience that *simultaneous* awareness of many cultures and many ages which used to be the mark of the very few.[60] [Italics added.]

McLuhan suggested that the organism battered by multiple sensory impressions (external communications) selects (internal response) what it will respond to and that external communications might be likened to Darwin's process of natural selection. Those communications louder, stronger, or better "bred" might survive weaker ones. Ranging from Plato's utterances on communication through Joyce's ability to "swallow the newspaper art form" in *Ulysses*, McLuhan concluded that:

> Just as history begins with writing, so, in a sense, it ends now with television. Just as there was pre-history when there was no linear time sense, so there is post-history now when everything that ever was in the world becomes simultaneously present to our consciousness.
>
> Printing greatly increased the scope of historical awareness; telegraphy and television completed the process by making the past twenty-four millennia equally present. This is to say that the media themselves act directly toward shaping our most intimate self-consciousness. Without our having any ideas about them whatever, they still deeply affect our idea of past and present, of ourselves, and of our relations to others.[61]

One of Shoemaker's many contributions to broadening the field of communication consisted of making Susanne Langer's two symbolic modes operationally possible. These symbolic modes, discursive and nondiscursive,[62] are similar to the two-layered structures so common to field theory. Langer's implicit "fusion" of the two exists in each organism, as Shoemaker pointed out in his extrapolation of the "psychobiological bases"[63] underlying Langer's concept of "Youth . . . is all potentiality."[64] Using Langer's concept as center, Shoemaker charted the curricular utility of Langer's symbolic modes for communication.[65] The chart contained concentric circles to suggest the dynamism of the curricular process. Concepts such as "Time," "Space," and "Memory" are outer fringes within which arts and sciences are dichotomized to discursive-nondiscursive constructs, but always existing in the organism's totality, which on the chart is represented by "Youth is all potentiality."

Shoemaker suggested methods for broadening curricula along lines implied by his chart in his detailed explication of such topics as "space and virtual space" and "time and virtual time," as these concepts affect and are affected by the student in his learning environment. Based on the sifting and winnowing of Langer's abstractions, Shoemaker provided what might be called a taxonomy of curricular objectives for future communication programs. Breadth, flexibility, dynamism, and feedback are some of the familiar concepts explicit and implicit in Shoemaker's prognosis.

Marshall McLuhan has made explicit some of Shoemaker's implications with a worldwide vision. McLuhan's *The Gutenberg Galaxy* focuses attention immediately on "field" with this statement:

> *The Gutenberg Galaxy* develops a mosaic or field approach to its problems. Such a mosaic image of numerous data and quotations offers the only practical means of revealing causal operations in history.
>
> The alternative procedure would be to offer a series of views of fixed relationships in pictorial space. Thus the galaxy or constellations of events upon which the present study concentrates is itself a mosaic of perpetually interacting forms

> that have undergone kaleidoscopic transformation—particularly in our own time.[66]

Communication is McLuhan's pivot for exploration of "interacting forms," and he has maintained (with convincing evidence) that today society is "confronting an electric technology which would seem to render individualism obsolete and the corporate dependence mandatory."[67] The confrontation with electronics is almost a stereotype of Europe's confrontation with the printing press—one of the first devices of mass media. Citing reactions of historians, writers, and dramatists to the impact of the printing press, McLuhan has developed a body of evidence to show that unusually perceptive artists (Shakespeare, Pope, Donne) were aware of the "closure" effect of mass print, particularly the imagination-destroying progenitors of what is now called "the press."

Moving to scientists' perceptions of the influence of the press on scientific thought, McLuhan has used quotations from cultural anthropology, physics, psychology, sociology, biology, and mathematics to support his view of contemporary society's need for an awareness of a unity of forms, an acceptance of dynamic interrelation with openness and indeterminancy as characteristic of this "oneness."

In literature, McLuhan has cited evidence implying that the printing press may have been the culprit behind C. P. Snow's "two cultures":

> It is the division of sense and the separation of words from their functions that Pope decries exactly as does Shakespeare in *King Lear.* Art and science had been separated as visual quantification and homogenization penetrated to every domain and the mechanization of language and literature proceeded.[68]

Quoting extensively from Alexander Pope's *Dunciad,* McLuhan has made clear the vitiating quality of mechanized mass media:

> Print, with its uniformity, repeatability, and limitless extent, does give reincarnate life and fame to anything at all. The kind of limp life so conferred by dull heads upon dull themes formalistically penetrates all existence. Since readers are as vain as authors, they crave to view their own conglomerate visage and, therefore, demand the dullest wits to exert themselves in ever greater degree as the collective audience in-

creases. The "human interest" newspaper is the ultimate mode of this collective dynamic.[69]

Opposed to this mechanized "literature," McLuhan has suggested, are such innovations as T. S. Eliot's "objective correlative," Joyce's "stream of consciousness," and the involvement of painters with solipsistic themes—which, as in modern literature, seek to involve the audience in an active, imaginative participation. Such immediate involvement is related to field concepts—observer viewpoint, feedback, simultaneity, relativity, indeterminacy, positioning, and others. "Corporate dependence" and "individualism" are both parts of modern man's field of electronic technology; the concepts tend to be opposed, thereby increasing tensions in a civilized world, but as McLuhan has implied, they form a kind of unity similar to "day and night," "yin and yang," "good and bad"; they must be recognized as constants.

Up to this point, communication has been viewed as a body of content, as a discipline with broad implications for teaching. The consideration of communication as a teaching "field" demands specific examination of some coordinative statements about its materials, methods, and underlying philosophy. One perspective on communication as a coordinate teaching field was provided by Lennox Grey and Francis Shoemaker in their study of *General Education in Relation to Vocational Technical Education in the New York State Institutes of Applied Arts and Sciences*, made at the specific direction of New York State's Committee on Institute Curriculums, which blueprinted programs that are presently basic to vocational-technical institutes in the state. Using precepts of general education derived from research and conferences and the Committee's plans in 1946 to increase vocational-technical education for returning veterans, Grey and Shoemaker identified from research reports and conferences five groups of courses as general educational possibilities.[70] Each of the five groups identified was described according to the "basic ideas" that gave it an individual character but at the same time related it to other groups in the overall vocational-technical pattern. The basic ideas for communication, for example, were described as follows:

1. Communication is a two-way symbolic process.

2. Human community depends on communication through symbols in the family, the neighborhood, the region and throughout the world.
3. The variable interpretation of such symbols is the basis of much of our misunderstanding.
4. Symbols of various kinds reinforce one another in the communication of information, ideas, feelings, values.
5. Skill in the arts of communication is essential for the individual's development—for social competence, for intellectual growth, for personal resourcefulness.
6. New mediums and arts of mass communication are providing more of our common experience than print provides.
7. New instruments and arts of communication now for the first time make possible world community, as well as much larger and more tightly integrated local community units.[71]

These basic ideas sound modern in the present world of international tensions—fifteen years after their prophetic taxonomy for communication programs were listed. But Grey and Shoemaker went beyond the mere listing of philosophic truisms. In a section of their study entitled "Outline for Communication Skills," they described methods for helping students to understand, to absorb, to apply, and thus to "learn" in the truest sense of the word the "basic ideas" of communication. The outlines started with a "Basic Idea," moved to "Problems and Projects," followed by "Illustrations and Development" and ended with "Communications (Reading, Writing, Speaking, Listening) Laboratory."[72] In each of the seven basic ideas of communication, Grey and Shoemaker made explicit not only the methods by which skills and understandings in the communication process take place but also the relationship of these learnings to other aspects of the vocational-technical institute programs. In essence the Grey-Shoemaker explication described *sans* name the technique of a field approach to communication that combines a philosophic and goal-based structure with a teacher-critic method to develop in students a technique for exploring their inner and outer worlds.

Shoemaker, discussing communication courses and humanities in the framework of general education in 1949, pointed out the unique identification of each of the disciplines and their common goal:

We have found, however, a common center in communica-

> tion courses in the biological-psychological-anthropological idea of communication as the process of self-realization in expressive interaction with society.
>
> We have detailed a comparable idea of aesthetic experience as unifying center for humanities courses dealing with literature, art, music, and philosophy. Major distinctions between the most advanced examples of both kinds of courses are two: (1) communication courses take specific responsibility for developing communication skills in varied mediums, while humanities courses focus on ideas and values; (2) communication courses tend to work with contemporary materials of local community life, while humanities courses tend to deal with more complex historical symbols. It seems important that further development of these two phases of general education programs be guided by consideration of their distinctive characteristics and their common goal.[73]

For the 1940's and a good part of the 1950's, modern communication inquiry became an organizing center for many high school, junior college, and college courses. Examination of an issue of *College Composition and Communication* (an affiliate of the NCTE) for the middle 1950's (such as the issue devoted to the annual Conference on College Composition and Communication) reveals articles dealing with linguistics, mass media, communication skills, and similar communication topics.[74] While in the 1963 issues of the *Journal of the Conferences on College Composition and Communication*, communication inquiry has not been completely abandoned, the table of contents shows a narrowing and segmentation of the communication area. Articles entitled "The Shame of Freshman English," "The Multiple Approach to Meaning," "The Phoneme of Content," "Abstract and Concrete Sentences," and "On Not Fracturing Errors" are typical of those published in the *Journal* in 1963.

The *Journal's* focus on individual "trees" may help the concern for the kind of "forest" implied by McLuhan in *The Gutenberg Galaxy*, but with McLuhan's intersect of "electronic technology," which in turn is based on communications research, it may be that the *Journal* has overspecialized. In a time when machines communicate with machines, when machines teach three-year-olds how to read, when machines write television plays and poetry (although the quality of their creations poses no threat as yet to human authors), when communications research is a concern of every discipline, teachers may perhaps properly question the narrowness of focus presently characteristic of influential spokesmen within the ranks of the National Council of Teachers of English.

Opposed to such specialization, Lennox Grey almost a decade ago proposed an "ecology of communication"[75] that recommended interdisciplinary approaches to this core tool of all disciplines.

Grey's proposal was prompted by reports made by the Interdivisional Seminar Staff on the Study of Communication and the Communication Arts at Teachers College in November, 1955. Staff members, who were also authors of the reports, included anthropologists, psychologists, mathematicians, scientists, and sociologists as well as specialists in various aspects of the communication arts. After studying their reports, Grey raised a question that is central to the education of preservice teachers of English:

> So we come to our decisive question: Can we, from the nexus points suggested by the articles in this issue and from practical experience of one department reaching out to many fields, develop a comprehensive yet economically focused interdivisional "ecology of communication" which will be intelligible to our students and their students, supported at every key point by significant educational research?[76]

In partial answer to Grey's question, Francis Shoemaker and Louis Forsdale pointed out in 1960 that eighteen selected campuses were striving for what Grey might call an "ecology of communication." Among these eighteen were the Massachusetts Institute of Technology, the Air Force Academy, the United States Military Academy at West Point, and the University of Miami—all attempting to broaden students' learning through communication supported "at every key point" by significant research.[77]

In connection with communication as a coordinate field, it is important to recognize two current phenomena in the teaching of English that may be considered tangential to communication but have communication objectives of accuracy, perception, and efficiency in the use of language. The first of these phenomena is the increase in the use of "casebooks" to teach freshman English at many colleges. Casebooks concentrate on a single literary work by presenting the work in its entirety, then a "field" of critical perceptions about the work, and finally suggestions for extending these critical perceptions through student papers and further readings. Kenneth S. Lynn, in *Huck Finn: Texts, Sources and Criticism*,[78] for example, presents the complete text of Clemens' work, follows it with critical essays by William Dean Howells, Van Wyck Brooks, Bernard DeVoto, Lionel Trilling, and others, and then makes suggestions for student papers and for further reading.[79] Depth concentration on a single literary work, many "observer viewpoints" for that concentrated experience, and the "indeterminancy" of the conclusions (as implied by further readings and papers on enigmatic passages) suggest the kind of openness and dynamism noted by McLuhan and others in describing the communication field.

The second phenomenon is the increase in the number of methods texts for teaching English, some of which consider the teaching problems concerned with mass media and some of which ignore them. Those methods texts that ignore the mass media tacitly support the recommendation of the Commission on English on narrowing English-teaching efforts to "language, literature, and composition." Among such texts are Albert Kitzhaber's *Themes, Theories and Therapy: The Teaching of Writing in College* (1963), which focuses strictly on the writing component of the language arts, J. N. Hook's revised edition of *The Teaching of High School English* (1962), which ignores the mass media, Edwin R. Sauer's *English in the Secondary School* (1961), which except for "semantics" also ignores mass media. Representing a kind of "middle ground" are texts such as M. Jerry Weiss's *An English Teacher's Reader* (1962), which devotes one section to mass media with an effective communication philosophy, John S. Lewis's and Jean C. Fisk's *Teaching English 7-12* (1963), Abraham Bernstein's *Teaching English in High School* (1962), and *Teaching Language and Literature* (1961), by Walter Loban, Margaret Ryan, and James Squire, which has both a chapter and a section devoted to communication media. Textbooks cognizant of the teaching problems with mass media in today's classroom include William Boutwell's *Using Mass Media in the Schools* (1962), a series of teacher-written articles and essays on handling specific aspects of communication media in the classroom, Neil Postman's *Television and the Teaching of English* (1961), a direct focus on television and its implications for teaching, Wayne Thompson's *Fundamentals of Communication* (1957), and Charles Kegel's and Martin Stevens' *Communication Principles and Practices* (1959), which attempts to combine "traditional" perceptions of English (Latin nomenclature, rubrics) with analyses of various forms of mass media.

Compared to those made by specialists in symbolic logic, psycholinguistics, and cybernetics, the pronouncements on communication made by specialists in English grossly understate its implications. Teachers of English must begin to broaden their reading to include journals from other disciplines such as *American Psychologist* and *Scientific American* to gauge the full range of communication as a coordinate field. Then, more English texts may in the future devote the attention to communication that is necessary in this era of electronic technology.

FOUR

EXTENSIONS OF FIELD CONCEPTS IN THE STUDY OF LITERATURE

In field theory in the sciences and in its extensions in the broadened "fields" of English, wide use is made of "symbol" as a concept. In physics, chemistry, and mathematics, the language of symbols is well known. In English, particularly in the linguistics and psycholinguistics of language-culture-area studies, the letters and words on a page are recognized as graphic symbols. In the coordinative field of communication, problems are posed by the ubiquitous symbol concept with its wide horizons circumscribed only by a time-space field. Seeking to make the symbol concept a useful tool for communication, Lennox Grey has identified three problems related to the use of the symbol by those aspiring to use the communication arts in teaching:

> One is *circumference*—how much territory to take in. This is the problem which first excites most students of the field as they think of concentric circles of communication expanding out from the local community through regional, nationwide, and worldwide communities.
>
> The second key problem is *sectoring*—how to cut this cosmic circle into manageable pie-chart segments that will show clearly and in proportion the areas of communication explored (and not yet explored) by workers in anthropology, political science, sociology, psychology, biological science,

physical science, history, geography, philosophy, art, music, language and literature, and others.

The third key problem is *center*—how to define or characterize the center where all expanding circles take their start and where all the segments and radii come to focus. Experts in many aspects of communication seem to be fairly well agreed that this center is the *symbol* or the symbolic process in man which enables him to take the impressions of gross experience, abbreviate them into manageable signs or symbols—verbal, pictorial, structural, gestural, rhythmical, tonal—and carry on communication with other men through them.[1]

It is the "abbreviation" characteristic of the symbol as a concept that has become so important in this time. From teaching machines to the novel as the microcosm of a cultural macrocosm, the abbreviation factor of the symbol is basic to a field theory approach to literature. Grey recognized the importance of this abbreviating quality when in 1944 he described the growth of humanities courses in American colleges:

> Fifty and more Humanities courses have been established since 1931 in American Colleges, to study notable works of world literature and of the other arts not as monuments but as means or symbols for communicating human culture.[2]

The process of symbolization, as Shoemaker has pointed out, tends to be individually different. From a teaching perspective, Shoemaker's description of the symbolic process is very important, for it suggests an increase in tension and awareness on the part of the organism that corresponds to psychological descriptions of learning:

> The symbolic process involves both *impressive* and *expressive* experiences for both the communicator and his audience. In an initial moment or period of impression, the individual becomes aware of an idea, value, or event whose meaning disturbs his current pattern of values. At the same time his organic impulse toward unity demands that he integrate the new experience into his pattern of alternatives. The process of repatterning his self occasions a heightened tension which we may describe as an emotional-intellectual response of the whole organism.[3]

Alfred Schutz, referring to the work of Ernst Cassirer, has

described an organism's specific concern with symbols as distinguished from signs and signals:

> Ernst Cassirer distinguishes signs, which are operators and part of the physical world of being, from signals, which are designators and part of the human world of meaning. The former, even when understood and used as signals, have, nevertheless, a sort of physical or substantial being, whereas symbols have only functional value. Signs or signals are related to the thing to which they refer in a fixed and unique way, whereas the human symbol is not rigid and inflexible, but mobile.[4]

"Mobile" in the above quotation is basic to a field theory approach to literature, and Robert Hartman, paraphrasing Cassirer, has pointed out the "unification" theme implied by "mobile":

> That primary fusion in the symbolic, this *primacy of symbolic* function, is the secret of all symbolic forms and all spiritual activity. There is no Outside or Inside here, no Before or After, nothing Active or Passive. Here we have a union of elements, which did not have to be constructed, but was a primary meaningful whole which belongs only to itself and interprets itself alone.[5]

"Meaningful whole," as it may apply to goals for high school students studying literature, and the novel as "cultural symbol" have been described by Shoemaker:

> The goal is to provide a sufficiently simple pattern of materials for students to observe the direction of change in the society. The goal is to make it easier to observe the growth-patterns of individual characters seen in their total context rather than in misleading excerpts.[6]

An example of "patterns in totality," according to Shoemaker, is contained in the "composite man" developed by George R. Stewart in his novel, *Storm.* "Composite man," in addition to other attributes, is:

> ... fearless because he is confident, in his flexibility, that he can meet any emergency. "The readiness is all," he says, quoting Hamlet. He therefore turns all his efforts to providing opportunity for increasing numbers of people to control part of their environment.... Students may see that in

such a life there can be no part that is ever settled "once and for all," to repeat this vicious cliché.[7]

In Shoemaker's "composite man" the abbreviating function of symbolic processes is evident. Teachers preparing to deal with broadened curricular English fields need to keep in mind the levels of perspective students bring to the classroom in their experiences with symbols. They need to remind themselves of a group of French writers labeled "symbolists,"[8] who did much to structure the ambiguity of much "symbolic" writing, and to remind themselves that Baudelaire's dictum, "Don't state—render," is operative in symbolic criticism today. They need finally to keep in mind that symbolism has a long history in literature and that in American society, according to Bradford Booth, World War I is a time-space focal point for "current" symbolism:

> One peak of symbolic writing centers around World War I. Before, during, and shortly after World War I such symbolic novels as the following appeared: Mann's *Death in Venice,* Joyce's *Dubliners,* Proust's first volume of *Remembrance of Things Past,* Mann's *The Magic Mountain.* Other works in the same symbolic vein included Joyce's *Ulysses,* Kafka's *The Trial,* Lawrence's *The Plumed Serpent,* Woolf's *To the Lighthouse,* Faulkner's, *The Sound and the Fury* and a kind of symbolic summit, *Finnegans Wake.*[9]

Study of the books mentioned by Booth is part of the background of many prospective English teachers, particularly those classified as English "majors." Booth has pointed out that the literary symbol is still another level of the symbol that the teacher-critic who aspires to deal with broadened curricular English fields must know. Quoting William York Tindall, Booth has written:

> "Conrad's vision," he [Tindall] tells us, "though no less symbolist than *A Portrait of the Artist,* differs from it in structure. In Joyce's book, narrative attended by images that enlarge it, is central; in Conrad's book, narrative and subordinate details are centered in image. Tied to narrative Joyce's image develops thematically in time, whereas Conrad's organization, more nearly static, is spatial in effect." The third type is represented by the work of Henry Green, who has won T. S. Eliot's praise. Green's *Party Going* seems centered in the symbol of the railroad station. But what at first appears

> centralized is later seen to be "a system of almost equal elements, cohering not by subordination to a great image or a narrative but by glancing reflections" or refractions. Green called his novel a "conspiracy of insinuations." Tindall quotes Yeats in "The Symbolism of Poetry" admiring the way a poem "flickers with the light of many symbols." The metaphor . . . is not without relevance to the over-all techniques employed by this important group of novelists.[10]

It is this "flickering" aspect of "symbol as center" that recalls Murphy's "becoming" and Wiener's "dynamism" of field theory in the sciences. "Image," as used by Tindall, is related to John Ciardi's "meaning in motion":

> Basically, a symbol is *something that stands for something else*. A traffic light is a fixed symbol: it uses three different colors to stand for three different commands. A dollar bill is also a symbol, but though it seems a fixed and clear symbol, it stands for a theory of wealth and of money-exchange that economists do not yet pretend wholly to understand. One can see, therefore, that even very simple symbols, upon careful reflection, tend to represent "areas of meaning in motion" rather than static equivalents. It follows that symbolism should offer a natural sort of language to the poet, interested as he must be to keep his "meaning" in motion.[11]

Still another level of criticism necessary for teachers in a broadened curricular English program has been described by Dorothy Sayers, who identifies two kinds of symbols: the "conventional" and the "natural."[12]

"Conventional," for Sayers, means the usual something for something else, but the arbitrary nature of the symbolic meaning is agreed upon by people using it. The letter *x*, for example, may represent an unknown in mathematics, a cluck and hiss in the alphabet, and other things. "Natural" symbols, by their nature, according to Sayers, image a greater reality of which the symbol itself is an image. An arch, for example, maintaining itself by a balance of opposing strains, is a natural symbol of that stability in tension by which the whole universe maintains itself.

Other writers give still other definitions of the symbol (Kenneth Burke, for example, uses "dynamic symbol"[13] almost synonymously with Sayer's natural symbol), and discussions of symbolism can be found in almost every discipline. Some idea of the range involved in the use of the symbol as a concept has been suggested by Wellek and Warren:

> It [symbol] appears as a term in logic, in mathematics, in semantics and semiotics and epistemology; it has also had a long history in the worlds of theology ("symbol" is one synonym for "creed"), of liturgy, of the fine arts and poetry.[14]

In addition to its wide use in English, the symbol as a concept is common to all aspects of formal, i.e., programmed experiences in education. Robert Ulich has described the international aspect of symbols:

> According to modern English dictionaries "symbol" is "that which suggests something else by means of relationship," or "a visible sign of something invisible." Consequently, it could apply to a picture, a national flag, the Christian cross, and Hitler's *Hakencruz.* We have "philosophy of symbolic forms" as we have various forms of "symbolism" in the fine arts and an enormous content of symbolic suggestion in modern propaganda and advertising.[15]

It is the widespread application and commonality of the symbol concept that makes it such a useful integrative tool for teachers. Grey's identification of the need for "sectoring" the "symbol-force" that shapes a field suggests that an area of symbolism that has direct application to a field theory approach to literature, namely, literary criticism, might be "sectored" and examined.

LITERARY CRITICISM

Literary criticism, Northrop Frye has suggested, has an overarching "fieldness" to it that includes all literature. In four important essays, he has attempted to describe critical modes—historical, ethical, archetypal, and rhetorical—and to discover a "comprehensive view of criticism."[16] To synthesize Frye's views would be presumptuous; they are too closely reasoned, and it would do violence to his critical scheme to quote him out of context. It does seem, however, that "form" as used by Frye has many of the elements of "field." This "fieldness" of Frye's approach is revealed in such passages as the following:

> The book attacks no methods of criticism, once that subject has been defined: what it attacks is the barrier between methods. These barriers tend to make the critic confine himself to a single method of criticism, which is unnecessary, and they tend to make him establish his primary contacts, not with other critics, but with subjects outside of criticism.[17]

In this statement Frye implies a "oneness" and a "wholeness" characteristic of the field concept. Frye is particularly concerned with symbols, as can be seen in his second essay, entitled "Ethical Criticism: Theory of Symbols."[18] Using the "symbol as archetype," Frye has suggested that it has an abbreviating effect that, coupled with the "theory of mythos," tends to be employed consciously or subconsciously in much modern literature, such as Joyce's *Ulysses:*

> The culture of the past is not only the memory of mankind, but our own buried life, and study of it leads to a recognition scene, a discovery in which we see, not our past lives, but the total cultural form of our present life. It is not only the poet but his reader who is subject to the obligation to "make it new."[19]

Frye's view is thus related to "observer viewpoint," McLuhan's "do-it-yourself literature," and Shoemaker's "Youth is all potentiality."

All prospective English teachers, somewhere in their program of courses required for certification, deal with literary criticism. Sometimes the method of this criticism will be implied and a function of a particular professor's perceptions. More often, the method will be identified as "historical," "New Critical," or "psychological," but always there will be some particular pattern for examining literature. A survey of some of these methods of criticism is necessary in order to establish a frame of reference for viewing a field theory method of literary criticism. Arbitrary and eclectic as the selection of the methods described has been, the survey reveals that there are as many literary critical methods as there are definitions of the symbol. Yet each approach to literary criticism has a degree of "fieldness."

The discussion of Frye's "archetypal mythos" as an attempt to define the boundaries of literary criticism introduces a problem critics have wrestled with in every historical era, namely, what criteria can be used to distinguish literature from a nebulous something else? Frye's solution has been to make literary criticism the field and "literature" one aspect of that field. Frye, wisely, has merely implied definitions of "literature"—"wisely" because what constitutes the "field" of literature is as arbitrary today with mass media and the "literature" of the film as it was when Thomas De Quincey was trying to "sector" and "center" the concept. Literature, according to De Quincey, was "everything printed in a book,"[20] and literary criticism was some method of judging, classifying, defining, or describing written and oral materials.[21] De Quincey did take exception to the restrictive aspects of "printed in a book" in pointing out that sermons from the pulpit and Shakespearean plays were literature long before they were bound for posterity. "Sectoring" the field, De Quincy classified two kinds of literature: "literature of knowledge" and "literature of power." Literature of power was further defined as containing topics of "general and common interest to man."[22] Written or oral, literature of power ought to be, according to De Quincey, the focus of literary scholarship. Cookbooks contain "literature of knowledge"; they add to one's information about cooking but do not supply the "general and common interest of man" contained in the "literature of power." De Quincey was not the first nor the last critic to employ the literary Aristotelian dichotomy for purposes of specialized concentration and analysis. De Quincey's critical writings reveal a pristine two-layered view of literature very much like the early two-layered view of phenomena in the sciences.

One hundred years after De Quincey's time, the dichotomous scheme is still evident in the attempt of Wellek and Warren to distinguish between literature and literary study—"one is creative, an art; the other, if not precisely a science, is a species of knowledge or of learning."[23] Literature as an art does not lend itself to study, Wellek and Warren have said, because the method suggested by proponents of the "literature-as-an-art school" involves a concept of "second creation." Second creation as a method of studying literature demands that the student redo, sometimes in another literary form, the piece of literature being studied. The second creation allegedly helps the student to "understand" literary forms, but, Wellek and Warren have maintained, such "understanding" is suspect because "individualism" is involved; furthermore, the second creation is "usually inferior."[24] Supporters of the "second creation" method say that literature cannot be "studied" at all; "we can only read, enjoy and appreciate it."[25]

Wellek and Warren have disagreed with the allegation that literature cannot be studied. They have said that there are essences in literature (as distinguished from their concept of "non-literature") that make Shakespeare, for example, "Shakespearean"—a unique quality possessed by no other person but Shakespeare. The biological concept of genotype-phenotype has implications for the "essence" concept described by Wellek and Warren—some unidentified but inherent irrational element that determines the unique properties of a given phenomenon. From their observations of this essence, Wellek and Warren have approached a field theory concept of what they describe as literature:

> All these distinctions between literature and non-literature which we have discussed—personal expression [second creation], realization and exploitation of the medium, lack of practical purpose, and, of course fictionality—are restatements, within a framework of semantic analysis, of age-old aesthetic terms such as "unity in variety," "disinterested contemplation," "aesthetic distance," "framing," "invention," and "imitation." Each of them describes one aspect of the literary work, one characteristic feature of its semantic directions. None is itself satisfactory. At least one result should emerge: a literary work of art is not a simple object but rather a highly complex organization of a stratified character with multiple meanings and relationships.[26]

Wellek and Warren have set up a taxonomy of literary criticism based on what they perceive to be the "function of literature."[27] Using extensive documentation, they have described some of the ways that literature is studied at colleges and universities in the United States.[28] Of the many conclusions possible from a detailed reading of *Theory of Literature,* at least three seem useful as structures for literary criticism: First, no one approach to the study of literature will provide the necessary depth required of teachers of literature in contemporary society;[29] second, no matter what series of approaches are used to study literature, a basic frame of reference for the study will involve "structure" and "materials" as a point of departure;[30] finally, literary study in today's world "must receive stimulation . . . from modern criticism and contemporary literature—from participation in literature as a living institution."[31]

The necessity for "participation" (Frye's "make it new") seems implicit in Howard Mumford Jones's assignment of literature's role in today's society:

> Literature takes nothing less than the universe for its province, inasmuch as it may deal with human beings, it may deal with animals, it may deal with nature, it may deal with any branch of learning and it may deal with God.[32]

Although acknowledging the breadth of literary themes, Jones has pointed out that the values in the study of literature are seemingly confined to the academic world:

> But that literary scholarship can still illumine human motives, enrich human enjoyment, develop sensitivity to beauty, and increase in some degree the wisdom of readers by revealing depth and variety in literary masterpieces—all this seems clearer even though these revelations are presently confined in the main to a minority of the population and to the academic world.[33]

Jones's statement suggests the need to broaden "literary scholarship" and perhaps to develop methods for studying literature from broader perspectives. Broad perspectives, according to Shoemaker, can be traced back to Plato, who considered works of art in their cultural contexts.[34] Just as Aristotelian precepts for literary criticism can be traced down through time so, too, can Platonic concerns for contextual relations in literary criticism. From the concepts of wholeness and interrelatedness in the trivium and quadrivium through Dante's fusion of knowledge from the pagan-Christian world to John Donne's "No man is an island" and the holistic views of Blake and Coleridge and others in the eighteenth century, there is a pattern of development that encourages organic perceptions—seeing the work as a totality—for the study of literature.

It is not surprising, therefore, to find twentieth-century authors concerned with "field-like" approaches to literature, using the work of earlier writers to illustrate unified methods for studying current literature. Blake's influence, for example, is widespread. The quatrain quoted below is alleged to have shaped the thinking of a range of writers and philosophers from Joyce[35] to Barrett.[36] It is closely related to Huxley's "one and many"[37] and the Tennyson-Whitman theme of macrocosm in microcosm:

> To see the World in a Grain of Sand
> And a Heaven in a Wild Flower,
> Hold infinity in the palm of your hand
> An Eternity in an hour.

L. A. Strong, in extending the "fieldness" of literary criticism, has described the influence of the Blake quatrain on James Joyce:

> This credo, the attempt to see the universe in the microcosm, sang happily in the ears of the writer who took Dublin as the type and figure of the world, and who, by concentration on its particular features, was to be made free of all the world had.[38]

Joyce is supposed to have tried to provide a gestalt, a totality of experience, for readers. Tindall, for example, using the "method" of "individual authority" has pointed out that in *Finnegans Wake* "the key is an acceptance of multiplexity. 'Whirled without aimed.' A cycle of birth, life, death-rebirth 'polarised for reunion by the symphysis of their antipathies.' "[39]

The reader's acceptance of "multiplexity" in approaching *Finnegans Wake* is in his reliance on Tindall's "authority" or "reputation" as a critic. According to Jacques Barzun, the reader learns little about Tindall's method but admires the critic for his "talent and tact."[40] Yet the "fieldness" implied by Tindall's "multiplexity" along with his urging of "wholeness" in viewing literature provide a yardstick—a taxonomy—for sectoring the field of literature. According to I. A. Richards, Samuel Taylor Coleridge's concept of "simultaneity"[41] also provides taxonomic levels of criticism. Coleridge wrote:

> One man's consciousness extends only to the pleasant or un-

> pleasant sensations caused in him by external impressions; another enlarges his inner sense to a consciousness of forms and quantity; a third in addition to the image is conscious of the conception of the notion of the thing; a fourth attains to a notion of his notions—he reflects on his own reflections; and thus we may say without impropriety that the one possesses more or less inner sense than the other.[42]

Auguring Tindall's "multiplexity," was Coleridge's statement that "Imagination . . . together with the power of reducing multitude into unity of effect"[43] is necessary to produce the total feeling of a poem. Coleridge was a literary ancestor of those twentieth-century critics who are concerned with totality in literary criticism.

The concern for totality is related to the ever-widening geographical focus of American literary criticism. During the colonial period and perhaps up through the Civil War, critics were concerned with "local color" in literature, i.e., the skill with which an author could describe or portray the Creole culture in New Orleans, life on the Erie canal, or the folklore of the lower Hudson River Valley, such as in Washington Irving's "Legend of Sleepy Hollow." Through the critical essays of John Crowe Ransom and others, the studies of "regionalism" widened the lenses of American literary criticism to sections of the country, such as New England, the Far West, and the South, as seen in novels like William Faulkner's *Intruder in the Dust.* As useful as these broader applications of local color are, they are somewhat limiting in today's world of swift communication, global ideas, and "best sellers."

Marshall McLuhan has described some of the new dimensions in mass media, communication, and literature:

> The first phase of the electronic revolution produced the headline among many other language changes . . . Edgar Allan Poe made the first imaginative response to this new medium. I think this is a key point for all of us in the field of English, since it concerns the meaning of the media for the teaching of English. I think Mr. Edgar Allan Poe has a lot to say to us because he invented simultaneously two new techniques of communication that were previously unknown in literature, or almost unknown—the symbolist poem and the detective story. Now the very peculiar property of these

> two forms is that the audience is expected to be co-author, co-creator. You are not given a completely processed package. . . . You are given a series of clues, and a series of parts with instructions, hints, and suggestions and the general over-all instruction, "Do it yourself."[44]

Applying the "do-it-yourself" concept to more modern times and the field of poetry, he has commented:

> Mr. Eliot constantly annoys people who ask him, "Did you, when you wrote this line in Sweeny," or some other poem, "did you mean so and so?" And Mr. Eliot always says, "Well, I must have, if that's what you got." This seems utterly baffling and unreasonable to the ordinary inquirer, but it is part of this basic attitude of "Do it yourself, you are the poet, too."[45]

There is of course a great audience for didactic critics—people who still want the "package of meaning" neatly tied and presented. McLuhan has also attempted to show the literary import of literature widened through mass media:

> This matter of what Toynbee calls challenge and response between language arts and the developing technology of the West is a totally unlooked at field; but you cannot study contemporary literature without becoming very much aware of this as a fact. The use of movies, of newspaper technique and many other media by Eliot, Joyce, and Pound is very well known.[46]

Tacitly granting the importance of mass media in newer concepts of literature, and even the important contributions to literary criticism a communication approach can make, Wallace Stegner has still maintained that:

> Art is the record of man acting, man as aware of experience; and though scientific discovery may well modify it by modifying man himself, it seems likely to affect only the forms, never the essence. As Albert Camus has said, in art "a profound thought is in a constant state of becoming. It adopts the experience of life and assumes its shape."[47]

Stegner's "essence" is similar to Frye's "form," as Frye uses it to delimit boundaries of literary criticism. Just as mathematics has it laws, e.g., commutative, associative, distributive, so has literary criticism. Once the law is expressed, the literature follows a pattern dictated by the law. In mathematics a changes depending on the law: commutative $a + b = a$, $ab = ba$; associative $a + (b + c) = (a + b) + c$, $a\,(bc) = (ab)\,c$. In literary criticism, time, place, and circumstance may change, but if the form is a hero myth, then Joyce's *Ulysses* will share with literature of the hero myth hundreds of years hence a form recorded by Homer. Defined in this way, "form" can exist in a pure state, just as mathematical models can, and, according to Frye, literary criticism can combine both "practical" and "pure" study. Frye has been quick to point out that these similarities between mathematics and his perception of literary criticism do not make the latter a science, but they suggest a "scientific" method for use in literary criticism.

But Stegner, commenting on the differences between scientific and artistic methods for literary criticism, has stated that:

> When a science and an art accost the same materials, the same apparent problems, it becomes very clear that they ask different kinds of questions. Examine a piece of literature in the light of communications theory; pose it as a model communication system, strive for the equation that will express its entropy, get all the reluctant variables under control and measure the intellectual and emotional output against the intellectual and emotional input: you may have demonstrated something, even something important, about something, but not about literature as an art. For it is the essence of art that it is different things to different people. Within certain fluid boundaries of general meaning a writer is, as Robert Frost has said, entitled to anything a reader can find in him.[48]

Stegner's citing Frost and McLuhan's citing Eliot with exactly the same implication suggests that at least their perceptions of literary criticism tend to lead to a common end. The work of both men has implications for programs of prospective English teachers: First, a wider range and greater depth will be necessary for programs of future teachers of English; second, and even more fundamental, structures and processes different in concept from "packaged meanings" must form the basis for future approaches to literary criticism. These two ideas suggest the outlines of the field of the teacher-critic.

Lewis Leary, has provided a perspective for the teacher-critic "field" in commenting on Jacques Barzun's essay on the "Scholar-Critic":

> Just as there is no longer reason for invidious distinction between the scholar and the critic, so there is also no reason to distinguish between the scholar-critic and the teacher. Whether the classroom-audience is made up of readers of a coterie magazine, graduates in a seminar, or a group of tenth graders, the task is the same: to communicate something which he knows and about which he is enthusiastic to an audience which does not know or properly appreciate. The enterprise is trifurcate: to discover as a scholar, to analyze as critic, and to communicate as teacher. No one of these activities is effective without the qualifying support of each of the other two.[49]

Leary has used "scholarship" along with other concepts to demonstrate how the teacher-critic fulfills his "trifurcate" duties. Leary's "scholarship" concept is related to "field," especially as it refers to the teaching of literature:

> For literature is so richly diverse that it submits finally to no party line, and scholarship is so various that it belongs to everyone with will intelligently to pursue it. What emphasis each places on that part of him which is scholar, or critic, or teacher will differ greatly as do the physical intellectual and emotional qualities which make men, who are so much alike, each so very different. . . . He [the scholar] may investigate historical background or biographical detail, be Freudian, Marxian, or just his own quizzical self; he may be intrigued by linguistics, which is the history of mankind; he may be concerned with structural analysis or the quest for mythic archetypes; or he may simply test in classroom or study the findings of other men.[50]

Leary has suggested that prospective teachers have the critical backgrounds for "linguistic," "historical," "biographical," "Freudian," and "Marxian" scholarship, that teachers know how to "test in classrooms the findings of others," and that there is some method that distinguishes each kind of scholarship. Leary is correct, although whether or not the prospective teacher recognizes that a given method is being used in his required courses is sometimes a discriminating test of the tyro's research skills.

Some literature courses in the backgrounds of prospective

English teachers do identify methods for studying literature. Q. D. Leavis, for example, dissatisfied with her interpretation of critical and scholarly approaches to literature, described an "anthropological method":

> I soon found myself committed to a method of investigation which I prefer to describe as "anthropological." It consisted of examining all the material that seemed to bear on this question [best sellers] in an unbiased but inquisitive frame of mind and concentrating on registering shifts of tastes and changes in cultural background, allowing such conclusions as I arrived at to emerge simply by comparison and contrast and analysis.[51]

Leavis' registering shifts in taste by comparison, contrast, and analysis suggests that her ability to recognize "shifts" developed perhaps from insights evolved through her study of literature. Students with her background might arrive at the same insights provided that they possessed her intellectual equipment. But what happens when her students' interpretations differ from hers? Possible answers to the question can be found in Leary's truism that "literature submits to no party line" and in David Daiches' concern for method:

> There is no single "right" method of handling literary problems, no single approach to works of literary art that will yield all the significant truths about them.
>
> Art is greater than its interpreters, and it should be clear from the preceding pages that not even the greatest critic has been able to pin down all its kinds of significance and values. All criticism is tentative, partial, oblique. This is not by any means to say that there are no standards of value, that we must fall back on personal taste, or vague impressionism or mere gush. We do, however, mean that no critical statement about a work of literary art can be a complete statement of what is and whether or not it is good. On the level of critical theory, it may be possible to construct a set of valid general principles; as far as practical criticism is concerned—criticism designed to demonstrate the nature and quality of a work and so to increase understanding and appreciation—it must always be fragmentary, indirect, approximate. It can never be a complete and wholly satisfactory description of what takes place in the work of art.
>
> Further, criticism, as T. S. Eliot once remarked, is not "auto-

telic"; it is not an end in itself, but a means to the greater understanding and appreciation of literary works.[52]

Lennox Grey has emphasized one of the "means" of criticism in demonstrating the implications of ecology as an artistic science or scientific art. Grey has pointed out the "humanities" aspect implicit in the books of the botanist-ecologist Paul B. Sears and the ecological perspectives in the account by John Steinbeck and E. F. Ricketts (novelist and marine biologist) of their explorations of the Sea of Cortez. Grey has also identified as ecologically oriented novelists such as Louis Bromfield and George R. Stewart and sociologists such as W. Lloyd Warner and has drawn principles from their work for looking at literature. Exemplifying some of these principles, Grey has quoted Sears:

> [Nature] works upon him [the individual], and he responds, through the medium of his culture. In this he lives, and moves, and has his being. It limits and compels him, true, at every step; yet it can be altered by his participation, his understanding, and his will, and his work.[53]

Steinbeck and Ricketts organized the same idea in these words:

> "Let us go," we said, "into the Sea of Cortez, realizing that we become forever a part of it; that our rubber boots slogging through a flat of eel-grass, that the rocks we turn over in a tide pool makes us truly and permanently a factor in the ecology of the region. We shall take something away from it, but we shall leave something too." And if we seem a small factor in a huge pattern, nevertheless it is of relative importance.[54]

"Pattern" and "relative importance" are the keys to Grey's ecological criticism of literature. As a teacher of teacher-critics, Grey has described the implications of an ecological criticism for helping teacher-critics to develop their own patterns of literary understanding and communicate them to their students:

> In going wide open [in exploring the ecology of the Sea of Cortez] . . . Steinbeck and Ricketts were not going at random. They went with a conscious ecological concern for the interrelations of living things with one another and with their environment, and with the finding of symbolic critical index or nexus points, where these interrelations might be most economically and strikingly observed.[55]

How "symbolic critical index or nexus points" in literary perceptions are arrived at, given an academic year or a college semester, will differ with the particular teacher and group of students involved. Grey has offered one method called "triangulation," where the triangle consists of "method," "outlook," and "literary application."[56] Specifically commenting on the teacher-critic aspects of the triangle Grey has written:

> The most effective means . . . for giving students [an image of literary audience] is . . . "triangulation" of John Steinbeck's *The Grapes of Wrath* (a best seller which also has literary stature), Steinbeck and Ricketts' *Sea of Cortez* (in which Steinbeck gives the "human ecological key" to *The Grapes of Wrath*) and Paul B. Sears' *This is Our World* (in which the Oklahoma-Oberlin-Yale botanist-ecologist spells out the "humanities" dimensions of his subject as well as the biological). The opening of *The Sea of Cortez* raises at once the question of the relation of old and new scientific methods and literary method, recalling Mrs. Leavis' conception of the "anthropological." (It also opens a vista in *The Grapes of Wrath* which persuades most students that they must go beyond the usual commentaries if they are to get at the art or creative achievement in works of literature to which people respond. This is particularly true for *The Grapes of Wrath* [or *The Red Pony* for high school use], which is commonly treated as topical, or regional, or proletarian literature, seldom as Steinbeck's effort also to see what an ecological outlook can mean for our literary view of the world, breaking through the older deterministic naturalism).[57]

Grey's "literary audience" is related to Leary's "classroom-audience," and it is interesting to note that the teachers to whom Grey addressed his essay were students in a course entitled "Literature and the Literary Audience." Teachers of English have perhaps always been aware of audience—Shakespeare's invidious allusion to groundlings may come to mind—but new perceptions of audience by Grey, Leary, and others emphasize the role of audiences in the criticism of literature. One dictum of Grey's literary ecology—"it is of relative importance"—implies that student audiences participate in interrelationships. Involvement in such relationships as the search for "significant transection points"[58] has:

> . . . always been intuitively the literary method: "I am a part

> of all I have met," whether in Homer or Tennyson, Emerson or Thoreau? Can we see it now becoming also a conspicuous modern method in philosophy (whether our key is Whitehead or Dewey), in biological ecology (Paul B. Sears, Rachel Carson) in ecological anthropology (W. Lloyd Warner), in educational research and inquiry (E. L. Thorndike's *Your City,* 1939; Riesman), in ecological literary and cultural criticism (Krutch), and in other fields?[59]

Grey's questions point up the existence of interdisciplinary nexi and sharing among the arts, sciences, and humanities in today's world. As early as 1938, Louise Rosenblatt suggested such an interdisciplinary sharing in classroom explorations of literature:

> My aim . . . is to demonstrate that the study of literature can have a very real, and even central, relation to points of growth in the social and cultural life of a democracy.[60]

Anticipating the totality and wholeness implied in McLuhan's "simultaneity," Frye's "form," and Grey's "ecology," she emphasized the spurious nature of specialized segmentation:

> Any theory about art that tends to break up the responses to literature into distinct segments whether under the heading "social" versus "esthetic" or "form" versus "content" is misleading.[61]

Her use of "form" differed from Frye's use of it as concept, but to the extent that she anticipated and recommended a fusion and totality in literary criticism, she augured Grey's formulation of an interdisciplinary ecology as method.

Ecological perspectives for teacher-critics are not confined to American literature. Authors who embody principles of ecology in their works are international. In common, these ecological writers tend to embody in their work the range of areas that includes linguistics, psycholinguistics, semantics, symbolism, communication, and, always to some extent, literary criticism, broadly applied.

In summary, principles and methods based on concepts of the Aristotelian "unities," the Platonic "contexts," or a range of sociological, psychological, or analytical structures (to mention a few of the "schools" of criticism) may be used to judge literature.

Judgments, some authors and critics contend, must be recognized as incomplete because of individual reader understandings and because of the impossibility of knowing everything about a given piece of writing. In spite of such indeterminacy, structures such as Coleridge's levels of inner senses and "critical appraisal" and processes such as Leavis' "anthropological method" and Grey's "literary ecology" do provide methods for increasing student awareness in the study of literature.

From the foregoing explorations of "symbol as center" and the symbolic process as tools for extending literary criticism, the following principles with application for a field theory approach to literature can be drawn:

> That the dynamic nature of symbols makes it difficult to say with certainty that a given symbol represents one and only one idea;
>
> That techniques for symbolic interpretations demand breadth of individual experience and opportunity to explore widely symbolism in all of its forms;
>
> That criteria for identifying the range of symbolic definitions (from Sayers' "natural" symbol through Richards' "concrete referent" to Frye's "symbol as archetype") suggest student study and application of various literary perceptual frames of reference;
>
> That "holism," "wholeness," and "totality" as concepts seem to be necessary background for symbolic interpretation of literature. Symbols tend to be planned parts of literature fitting into preconceived author-structures. Evidence of the designed nature of literary symbols must exist in a consistent and planned manner congruent with the total piece of literature. Failure to identify such planned patterns tends to make the sharing of literary experiences solipsistic.

Consideration of the common backgrounds in literary criticism shared by teacher-critics reveals the range of techniques for literary criticism they have been exposed to—a technique-range with "authority" at one end of a continuum and "simultaneity" at the other end. The continuum itself tends to be a technique, a "method interpretation," though few spokesmen from the literary criticism would accept the classification. Grey has demonstrated through his historical and evolutionary discussion of literary methods—anthropological, ecological, and triangular—that with "fieldness" as a base, broader "do-it-yourself" student perceptions may be possible.

The teacher-critic needs to explore, from an ecological perspective, some of those authors Grey has identified as "ecological" novelists. One of these, George R. Stewart, published several books that can be criticized by means of field theory principles by applying ideas of "fieldness" in English. Among Stewart's books are *Names on the Land, Man: An Autobiography, Storm, Fire, Earth Abides, Shepherd's Rock,* and others. *Storm* makes explicit and particular many of the generalizations noted thus far in this book.

FIVE

FIELD APPROACH TO *STORM*

THE FOREGOING DESCRIPTIONS of field theory principles and methods in the natural sciences, the social sciences, and the humanities suggest principles and methods useful for a field theory approach to *Storm*. The first principle noted in the description of field theory in physics was the influence of perception (observer viewpoint) on man's behavior in his environment. Early in his involvement with an adaptation to environmental forces, man becomes aware of entropic forces at work in the cosmos. Almost simultaneously, however, he recognizes that mankind as a collective, and each man in particular, is a potential enclave where entropic forces are temporarily offset in cosmic time. From these perceptions, each man fashions an "image" of his self-in-environment, and his attempts to achieve a balance (homeostasis) between his image and the changing environment become a field of life space with ever-changing boundaries. The dynamism in man's life-space field involves other field theory principles of relativity and feedback, with relativity functioning in a historical time-space perspective. Depending on the historical epoch in which an individual man appears, he adapts his self-image to his environmental feedback.

Communication, particularly through language, is the medium through which man tends to alter and be altered by his environment. Language sometimes limits man's perceptions of his environment. In spite of such limitation, man's skill with language as part of his organismic growth tends to expand his image of his self-in-field until he begins to perceive the ecological principle "that *all* is important," that his life-space field is irrevocably bound to that of his fellowman, and that potentially his every act can alter as well as be altered by all other forces in the universe. The total impact of man's awareness of these field theory principles is a conception of the wholeness, the completeness, of his time-marked passage in the cosmic scheme of things. These are the basic principles of field theory in science and the humanities that suggest a field theory approach to literature.

Of course, not all men perceive life-space with the degree of awareness noted above, but there are many ways for men to increase their levels of awareness. In almost every society, the social institution of education is singled out for this purpose. Literature as part of every educational system entails mankind's belief in literature as useful for the individual. The field theory principle of simultaneity is embodied in the study of literature because significant literary works embody the cultural values of a time epoch as well as the author's participation in the ecology of his culture areas. Wrestling with the problems of form and expression within the confining language, authors strive for linguistic structures and processes that will afford them a kind of homeostasis for recording the flux of mankind's aspirations. The organization an author achieves is one of the antientropic forces that sustains the culture and, indeed, the one that lets it burst its perimeters of habit to sample new systems of value and behavior. Only as the reader, recognizing not only his own viewpoint but the complementarity of additional viewpoints (such as the author's), makes an effort to state for himself the significance of the form of the work does any significant feedback become effective.

The novel, as literary work of art, symbol of culture, or aesthetic experience for centralizing cultural disparities, tends to embody ecological principles, to exemplify complementarity, and within temporal limits to reveal through thematic montage simultaneous extensions of all art forms. Ability to discover myriad facets of the novel as a work of art tends to be a function of individual perception. That "beauty lies in the eye of the beholder" is a truism that implies that a teacher of literature must imaginatively structure his students' involvement with a work of art if they are to increase their appreciation of the novel as an art form.

There are no "methods" that are everywhere applicable for getting students involved with the art of literature. Field theory as a concept rules out "a method" or "the method" for individual involvement in actually "experiencing" literary awareness. "Dynamism," the constant flux of fields in time and space, "participant-observer," individual involvement in a field changes both field and observation, and other field concepts imply that a variety of more or less viable patterns are available to teachers for involving students in new literary experiences.

Describing a generalized source for such viable patterns, Leary has written:

> Ideally . . . our scholar-teacher-critic is a skilled professional, trained as effectively for what he is to do as is the professional in any other area, law or medicine. He has learned techniques of presentation [methods]; he has studied the history and background of his subject, so that he knows it of itself and can relate it to other fields of knowledge; he is acquainted with the best that has been thought and said about it, not only last year, but this year also; he keeps abreast, that is to say, with current interpretations, new trends, and with the latest opinion and research. . . . It seems reasonable, then, to suggest that the teacher of literature, on whatever level, who overlooks the criticism of T. S. Eliot or the fictional techniques of Henry James, Joyce, or Faulkner is roughly equivalent to the teacher of physics who ignores the quantum theory or the family doctor who knows nothing of Salk vaccine. And Shakespeare or Goethe, though here the analogy is less apt, is the Blackstone, the Newton, or the Pasteur whose elemental truths are daily tested.[1]

The "professional" English teacher Leary has described seems to operate from a field that has characteristics related to field theory as a concept. "Dynamism," for example, is implicit in the fact that Leary's professional teacher recognizes that the completion of course work or degrees is not the final word on the teaching of English, that the interrelatedness of English to other broad fields of knowledge is continuous and reciprocal to the teaching of English, and that, without naming them, "feedback," "complementarity," "simultaneity," and other concepts are all critical-teaching methods that are marks of the professional. Leary's description tends to characterize English teachers with years of classroom experience, and it is from the "professional's" viewpoint that a field theory approach to the teaching of *Storm* arises. Chapter Six of this book explores means for providing pre-service English teachers with similar perspectives through their undergraduate programs.

Storm has been deliberately chosen to exemplify the field theory approach to a novel; it is contemporary, it has been adapted for television ("A Storm Called Maria" on Walt Disney's *Wonderful World of Color*), it is referred to in many high school anthologies, and it has an unusual and arresting structure that makes it an excellent source for extending a student's involvement with contemporary literature. "Contemporary" is a prerequisite for applying field theory concepts to literature. *A Tale of Two Cities, Silas Marner,* and other so-called classics lack the constellation of principles associated with modern field theory. But this does not mean that classical authors were ignorant of the scientific discoveries of their time. Milton's use of telescopic perceptions and Swift's use of scientific backgrounds in his *Voyage to Laputa* reflect, according to Marjorie Nicolson,[2] deliberate incorporation of scientific principles. The point here is that concepts used to describe field theory suffer similarities to concepts long extant in literary criticism. One effect of this seeming commonality is that the concept of "totality" as defined by field theorists may seem to be the same as "unity" as defined in Aristotle's *Poetics.* The two are not synonymous: Aristotle's "unity" was rigidily circumscribed to fit a form (drama), a time order, and a hierarchy of values; field theorists' "totality" rules out such proscription, holding that total impact on observer experience is "simultaneous" and not restrictive as to form.

Unless the differences between field theory concepts and their "look-alikes" from literary criticism are understood, a field theory approach to literature may seem to be nothing more than a new vocabulary for old literary concepts. Were this true, then a field theory approach could be used to examine the *Odyssey,* the *Divine Comedy, Paradise Lost,* and other classics of the past. No doubt, some readers will insist that field theory is one other exemplification of the cliché "old wine in new bottles"; if so, the earlier chapters of this book should be reread with careful attention to the origin of the field theory concepts and the phenomena which gave rise to their formulations. There is, of course, some overlapping of concepts, but it is doubtful that "relativity," "entropy," and "homeostasis," as field theory concepts can be found in the works of Voltaire, Fielding, or Dickens, anymore than the sort of contemporary themes explored by Salvador Dali, Marc Chagall, or Jackson Pollock can be found in Gainsborough's canvases.

Because the methods used to present a field theory approach to *Storm* exemplify in themselves the concepts of "observer viewpoint," "simultaneity," "totality," "perception," and similar principles, they are explained here: The reader in a field theory approach to a piece of literature is expected to participate in the author's experience. This fact of literary enjoyment is part of all "schools" of literary criticism, and the following approach to *Storm* is in the realm of the "do-it-yourself" type of literary experience. Possible explication of what the author meant by this passage and how it relates to Einstein's relativity or Wiener's cybernetics is left to the end of the exploration of *Storm*. Answers to questions raised in the development are to be supplied by the readers; they will be neither "right" nor "wrong," but will simply suggest the kinds of responses students and teachers might make as they react to *Storm*. Principles from the earlier chapters are signaled by quotation marks, italics, or context but are not reviewed in order not to interrupt the flow of the narrative. Readers in doubt about particular concepts can check them in earlier chapters or look to the summary of the *Storm* exploration at the end of this chapter. In a sense, the reader is called upon to play the role of a teacher using field theory to seek a rapprochement between critical method and teaching method in his use of *Storm* with high school classes.

The point of view for the involvement of students with *Storm* entails recognition of their daily experiences with weather from which they can approach the reading. (Perhaps they know only little of weather principles, but certainly they possess the usual interest in "the weather.") The feedback to students based on the "weather" viewpoint and perception presents the simultaneity of culture through several media: newspapers, magazines, radio, films, television, and additional communication forms. Simultaneous feedback also tends to structure the students' realization of the author's participation in the ecology of his culture area and provides them with experiences that increase their awareness of the *complementarity* principle. Students' appreciation of the literary art form demands involvement with the author's struggle to "position" the events of cultural experience in some order or form that affords him a kind of *homeostasis* with the dynamic flux of cosmic events. Each author's form for ordering experiences tends to be a function of his unique cultural perceptions, but more than that, authors tend also to realize how their perceptions shape and are shaped by their participation in their milieu. To the extent that authors can give form and order to events, and to the extent that students can participate in this ordering experience and state for themselves the significance of the order, antientropic forces that sustain man's unique cultural heritage may be said to exist. It is the total form of the novel as literary symbol that makes it an "art form." Students' involvement with stages of this literary art form tend to go beyond *entropy* and to provide them with new experiences, new values, new behaviors for seeing into cultural tomorrows.

"Wholeness," "totality," "gestalt," and "unification" as field theory concepts mean, by definition, that all facets of a given phenomenon contribute to an understanding or analysis of the phenomenon. With reference to *Storm,* the concept of "wholeness" demands that such things as flyleaf quotations, introductions, prefaces, and similar matters be examined. On the title pages of all editions of *Storm*[3] the following quotation from Sir Napier Shaw's *Manual of Meteorology* appears: "Every theory of the course of events in nature is necessarily based on some process of simplification of the phenomena and is to some extent therefore a fairy tale."

The concepts of relativity and indeterminacy from physics and mathematics seem reflected in Shaw's "fairy tale" description of attempts to simplify theories of natural phenomena. Shaw's qualification may also have shaped Stewart's note:

> The characters of this book—including Maria—are imaginary.... Although the scene is largely California, the story is not a local-color study, and for simplification a few alterations of setting have been introduced.[4]

Consciously or otherwise, Stewart indicates to the reader that he will be working with "simplification" at various levels of interpretation in his pattern of narration. A process of selection, of sifting and choosing the order of events that form the pattern of narration, also alerts the reader to look for the "alterations of setting [that] have been introduced."

Six years after the first publication of *Storm,* Stewart discusses his reactions to readers' questions about enigmatic sections of *Storm:*

> Re-reading the book now after some years, I find a number of things that I might say about it, but there is no need to try to put leading-strings on a reader. If you find the attitudes a little grim, however, you should remember that the text was largely written during those grim and terrible months of Dunkirk and the fall of France.[5]

> There is of course no complete or final explanation. No writer, I suppose can remember or identify altogether the sources of his ideas. But to work at the conscious level, I should say, first of all, that I had lived for fifteen years on the slope of the Berkeley Hills looking Westward to San Francisco Bay and through the Golden Gate to the horizon-line of the Pacific.[6]

Although he lived in California, Stewart's awareness of a storm as a dramatic vehicle for a book did not occur to him, he remarks, until he read of the California storms in Spanish while on a Mexican holiday.[7] Perhaps subconsciously Stewart illustrates how changed perceptions (Spanish language reports of California storms) in a changed environment (Mexico) sometimes lead to differing "observer viewpoints."

Concerning the pattern of the novel, Stewart provides the reader with a historical literary "set":

> This story, as originally conceived, fell into a familiar enough

pattern, that is, the adventures of many unrelated or slightly related people all happening to be affected by the same event.[8]

By his use of "familiar enough pattern," Stewart brings to the reader's mind *The Canterbury Tales, The Bridge of San Luis Rey,* and similar narrative patterns in which a single event in time becomes the vehicle for exploring total life space. But Stewart may be doing more than using the words "familiar enough pattern" to make the reader recall other "patterns" of narration. He may be suggesting that the reader seek "familiar" patterns in contemporary culture in the structure of *Storm.* At even a higher level, Stewart suggests that authors are to some extent the products of a wide and timeless literary environment where a given literary work is perhaps a *microcosm* of global literary history.

Beyond these backgrounds, Stewart tells of the research and legwork that went into the writing of *Storm.* His quote from Shaw's four-volume *Manual of Meteorology* and his detailed descriptions of meteorological phenomena imply extensive secondary research on storms. Stewart indicates his primary research sources in his Dedication section, where information gathered from his visits and vigils with men of the California highway division, highway patrol, water resources, telephone and telegraph companies, and other organizations is gratefully and admiringly acknowledged.

Finally in his Introduction in the Modern Library edition, Stewart makes a statement that seems somewhat enigmatic because it relegates human beings and their troubles and triumphs to the "edges" of the storm, "Maria."[9] Stewart states that "Maria" is the protagonist, but a field theory analysis of *Storm* suggests that "Maria" is perhaps the antagonist. The reasons for this judgment are based on the field theory approach that comprises the rest of this chapter.

One of the techniques or methods Stewart makes the reader aware of throughout *Storm* is that of the "overview"—a method of presenting thematic contexts within which the events in a given "Day" of *Storm* occur. Using the field theory principle of complementarity, i.e., microcosm contains all of the elements of macrocosm, the reader must look at Stewart's macrocosm, his view of world culture that is contained in the microcosm, *Storm.*

Events in the world of the late 1930's threatened human existence, even as the human species is threatened today. Diametrically opposed philosophies—freedom or slavery—ramified into a series of opposed value systems. Although World War II was fought to seek a resolution of these values, Americans are today facing essentially the same conflict of values; the only difference is that the so-called Communist bloc has replaced the Axis powers. The opposed ideologies of the 1930's and of the 1960's are framed in words and tend to affect all of man's social institutions. In essence, the universality of Stewart's theme in *Storm* applies to all mankind, from the freedom-loving Greeks to the harassed freedom-riders in the modern world. Table C attempts to identify some opposed perceptions of the two ideologies, and the following discussion of *Storm* will reveal how these perceptions of Stewart's world of the late 1930's and early 1940's are exemplified.

TABLE C

PREWAR PERCEPTIONS	POSTWAR PERCEPTIONS
Mercator map projection	Polar map projection
State autonomy	Regional planning
Machine production	Men and machines
Individuals in competition	Group dynamics
Police state	Service state
Rugged individualism	Cooperative individuality
Authoritarianism	Delegated responsibility
Pure science	Common concern for arts and sciences
Aesthetics	
Atomism	Simultaneity

Stewart never states that he is illustrating changing conceptions in cultural values; instead, using the symbolist technique of "rendering," he tends to present events in ways that suggest configurations where past and present are mixed in a total field.

All of the foregoing materials preface the body of Stewart's *Storm.* The kinds of exploratory questions raised in the reader by Stewart's design—the flyleaf quotation, the Introduction—and the consequent speculation about the world of the late 1930's might be called both a critical and a teaching method. This questioning begins as soon as the reader interacts with his initial contact with *Storm.* Man, seeker of patterns, wonders about the title of the novel, the quotation, the Introduction, and, in leafing through the novel, the unusual design. This same questioning occurs to the teacher who hopes to use *Storm* in the classroom, but the teacher also asks himself how he can help students to raise such initial organizing questions. Together, the first perceptions of *Storm* and the questions raised as a result of the perceptions provide the reader with a psychologist's "ground," or more commonly "background," that becomes part of his field. In psycholinguistic terms, the nature of the prefatory material to the body of *Storm* provides psychological "cues" or "sets" that pattern reader responses before, during, and after reading the novel. In terms of method, critical and teaching, these psychological cues should be discovered, speculated upon, and noted for later corroboration.

Leafing through *Storm* from beginning to end, the reader becomes aware of a definite structure. He finds twelve sections, titled "First Day," "Second Day," and so on through to the "Twelfth Day," the final day of the storm and the close of the book. Within each of the twelve days are kaleidoscopic subsections headed or titled simply by arabic numerals. The days and the number of sections in each day run as follows:

Day	1	2	3	4	5	6	7	8	9	10	11	12
Number of Sections	6	8	10	11	10	14	15	14	15	10	4	12

There are no transitions between sections of these days; instead Stewart uses double spacing. Even a cursory persual of *Storm* reveals that up to the "Eleventh Day" the subsections get longer and seem to have less of a patchwork appearance. But then in the "Twelfth Day" the author returns to the patchwork pattern of the earlier chapters with a curious difference: subsections "9" and "11" of the "Twelfth Day" are quotations;[10] "9" from *Hamlet* and "11" from the Bible. Stewart's somewhat unusual format makes one aware of kinds of first facts that skilled readers note immediately—and ask themselves about. Is the structure of

Storm planned for kaleidoscopic pattern? Was Stewart's planning conscious or merely a chronological narration of events as they occurred? What is the significance of the "objective" numerical sequence to sustain the "literary" narrative? Given a range of days for storms to exist, why did Stewart select twelve as the number for the life of his storm? How do both literary quotations and simulated newspaper reports fit into Stewart's pattern? What significance, if any, exists in the fact that each day's events are reported in separate subsections—and that the "Eleventh Day" has only four subsections?

As the reader moves through the seemingly unrelated sections of the "First Day," he receives the impression that he is looking at "stills" of sections of a montage of verbal photographs. What will the *total* montage be? From the "First Day" through the "Eleventh Day," the "photographs" flip faster until by the "Eleventh Day" Stewart makes the reader put the "stills" in a logically articulated "motion" where all are related. The "simultaneity" concept seems clearly illustrated by Stewart's "Eleventh Day." Almost any reader with field theory orientation would tend to see the photomontage in Stewart's structure and raise the necessary questions about *Storm* and its myriad meanings prior to a detailed examination of the book. Answers to a few of these questions can be found in the prefatory material to *Storm*.[11] Questions about whether or not the structure of *Storm* was planned, for example, seem to be answered implicitly in Stewart's statement that he "introduced alternations in setting" and in his 1947 Introduction, in which suggests he had a definite order for describing "Maria's" progress. Some questions about *Storm*, as Stewart implies, can perhaps never be answered,[12] but others can possibly be answered by a detailed examination of the processes contained in a field theory analysis of the novel.

Approaching the book in a field fashion, the reader examines the flyleaf inscription, the title page, the Dedication, and the Introduction and gleans insights from a cursory overview of the content from cover to cover. The technique or method used in this overview demands that the reader pause here and there and notice Stewart's readiness for wordplay, his infinite attention to multiple meanings. One result of this eclectic browsing, and the awareness of Stewart's perspicacity it brings, is that the reader is given a psychological *set* to use the close-reading methods of modern criticism. Where a given reader stops to explore a paragraph or so in detail depends on his background. A teacher might stop at the following paragraphs from section "4" of the "Seventh Day":

> Theoretically, the J.M. knew that such things could happen. At the Institute he had even heard a visiting specialist in dynamic meteorology read a paper on the synoptic preliminaries of a polar outbreak and demonstrate mathematically the sources of energy involved. Nevertheless, when he saw the map that morning, the J.M. almost gasped. To know that all this was in the actual process of happening was very different from thinking of it as equations—and at the same time to realize that as part of the Weather Bureau he carried his share of responsibility for charting it and forecasting its progress. He felt as if the government of the air had suddenly been overwhelmed by revolution.
>
> In the orderly hemisphere of the text-books there was a high-pressure area over the Pole and another near the Tropic of Cancer in what were known as the "horse latitudes." Between the two, in the temperate zone, a succession of storms moved steadily from west to east. South of the subtropical high pressure was low pressure again, and the trade winds blowing from northeast to southwest.
>
> But now, in two great tongues of cold air, the polar high pressure had broken clear through the chain of storms.[13]

Perhaps the word "theoretically" is the graphic symbol that acts as stimulus to a teacher. Contrast between the "classroom" and "reality" might draw a teacher on into the paragraph. The *pattern* and organization of words might sustain a teacher's interest. Words such as "equations" coupled with "responsibility" raise scientific spectres of Hiroshima (Hiroshima itself coming from the reading perhaps of the "grim days of Dunkirk" in the Introduction). Then the unusual "government of the air" in context with "revolution" raises questions because the coupling of the two ideas with reference to air seems unusual. "Hemisphere of textbooks" tends to raise new *perceptions* of textbooks and coupled with metaphorical language such as "horse latitudes," "tongues of cold air," and "chain of storms" suggests that multiple meanings are implicit in these paragraphs. The paragraphs for a teacher and a reader with different perceptions imply a *microcosmic* sample of the *macrocosmic* book. With these preliminary techniques for a field theory approach to *Storm*, the reader can now begin to look at the body of the book in detail, beginning with the "First Day." Procedures for such a "detailed" examination of *Storm* follow the general procedures used throughout this book: an overview to discover structures and descriptions, a search for interrelationships between structures and processes, and an exploration of the ways separate parts are articulated to imply *wholes* greater than their sum.

"FIRST DAY"

The "First Day" of Stewart's *Storm* deals with elemental forces: macrocosm and microcosm, polar and tropical air masses, man as a collectivity and as an individual, land and water, scientific theory and practicality. As broad as these dichotomies are, they contain, through Stewart's detailed explication, a caution about treating them only as extremes, as "either-or" absolutes. With his opening description of the earth's course around the sun, for example, Stewart leads the reader to think in sweeping rhythms of *time-space*:

> Continuously, in the succession of day and night, season and season, year and year, the earth had received heat from the sun, and again lost into space that same amount of heat. But this balance of the entire sphere did not hold for its individual parts. The equatorial belt received yearly much more heat than it radiated off, and the polar regions lost much more heat than they received. Nevertheless the one was not growing hotter while the others sank toward absolute zero. Instead, at once tempering cosmic extremes and maintaining equilibrium with the sun, by a gigantic and complex circulation, the poles constantly cooled the tropics and the tropics reciprocally warmed the poles.... Cold currents bore icebergs toward the equator, and warm currents moved poleward. But even these vast rivers of the oceans achieved only a small part of the necessary whole.[14]

Similarly, Stewart notes that California's unfortunate drought led to a *balancing* upsurge in the price of barley on the Chicago exchange.[15] Cold land-air pushes and mixes with warm sea-air, and anonymous men performing routine duties aboard a ship en route to the China Sea note the air mixture.[16] In other incidents connected with the "First Day," Stewart suggests that parts and wholes intermingle and that even insignificant daily routines (a ship's officer recording temperature and pressure) may have contributions to make to unforeseen *totalities*.

Another device Stewart employs in section "6" of the "First Day" is the use of titles instead of names for his "main" characters. "Junior Meteorologist," "Chief," "Superintendent," "General," or abbreviations for the titles, e.g., J.M., seem to be a planned contrast to other characters who are named, and Stewart is consistent in this title technique throughout *Storm*. Stewart describes the Junior Meteorologist (familiarly "the J.M.") in some detail, leading the reader to think of him as possible protagonist, though the impersonality of naming-by-function leaves an open question of whether "man" in nature may not be Stewart's central figure. But as a character, the J.M. discovers and names Maria; as a character he changes from an impatient, just-out-of-college theorist in meteorology to a scientific humanist, a more tolerant, experience-tempered predictor of meteorological phenomena.

In a symbolic frame of reference, the J.M. might be Stewart's symbol of the sciences in the modern world, using meteorology as the *microcosm* of scientific advances. The J.M., later chapters reveal, is contrasted with two prior generations of meteorologists —his "Chief"[17] and "the old man."[18] The old man tended to predict weather almost by intuition; the Chief, hired by the old man to "sweep out the office,"[19] learned weather prediction through experience and profited from advances in *communication* (mainly teletype messages from increasingly numerous weather stations); the J.M. learned his meteorology in college, where weather was considered a branch of physics.[20] In contrasting the perceptions of these three characters toward meteorological phenomena, the reader senses that Stewart is revealing the debt of modern science to the past as well as to knowledge acquired from pragmatic experience—and by extension the relation of theory and experience, on which science will develop in the future. Stewart's deliberate choice of these three characters and their occurrence in time places the reader inescapably and consciously in a "time-space" field, again a "ground" the reader is alerted to explore as he moves on through *Storm*. Within these first few pages, early intuitions about "objectivity" and "literary" narration begin to be fulfilled. The J.M. and other characters in *Storm* reveal a poetic tendency toward science in their metaphors, word choices, and perceptions. The J.M., for example, views a weather map and perceives a "gigantic dog's head."[21] Noting the first pressure change suggesting Maria's "birth" in the Pacific Ocean, he "drew a black line in the shape of a tiny football."[22] Alert to these figures, the reader may ask whether Stewart might not have described the shape of the black line quite as well as an "oval," "ellipse," or "egg." If his purpose is wholly scientific, the answer might be yes. But if Stewart is also aware of his "game-minded" American audience, may he not be inviting the reader to share the J.M.'s sportive attitude toward his work? At least he is sensitizing the reader to bridge an ancient dichotomy—of work and play, and, later, of product and process, science and art.

Still leading the reader to processes in the "First Day," Stewart draws an analogy between the "embryonic" storm and a child:

> As a baby possesses the parts of the adult, so the baby storm displayed as in caricature the features of a mature storm. The red line symbolized the "warm front" along which the southern air was advancing and sliding over the northern; the blue line symbolized the "cold front" where the northern air was advancing and pushing beneath the southern. The black line shaped like a football was an isobar, indicating a barometric pressure of 1011 around the center of low pressure, symbolizing also the complete circuit of winds around that point. As baby is without teeth, so also the storm was lacking in some attributes of maturity. But just as surely as a baby is a human being, so also was his new discovery a storm in charming miniature—provided always that he [the J.M.] had rightly analyzed the situation.[23]

Having established an analogy between the little storm and a child, Stewart seems duty-bound (for the sake of consistency) to follow up the comparison in later descriptions of the storm.

Commenting on theory and practicality in the art and science of meteorology through the J.M.'s perceptions, Stewart writes:

> ... equations now flashed into his mind with photographic exactitude; they dealt with velocities and accelerations, with the Coriolis force, and frictionless horizontal, rectilinear flow. They contained such delightful terms as $\frac{1}{2}A_i t^2$, $\triangle T^{o,o}$, and $2mv_w sin\emptyset$. To a well-trained mathematical meteorologist they were more beautiful than Grecian urns.
>
> He shrugged his shoulders. The local Weather Bureau had to deal in immediate practicality; there was little need and no time for mathematical abstractions.[24]

Stewart's metaphor of "mathematical equations" and "Grecian urns" suggests the existence of a "new field" comprised of both science and art. Art, he suggests, is not necessarily confined to "the fine arts"; instead, man doing his job well with enjoyment, imagination, and exactitude is an artist regardless of his profession. *Time,* for Stewart, is important to any art that must deal with a collective—human society. Artists able to communicate with their society are fortunate; other artists, Einstein and Van Gogh, for example, have to wait for society to catch up with them. The J.M., forced by the needs of a social institution, the Weather Bureau, must put aside some of the imaginative aspects of his art and use the language of his society to achieve social action. Language, in this context symbolic and metaphorical, again seems to occupy Stewart in the "First Day" of *Storm.*

Concern for process as it seems to operate in a field theory approach to *Storm* implies that greater consideration be given to a discussion of the "First Day" and the "Twelfth Day." A rationale for greater considerations for beginnings and endings of some kinds of novels rests on the assumption that some authors use their first chapter as a *microcosm* of the novel as a whole. These same authors tend to summarize and resolve conflicts in their final chapters. Consequently, Stewart's decision to include the ideas and themes noted in connection with the "First Day" seems to be deliberate. Why, for example, did not Stewart begin dramatically with the storm at its height *(in medias res)* and then use the flashback technique to describe Maria's beginnings? One of the many answers to the question is that Stewart seems to have a planned pattern for presenting Maria's progress through a process that his individual perceptions dictate as most effective for his literary audience. Another answer is implicit in Stewart's decision to eschew conventional literary form for what might be called a scientific-descriptive technique in his writing. Speculating on the reasons for this choice of technique, the reader might infer from Stewart's contexts that only those narratives that deal with the actualities of wrestling with science will be really significant tomorrow.

"SECOND DAY"

Beginning with the "Second Day" and continuing through to the "Twelfth Day," Stewart starts his first section of each chapter with some reference to man. As the reader observes this, his feeling that man rather than Maria is the protagonist is strengthened. Appropriately enough, when man emerges as the first topic of importance eleven out of twelve times, the laws of statistical probability state that this "could not be due to chance." In this frame of mind, the reader comes to this passage:

> In his pre-natal months, indeed, man is aquatic. But thrust forth into the atmosphere—small and red—he sucks in a first breath spasmodically, and owes his allegiance to air. Seventy years later, a nurse stands by an old man's bed, waiting for what is known as "the last breath."[25]

What level of critical appraisal does Stewart reveal with his play on the ripples of meaning from the *semantic* stone "air"? How does Stewart through these same meditations on "air" suggest that his choice of metaphor, e.g., "dog's head," "tiny football," are deliberate? Answers to these questions are both enigmatic and individual, depending upon the reader's *frame of reference.* Yet there seems to be evidence from Stewart's implicit comment on semantics that the words he uses are deliberate and chosen to fit a planned structure.

Speculating on the seemingly insignificant aspects of natural phenomena and the sometimes far-reaching effects of these cosmically minor shifts on men, Stewart writes:

> A thunderstorm in hay-time may overthrow a ministry, and

> a slight average rise or fall of temperature may topple a throne; a shift in the storm-track can ruin an empire. In the twentieth century a temporary variation of rainfall put Okies upon the highway by the hundred-thousand, just as in the third century a similar shift might in a single year hurl the Huns against the Chinese frontier and set the blue-painted Caledonians swarming at Hadrian's Wall. In the mass as in the individual, man is less a land-animal than a creature of the air.[26]

From this generalized concept of man, Stewart moves in section "2" to specifics—to characters as individuals and to men-in-the-mass through their reading of the daily headlines. The individuals are the Chief and Tom. The Chief, like other leaders throughout *Storm*, is never named; Tom, on the other hand, is relatively typical of minor "characters" who seem to "pop" in and out of the book. "Characters" is in quotation marks because these minor individuals in *Storm* seldom have last names, e.g., Rick the lineman, Whitey the chartman, and seem to be stereotypes of individual men performing individual jobs in any society at any historical time.

The personality characteristics that make individuals unique seem to be lacking in these minor characters. Stewart seems to have a deliberate purpose in stereotyping them. That some of these minor figures appear in special sections of the novel seems to show that rather than popping in and out—a first-glance inference—they appear in planned patterns.[27] One possibile explanation for this stereotyping is that the J.M., the Chief, and others *are their jobs* while the minor characters are named "Rick the lineman" and the like because they have yet to give their *total* selves to their occupations.

The existence of man the collective is suggested by the Chief's reaction to the headlines in the local San Francisco paper. The headlines deal with "rumbles of war, labor crises, political strife." Reflecting on the headlines, the Chief "felt a stirring of pride at his own international profession in which you were pitted against natural forces, not your fellow men."[28] Do the Chief's reflections suggest still another reason why meteorology was selected as the science for symbolizing a theme of *unification*? Stewart goes on to illustrate in the same section "2" the extent of internationalism in weather-reporting. Alaska, New Zealand, Tokyo, Capetown, Athens, and the Arctic are locations of some of the weather stations the Chief calls to mind in reflecting on the internationalism of his profession.[29] Coupling storm and war as he does in this section, Stewart "plants" an idea of the relationship between the two that is extended later. For the present, this coupling extends the "Dunkirk" reference from the Introduction section.

Suggesting the role of *perception* in human understanding, Stewart, through the Chief, comments on the Chief's *viewing position relative* to Whitey, who is making up the weather map:

> The Chief slipped into his chair. In this position he was opposite Whitey, and saw the map upside down. But he had long since adjusted himself to this position so as to avoid joggling the chartman's elbow and having to peer over his shoulders. After all, as he liked to demonstrate with pencil and paper—ϛ is just as easy to read as 5 once you get used to it.[30]

For a teacher-reader, preparing to deal with values in literature, is this flexibility something to draw to students' attention—and to foster? Can students "see" a *unified* perspective as Stewart goes on to have the Chief "see" in the following context? "As a wave moves through the water without carrying the water along with it, so the storm center and the two fronts moved through the air, yet themselves remained a single unit."[31] Stewart's simile seems apt, for it implies the characteristic *two-layered-field-to-one-layered-field process.*

Stewart takes up another theme in this section, one that he develops at length throughout the book. This theme might be called the "public collective," defined as group effort for the general welfare, versus the "private collective," defined as group effort for personal gain. Starting positively with the "public collective" and a somewhat historical perspective, Stewart traces the efforts of collective man to make a trail into California. Donner Pass—trail of covered wagons, railroads, automobiles, telegraph wires—became a "main channel of world *communication*" largely through man-in-the-mass.

Switching back to man the individual, Stewart introduces the Road Superintendent. Like the Chief, he is a conscious center for *interrelationships*: He habitually calls out to himself the myriad state names on license plates on the cars that sweep past him on U. S. Route 40 as he goes about his job of keeping the "Pass" open in all weather. Of the many comparisons possible, Stewart likens the Road Superintendent to Casey Jones, "the epic of the American working-man."[32] Is Jones, and by inference the Superintendent, a symbol of collective man, of man contributing his best along with other men until the end result of all the contributions is perhaps the modern-day United Nations "one-world" ideal?

When the Superintendent goes about his duties and reads the license-plate names, Stewart places the state names in block capital letters—a graphic visual device. Stewart could as easily have capitalized the first letter of each state's name in a somewhat conventional way. Why place them in block capitals? Speculation suggests that Stewart may be using this device to reinforce the communication aspect of the highway system and to emphasize that modern communication, such as the highway U.S. 40, gives new meaning to Donne's "No man is an island." Flowing into and out of California are people affected by and in turn affecting the California region. Enough states are called off by the Superintendent to suggest that almost every state in America shares, intentionally or unintentionally, in the welfare of every other state. Pushing the analogy, Stewart, through his Introduction, implies that international states might profit by a recognition of these symbiotic influences.

Stewart (perhaps consciously) makes the reader aware of his literary heritage in building into the Road Superintendent the "tragic flaw" or, in the Greek dramatic reference-frame, "hubris," of placing more value on machines than on men.[33] Later on in the book even the vaunted machines are buried in the snow, high up on Donner Pass. The same snowslide that buries the machine and men together almost buries the Superintendent. After ordering a rotary plow up to uncover the buried plow, the Superintendent wonders if he should use a hand shovel to try to dig out the men trapped in the plow under the snowdrift. He decides such a gesture would be futile and foolish *(irrationality)*, returns to his partially buried car, and then ponders on the wisdom of his decision. Stewart has the Superintendent's reminiscences take the following form:

> The Superintendent was thinking back some years to the time when he had been in high school. One teacher had made him read a lot of poetry, and he had always had a sneaking liking for the stuff, although he would never have confessed to it to the other boys. The trouble was that things people did in poems were so often silly, even though the words were fine.
>
> There was one poem he remembered now, while he sat in his car waiting for a rotary to come up. It was about a man who went through a lot of terrifying experiences and finally came to some place where he saw a tower, and just then he was going to be overwhelmed by some great mysterious power, far too big to fight against. Then the man got out a little horn, and blew defiance against the great mysterious power. The teacher had called it a magnificent gesture, and said something about the dignity of man, but the Superintendent remembered that he had always thought it pretty undignified to go blasting into a horn in a situation like that. Take the way it was now. If this was a poem, he probably should get out and start shoveling snow. Would that be a magnificent gesture, or just ridiculous—in the face of a storm that covered all California? Only machines could clear that road, and he might as well settle himself and keep calm and wait for them.
>
> He leaned back comfortably. Stolidly he lighted a cigarette. He had a fleeting suspicion that perhaps the cigarette itself was a gesture. "Well, anyway," he said to himself, "it's time I was having a smoke."
>
> But as he pulled in on the cigarette that feeling of deep depression came over him again. He had lost the road! The storm had been too much. It had worn down the men and beaten even the machines.[34]

A grim irony seems to be operating in Stewart's description of the Superintendent's value system, for the reader is later told that Peters and Swenson (the two trapped operators of the rotary plow) actually make their escape by digging themselves out with hand shovels.[35] The tendency of all leaders throughout *Storm*, men described by their titles and nothing else, is to place their faith in collective man as he is represented through particularly fine "work crews." But work crews in these leaders' frames of reference tend to be indistinguishable from "materials." The Superintendent, for example, makes only an academic distinction between men and machines. The same academic distinction is made by "the L.D." (the Load Dispatcher) in power-line communications, the General in flood control, the Chief in the Weather Bureau. Yet Stewart's plan reveals that it is man the individual, man identified by name who through the performance of his work to the best of his ability maintains the vital communication systems of civilization. Always blending, Stewart uses other individual men to set blocks to this vital system of *communication.* Observing this consistent pattern of blending throughout *Storm* raises a question: Does Stewart through this process in a sense augur the later preface to the charter of one of the UNESCO sub-committees, which opens with "Since war begins in the minds of men, it is in the minds of men that the defenses of peace must be constructed"?[36] Man, since he creates war, has the power to destroy war. In Stewart's frame of reference some men seem to ignore their responsibilities to society; other men go beyond their social responsibilities to keep the vital communication system of society alive, but society considered as a totality always implies the presence of both elements.

The J.M. on the "Second Day" continues to note Maria's growth and progress and is reminded of one of his professor's sayings: "A Chinaman sneezing in Shen-si may set men to shoveling snow in New York City."[37] One of the cities in the path of the "Chinaman's sneeze" is San Francisco. Stewart closes his "Second Day" by describing and implicitly symbolizing San Francisco as follows:

> A proud City, set upon hills, pearl-gray in the winter sun, swept clean of smoke and dust by the steady wind from the sea. Last warder of the West, a City looking forth upon that vast water where West in the end became East, space so wide as if to defeat Time the ancient, and cause the calendar to lose a day. A City bearing the Phoenix for its symbol, proud that like the Phoenix it had more than once sprung to life from its own ashes. A City of towers and banners.[38]

Stewart's perceptions of West blending into East, of Time (personified as "the ancient"), and of the Phoenix make the reader aware of space-time perceptions and place San Francisco in world perspectives. Through similes and metaphors Stewart describes the city in terms of castles and feudal strongholds, with banners representing various businesses—banks, telephone and oil companies—then switches the reader to the national emblem ("floating modestly over the squat Customs House"). Stewart goes on to say, "One might have said that these [banners and companies] and their like were the rulers of the City and the World."[39] Then, qualifying the "might have said," Stewart writes:

> Yet one might well look again. Was it perhaps by some inter-company agreement that all the banners streamed off to the southeast? No, not the Board of Directors, not even the stockholders voting as one man, could make their flag fly to the north. The Chief Engineer himself could not contrive that miracle.[40]

Besides feudal castles and business enterprises, what else might these "banners" suggest? In the manner of Steinbeck in *The Grapes of Wrath*, Stewart seems to be introducing an idea—perhaps a theme—on the relationship between representative government (symbolized by the national emblem) and the impersonal organizations that minimize the individual. Later on in the book, for example, Stewart describes the various attempts of private collectives to stave off the periodic floods of some of the California rivers, to the detriment of their unorganized fellow men:

> At last, although the white men hated the very sound of the words, they began to talk more and more of "the government" and "regulation." Then finally came engineers who looked shrewdly not at one part of the River, but at the whole. They measured snow and rain, and the depth of streams. They surveyed; they calculated with many figures how high the levees must be and how wide the channels between. Gradually even the fiercest fighters among the white men came to see that the River (which was always the whole River) was too great for any man or any company of men. Only the Whole People could hope to match the Whole River. So, after many years of disaster, the white men began to live in a truce with the River.[41]

"THIRD DAY"

The "Third Day" of *Storm* opens with a description of the sun's movement in terms of the forces of "light and darkness." Words such as "battle," "armies," and "front" recall Stewart's Introduction, where he points out that the battles going on in the world in 1940 and 1941 might have given a grim (but subconscious) theme to his book. The word "front" to describe a weather system, Stewart says, evolved about 1914 as a transfer from World War I terminology when the term was "on everyone's tongue."[42] Speculating on the *ecological* origin of the term, Stewart writes:

> Had the discovery been made in more peaceful years, men (who involuntarily try to humanize nature) would perhaps have derived a term from marriage rather than war. This comparison also is apt—love, as well as hate, arises between unlikes, and love like hate breeds violent encounters. Best of all would be to use words unrelated to human feelings. Those great storms know neither love nor hate.[43]

Exploring *transection points* of words and their origins in man's *life space,* Stewart makes the reader aware of the images he uses, the etymology he explores, the psycholinguistic and semantic patterns he applies. Consequently, Stewart's use of visual devices such as "MINNESOTA" on license plates, "Whole People" and "Whole River" in the passage on the California rivers, seem to be conscious attempts to communicate something important to the reader. "Important" is assumed, because capital letters are used with "proper," i.e., important, ideas. Or are there other fields that may be explored in speculating on Stewart's use of unusual capitalization throughout *Storm*?

Stewart's "Third Day" introduces the reader to still another seemingly enigmatic process in the literary structure of *Storm.* The process consists of describing incidents that seem to have no relationship to the narrative pattern of the novel. The novel is entitled *Storm,* and in the "Third Day" of the narrative Stewart devotes a section to an owl that accidentally electrocutes itself.[44] After the electrocution, a wildcat picks up the body of the owl and makes a meal of it.

What does the owl have to do with the imminent storm? Or

what, for that matter, do the sections of the "Third Day" devoted to a report of a telephone conversation between a man named Jim in San Francisco and a man named Pete in Colusa,[45] a waitress calling from Reno to tell her sister in San Francisco that she will be coming to San Francisco for the weekend,[46] or a Victoria Island fur-trader who decides to stay inside because of the unusual cold?[47] It is not that these incidents are in themselves illogical: Pete wants to take a shortcut to San Francisco to sell Jim some flour; the waitress, Jen, wants to introduce Max Arnim, her boyfriend, to her sister, Dot; the Victoria Island fur-trader knows that little can be accomplished in extremely cold weather. The reader questions their purpose within the context of the "Third Day" because of the seemingly[48] more logical description of the old man's visit to the Weather Bureau and the introduction of the Load Dispatcher, the General Manager of the Railroad, the Chief Service Officer at Bay Airport, and the District Traffic Superintendent of the telephone company, who share in common discussions of the weather in relation to their particular jobs. Direct reference to the storm in the "Third Day" comes from two sources: the J.M.'s plotting of its progress and the discomfort of passengers whose ocean liner on its way to Hawaii passes through the air mass that will make up part of the storm. In addition to creating suspense, Stewart appears to use the *elliptical (indeterminacy)* process of character presentation for other reasons. One possible reason might be to emphasize the point that no man knows what each day will bring. Statistical probability says that given certain standard patterns certain expectations in the "tide that governs the affairs of men" can be anticipated. But probability, because it is actuarial and statistical, also warns that there is a standard error involved—a rational bowing to irrational elements—that, considered en masse, behaves in predictable ways. Yet, the existence of standard error, considered individually, means that no one knows with certainty what will happen, except that in the cosmos every act has some consequence. Stewart in the "Third Day" makes the reader aware of the "simultaneity" of the seemingly unrelated acts of individuals in a cosmic whole.

Such cosmic consequences are also uppermost in the minds

of the leaders described in the "Third Day." The Load Dispatcher, for example, is aware that a passing cloud may have a consequence relative to his control of the flow of electricity:

> If a sudden cloud appeared, twenty thousand office-workers might casually turn on the lights, and the L.D. was responsible that those unexpected lights should neither flicker nor be dim. If the evening was warmer than usual, five thousand old ladies might decide not to plug in the electric heater, and the L.D. was responsible that this unused energy did not flood the system and disarrange the delicate continuous process in operation at the Consolidated Paper Mill.[49]

But these kinds of phenomena are not the only ones recognized by the Load Dispatcher and other leaders throughout *Storm.* They also recognize the need to consider and accept "good" and "bad," "positive" and "negative" as perennial in their fields of endeavor *(entropy).* When man is born he begins to die; the beginning of summer is the beginning of winter in terms of amount of daylight; the sprouting of a plant is a signal for its decay. The Load Dispatcher comments on his understanding of these elemental forces:

> As often, he thought of the paradox in which he was involved. In the long run, not only Power-Light but also the whole state depended upon the water furnished by the great winter storms; yet these indispensable storms were his chief problem, and sometimes he caught himself, against all rationality, wishing for a dry year.[50]

Against such elemental forces, Stewart says, man uses knowledge—knowledge gained from the heritage, the sacrifice, the experience of his ancestors. The characteristics of this knowledge are a recognition of man's fallibility and a questioning of closed systems of explanation. Seeming to exemplify this philosophy is the Chief Service Officer at Bay Airport, who as the son of a Methodist minister used to say that he was second-generation in the flying business since his father was a "sky-pilot." The father's influence on the airport "Service Officer" is described by Stewart as follows:

> The sermons and Bible-readings of his youth had left only a few perceptible and curious tokens upon him. For one thing, he was fond of the expression "act of God," but since he con-

> fined it to disasters he must apparently imagine God as practicing sabotage.
>
> This conception was borne out by the few biblical verses which he liked to quote. "Get this!" he would say to some youngster who was in training. "This is the one business you can't take any chances in. Why?—because the Lord's working against you. It says so in the Bible. 'Praise the Lord from the earth, ye dragons, and all deeps——Fire, and hail; snow and vapors, stormy wind fulfilling his word,' 'Fulfilling his word,' that means they work for him. Dragons and deeps you can maybe forget about. But fire. That's lightning, and all kinds of electrical disturbances that go with it—static that mixes up the radio beams and gets a pilot lost. Hail and snow—that's icing conditions. Vapor means fog and low ceilings. Stormy wind means turbulence. Remember that verse and you've got all the inside of what a storm means to the air lines."
>
> He would pause a moment for effect, and then go on: "What's more, who is it that the Bible calls the prince of the power of the air? Why, the Devil! And, believe *me,* when you got the Devil and God workin' against you, you got to watch your step."[51]

The Chief Service Officer, to offset his perception of "God" and the "Devil," as enemies of pilots, used "every good principle of meteorology and aerodynamics."[52] Unlike other leaders in *Storm,* he recognizes individual men as being essential to his operation. Although he treats these men as a collective, pilots, he notes: "If you have a good plane and a good pilot, he can most likely come through anyway."[53]

Choice of *communication* systems to exemplify man's relations to nature seems to be an idea Stewart plants in the reader's mind at this point in the book, implying that the idea will later be demonstrated. Highways, railroads, the telegraph, the telephone, and electrical power systems share in common the fact that they are bound to the earth, to the geography of a region. The highways cannot deviate from an engineered course, the telephone, telegraph, and power lines are fixed to the hills and valleys in which they are established; the railroad must stay on the laid track. While some *opportunities* for relays and rerouting exist in all of these systems, they still tend to lack the kind of *flexibility* available to the wireless and to airplanes, which are capable of making adjustments in terms of information received.

Stewart explores another aspect of the communications concept of the "Third Day" through the J.M.'s reflections on his relations with his colleagues in the Weather Bureau:

> They were jealous of him, he reasoned—of his training. Even the Chief must be; the Chief hardly knew enough mathematics to figure *theta-e*. And Whitey would never rise higher than Observer; he had tried the Civil Service examination three times and always failed the mathematical part. Mr. Ragan had been a promising youngster once—had even published an article on cyclone tracks; but he had died above the ears about 1915, and been a routine worker ever since.[54]

Having pigeonholed the defects of his fellow workers, the J.M. goes on to reflect on his loneliness that, he feels, comes because "he always seemed to be giving the cold shoulder to the boys in the office."[55] The J.M.'s thoughts are interrupted by a telephone call from a woman who wants to know if she can hang out her washing safely. Using his most ironic voice the J.M. assures the woman that she can hang her washing outside, but the incident makes him bitter. Trained in meteorology to plot weather systems, the J.M. must give mundane answers to the public's questions "about hanging out diapers—he was sure it was diapers!"[56]

At this point Stewart makes the reader aware of the communication problem posed by the increase in abstract knowledge. The J.M. wants to use meteorological terms to communicate weather data, but to the diaper-hanging housewife the meteorological terms would be a foreign language. Besides, after the J.M. had explained air-mass data to her, she would probably have asked, "Does all this mean that I can hang out my wash?" Housewives are part of the everyday world—in some cases the largest part. Abstract knowledge is useful only when it gets close to the individual's field-ground end—utility. "Pure" science, "pure" mathematics, and "pure" scholarship, Stewart suggests, lead to isolation from people. How well, Stewart seems to ask, does *theta-e*[57] communicate to the general population, or to the J.M.'s fellow workers? Relativity of time and place are implicit in the answer to this question, at least as far as Stewart is concerned.

On the college campus, with fellow students and a professor in mathematics, *theta-e* is a common tool for the computation of meteorological data. In the Weather Bureau (a different frame of reference), *theta-e* is vaguely known to the Chief and not known at all to his fellow workers. Use of the concept by the J.M. makes everyone in the "Bureau" uneasy. The concept tends to become a divisive force; it is strange, it is not understood, and because it is not understood the J.M. is looked on as acting superior, cold, and aloof by his fellow workers. But the J.M. is learning to adapt to change. Presumably, at conferences back at the campus, with other college-trained meteorologists, lively discussions and computations using *theta-e* may be expected. In the Weather Bureau, except on an individual basis, such computations must be put aside for reality—the daily effect of weather on people. Perhaps this is why Stewart alerts the reader to the J.M.'s growing recognition of the public collective by concluding the J.M. section of the "Third Day" as follows:

> He [the J.M.] pulled open his drawer and saw the well-worn leather case containing his slide-rule. Reflectively rubbing a finger-tip across it, he noticed that he left a track in a faint film of dust.[58]

"FOURTH DAY"

Stewart opens the first section of the "Fourth Day" with a historical comment on man's relations with weather. From this historical description the reader learns of the origin of some weather proverbs that, Stewart says, society preserved not for their sagacity but for their "catchiness."[59] Stewart again demonstrates that his use of words, of language, is deliberate and exact:

> But language, which always said too much or too little, was also a great corrupter of knowledge. He who handled words most cunningly was seldom the wisest, but the catchiest proverbs, not the truest, survived. (So even yet those who speak English say:
>
> *Rain before seven,*
> *Clear before eleven.*

But those who speak other languages do not say that particular foolishness, not because they are wiser, but because in their speech the two numerals fail to rhyme.)[60]

Also in the opening section of the "Fourth Day," Stewart makes the following statement, which seems to imply a concern for the *unification* of knowledge, characteristic of field theory in the social and physical sciences:

> And since the storm knows no boundary of race or continent, men of all nations perforce have labored together to learn the ways of weather. Torricelli, the Italian, invented the barometer. Halley, the Englishman, mapped the winds. Franklin, the American, audaciously grasped the idea of a revolving and traveling storm. Coriolis, the Frenchman, discovered how the earth's own rotation shifts the wind. Buys Ballot's Law derives from a curiously named Dutchman; Dove, the German, stated the laws of storms; Bjerknes, the Norwegian, probed their nature and explained their life-history.[61]

Storms are not the only phenomena that have occupied the mind of collective man; advances in knowledge have generally been the product of international and interdisciplinary exchanges. A final statement from the opening section of the "Fourth Day" seems to extend the implication of this fact and to be particularly relevant to the future of mankind: "Ahead, if man can but conquer himself, lies every hope of greater victory."[62]

The second section of the "Fourth Day" exemplifies a technique that by this time the reader has learned to interpret as foreshadowing, a device whereby the incident reported implies later consequences. The technique derives from Stewart's earlier descriptions of various leaders—Load Dispatcher, Chief Service Officer—and their concerns with the relationships between weather and communication. Stewart's "Fourth Day" foreshadowing reveals: a tree bole perched on a hillside within which the "slow fire of decay" has been burning since 1579; a two-by-four jostled off of a truck and perched on the edge of the road; a switch box penetrated by a .22 rifle bullet fired by Dirty Ed and his friends; and Blue Boy, Tony Airolo's boar, who "worked his way across a hillside far above the railroad tracks." Having met the Road Superintendent, the Load Dispatcher, and similar men concerned with communications of all types, the reader begins to sense that these forces have a Damoclean relationship to the forces of readiness controlling the fair-weather communication systems in California prior to the storm's arrival.

The third section of the "Fourth Day" continues the human analogy of Maria by pointing out that she has reached maturity—a maturity roughly corresponding to that of a man of twenty-five. Stewart reveals the life-in-death and death-in-life field:

> But to speak of a healthy man of twenty-five as dying although in some ways justified, would be counted an overstatement. The man is no longer growing, and his physical condition probably shows a decline. Nevertheless, most of his life and his best years of power lie still ahead. So also the storm actually contained within itself an amount of energy which in human terms was the equivalent of many millions of kilowatt hours.[63]

The fourth section of the "Fourth Day" depicts two views of man and his reaction to the local weather conditions shortly before Maria arrives on the West Coast. Again, Stewart makes the reader aware of the contrast between the private collective, the organization, and man the individual as both respond to the same weather phenomena *(relativity)*. Oscar Carlson, the individual man, the farmer, receives a letter from the bank telling him that he must pay his overdue interest. Oscar cannot pay and cannot get credit to tide him over the drought, so he hangs himself.[64] The Secretary of the Trade Association, on the other hand, prides himself on his "scientific detachment." Observing that consumer buying is down, the Secretary reports that a Mid-Winter Buying Week is planned to offset this slump. The Secretary also reports that the causes of the slump are attributed to "augmented taxes, the relief situation and a deficiency of precipitation."[65] Oscar Carlson's plight to the Trade Association is a statistic; to the university-trained Secretary of the Association, Oscar Carlson is an actuarial number, to some extent accounting for the drop in consumer buying. What ecological implications does Stewart suggest by putting these two incidents together in a separate section of the "Fourth Day"? The possible answers to this and other questions arising from the form and structure of *Storm* are less important than the reader's raising of the questions in the first place. The Oscar Carlson incident, for example, might have occurred almost anywhere in the first four days of Stewart's descriptions. The incident of the Trade Association's Report might also have occurred anywhere in the first four days. Or, depending on the reader's frame of reference, perhaps the description of the two incidents in close proximity in a separate section of the "Fourth Day" is part of a careful plan. Exploring the relationship between the two incidents tends to broaden the reader's perspectives and to kindle his imagination. Solipsistic feelings and meanings may result from such an exploration, and because these meanings are solipsistic, they may be nondiscursive. Since the two incidents occur together in a section separated from other sections, Stewart may be attempting a communication in which both seemingly separate events are to be regarded as a totality—possible outcomes, "good and bad" respectively, of a natural event, the weather. But the weather is only "good" or "bad" in terms of human perception, for weather behaves in accordance with predictable natural thermal patterns. Having established the "naturalism" of weather, Stewart makes the reader see that while there are chance elements that may affect weather prediction for a local region, macrocosmically considered, weather is a direct function of the sun-based structure of the planetary universe. Weather is impersonal, and man, to cope with it, must ready himself to deal with its impersonal but ordered laws.

After the "Fourth Day," only four new characters are introduced in *Storm*. Two of these characters, the General[66] and Big Al Bruntton,[67] seem to be major characters. The other two characters, Mr. Reynoldhurst[68] and Pablo, the Mexican track-walker,[69] seem to be part of Stewart's *deus ex machina* technique for explaining telephone relay systems and the reason for a streamliner's derailment. "Seem to be" is used because within larger configurations in *Storm* both minor characters can also be regarded as symbols of the dignity of man—in this case, men who do their jobs well and take pride in their work.

"FIFTH DAY"

Beginning with the "Fifth Day" and carrying through to the end of the book on the "Twelfth Day," Stewart brings the events, themes, and characters noted in the first four days of *Storm* to time-bound climaxes and conclusions. Exceptions to the above generalization, as already noted, are the General, Big Al, Mr. Reynoldhurst, and Pablo. "Time-bound" is coupled with climaxes because Stewart leaves the reader with the impression that the end of the storm by no means ends man's conflict with natural phenomena. The Road Superintendent, for example, gets his equipment ready for the next storm; the Chief Service Officer at the Bay Airport plans to shake up his personnel in anticipation of the next storm; railroad engineers redesign a culvert so that dead boars will not obstruct the flow of water and wash out tracks.

Stewart makes the reader aware of conclusions in a different way: Rick the lineman lies in his coffin; the bodies of Jen and Max are found below a cliff. Although these and other conclusions, e.g., deaths brought about by the storm, seem pretty final, Stewart suggests that this too is normal and for those deaths other lives are beginning—that in all of this cosmic process there is an order and a time. Even as the last of the storm, Little Maria (Maria's "baby"), sweeps out to sea from the East Coast of the United States, other isobars are forming in the China Sea. Each place, location, and characteristic of the isobars is different, but a storm's pattern of growth, maturity, and demise follows principles dictated by the movements of the planets in relation to the sun.

Stewart makes the reader aware of relativity by the way he handles climaxes and conclusions. Relativity in Stewart's frame of reference seems to focus on the world's value systems prior to and during the opening phases of World War II. In some ways, Stewart anticipates intellectual movements toward unification made somewhat more explicit by Hartmann in 1942.[70]

In microcosm, Stewart makes the reader aware of prewar, postwar value systems with his comparisons of Mercator and polar cartography. Mercator projections in cartography stem from the sixteenth century's great concern with land masses in the temperate zone. In Mercator's frame of reference (1512-1594), rectangular areas of the earth's surface are marked off with the meridians as parallel straight lines spaced at equal intervals and the parallels of latitude as parallel straight lines intersecting the meridians at right angles but spaced farther apart as their distance from the equator increases. Mercator maps become increasingly distorted toward the poles. Mercator's projection was probably quite reasonable for his world of cultural, philosophical, political, and historical values; polar influences on weather and communication routes were not known, and the poles were probably relegated to fringe areas of sixteenth-century-man's considerations. Polar projections proved valuable, however, for air flights on curved paths from America to England, and in the twentieth century made Russia's proximity to America strikingly apparent. Stewart makes the reader aware of the influence of the poles on weather in the opening section of *Storm,* and he continues to emphasize polar influences throughout the book. Polar projections tend to show that from the poles "one world" joined together geographically and subject to common thermal forces is a supporting reality for today's philosophic "one world" represented by such organizations as the United Nations.

Other examples of Stewart's comparison and contrast that imply thematic continuity might be found in the fact that all of his leaders—the L.D., the CSO, the DTS, the Chief, the General—through delegated authority and regional planning have at their fingertips flexible alternatives for emergencies in their respective fields of work. Dams in the river, levees around the city, relays for power and telephone systems, alternate airports and air lanes, spare equipment and sidings—all of these utilize knowledge obtained from governmental studies and studies by private concerns. These studies share a common method: Begin by viewing the total region; then examine possible trouble spots depending on the respective enterprise involved; finally, suggest not only means for handling trouble in a given sector of the region but also for planning alternate resources that might be used should the original facilities for handling trouble fail.[71]

Character development is another technique Stewart uses to point up his themes, but the reader must recognize that all of his techniques are woven together and that to treat them separately distorts their contextual blendings. The old man, the Chief, and the Junior Meteorologist particularly illustrate the character technique of thematic development. The Junior Meteorologist is the only character who appears in each day of the storm and is the only character who shows a marked change from the opening pages of the book to its conclusion on the "Twelfth Day." Thematically considered, the J.M. tends to represent a selfish and intolerant individual. The "Second Day" description of the J.M. reveals his imaginative approach to his job. From this description, the reader can infer that the J.M. is competent and devoted to meteorology, particularly since meteorology as perceived by the J.M. is a common concern of mankind and is international in its perspectives. Having established the J.M.'s superiority, Stewart makes the reader aware, in the "Third Day," of the J.M.'s battle with reality by having him participate in the "public service" aspect of the Weather Bureau. The public service consists of explaining the procedures and techniques of weather forecasting to a visiting group of students. Feeling that the students would not understand modern meteorology, the J.M. resorts to explaining weather in terms of an outdated theory and then rationalizes his action on the premise that the students would not understand the more current air-mass theory. The "public service" experience makes him more aware of the problem of communicating with laymen. In this same section, Stewart has the J.M. meet the old man, a former chief in the Bureau and a predictor of the weather for Grant's inauguration. The J.M. regards the old man with some contempt, feeling that the old man's methods for weather-forecasting were nothing better than guesswork. By the "Fourth Day," the J.M. and the Chief have arrived at a mutual-respect stage—each for the other's competence in doing the tasks related to meteorology. Through "feedback" and communication with other staff members in the Weather Bureau, the J.M. by the "Fifth Day" has learned to develop a tolerance for the old man. The J.M. learns the responsibilities connected with forecasting and in retrospect recognizes the courage of the old man in making forecasts in the old days when so much of forecasting was left to chance and shrewd guesswork. The J.M.'s increasing skill and enjoyment in his work are pointed up in the J.M.'s comparing "real" weather to a "paper on weather" he once heard during his college days. By the "Sixth Day," Stewart has the J.M. come to the realization that perfect storms in terms of predicting expected behavior exist only in textbooks. In reality, storms always contain elements of chance, as Maria's unusual behavior makes the J.M. realize.

It is at this point in the J.M.'s character development that the reader may begin to ask whether it is coincidence that the J.M.'s growth in social maturity and the storm's growth (described as an analogy to human behavior) match almost point for point *(complementarity)*. Maria as a baby storm, insecure, blusters about in fitful gusts, not as yet a blend of all the elements that identify it as an individual. In Maria's growth process there is a settling down whereby "intrusions" such as land masses and scattered local fronts are tolerantly absorbed in a "mature" way. By the "Seventh Day" the storm has become like a "middle-aged person too individualized to fit any rules." The extent to which the J.M. begins to recognize individual differences and develop tolerations for them seems to parallel directly his ability to recognize anomalies in Maria—anomalies that do not fit pat definitions of storms and storm behavior.

Switching perspectives, Stewart has the reader view the J.M. on the "Eighth Day" through the musings of the Chief. "Cause and effect" are convenient words, but they "tend not to mean much," the Chief muses, especially for the J.M., who has the book learning but needs much more before he can become a weatherman. The J.M. on the "Eighth Day" is aware of his Chief's doubts and begins to see the broader perspectives of his job.

On the "Ninth Day" Stewart has the J.M. make an important decision: to turn down an offer to join the airlines as a meteorologist. His decision is based on the fact that the primary concern of the Bureau is with weather, whereas the concern of the airlines is with airplane flights, weather being considered an incidental necessity for routing such flights. By the "Ninth Day" the reader sees the J.M. as a man who has learned to see the positive aspects of his fellow workers.

On the "Tenth Day" Stewart has the J.M. discover the "pattern" of weather systems. He is struck by the order and balance of air masses based on accurate worldwide communication of weather phenomena. In sharp contrast to the J.M.'s perceptions, the layman sees the weather as a "crazy quilt" of disconnected events—an inexplicable mystery. On the "Tenth Day," the J.M. also reveals a compassion for the old man—a sharp contrast to his earlier disdain.

The storm's end for California is predicted by the Chief and the J.M. on the "Eleventh Day." But even with Maria's end in sight, other isobars are forming on the world weather map, and the pattern of weather continues. The J.M.'s concern for the hospitalized old man mounts.

Stewart has the J.M. on the "Twelfth Day" refer to the old man as the "Old Master"; the J.M. is sincerely grieved by the Old Master's death. The J.M. listens and seems to absorb his Chief's comparisons of storms and men. Tacitly, the J.M. agrees with the Chief's admiration for the Old Master's service to the public in forecasting weather with so little scientific data. Following the eulogy and philosophic discussion with the Chief about the Old Master, the J.M. returns to his weather map with greatly changed perceptions to seek other football-shaped isobars in the air paths of the world.

Stewart makes the reader aware, through the continuity of the J.M. as a character, that he is taking a slice of mankind out of time. The reader perceives character changes in the J.M. that are symbolic of other changes developed in the twelve days of *Storm* through other methods. The J.M. is not named so that the reader might speculate about him and his speculations bring to mind Kafka's Noman or the morality plays' Everyman. The changes that occur in the J.M. from the first to the twelfth day tend to represent in microcosm the changes noted in the prewar-postwar themes outlined previously.

To discuss one of those earlier themes, flexibility versus rigidity, it is necessary to combine both structure and process as commingled in *Storm* for a realistic appraisal. Structure[72] ranges from a series of tight little sections separated by numbers and spaces to combined ideas running for pages under section "3" of the "Eleventh Day." "What," Stewart makes the reader ask, "is the implication of this movie-like process?" One possible answer to the question might be that the logic-tight compartments, the "still" pictures, in the early days of *Storm* tend to represent rigid, complete, self-centered little worlds. The Load Dispatcher, for example, has no idea that an owl's electrocution will be a major cause of power failure. The flour salesman has no idea that a shortcut will lead to his death. Stewart suggests through structure that few people consider the cosmic effect of their acts. But then Stewart in section "3" of the "Eleventh Day" seems to make his "still" pictures take motion. Time is speeded up, and isolated earlier incidents are no longer isolated but become part of a moving picture where the ecologist's "all of it is important or none of it" becomes the dominating theme.

Another process Stewart makes the reader aware of in the structure of the "Eleventh Day" is exemplified by his description of Big Al Bruntton, the pilot. Stewart contrasts Big Al and his airplane with the "crack streamliner" as polar extremes of flexibility. The streamliner, bound to a fixed path, the track, is delayed by a track washout. The washout occurs in spite of trackwalkers, men specifically hired to see that the track remains clear at all times. But the best laid plans of the railroad officials are thwarted by a boar who plugs up a culvert with his carcass and causes the tracks to be washed out by the resultant flood of water from the storm. Big Al is thwarted, too. Airline communications are out, but unlike the train the airplane has some flexibility and though blown off course is still able to reach its destination.

Stewart emphasizes that the airplane alone is not responsible for riding out the storm. Big Al, the pilot, with his flexibility in decision-making—to return to Reno, to continue on toward San Francisco, to change altitude, to risk icing on the wings, to frighten the passengers—is the key to survival. Because of Big Al's decision and his selection of alternatives, the plane comes successfully through the storm.

Although Big Al has doubts about his decision, the personnel on the "crack streamliner" have no such doubts. A porter replying to a question about whether or not the train is on time replies, "Dis train *ah-ways* on time, suh!"[73] Other personnel on the "streamliner" seem to share the porter's viewpoint. Is Stewart suggesting a closed system of thinking by his italicizing of "*ah-ways*"? That the General Manager of the railroad recognizes irrational elements that may affect the schedule of the streamliner seems apparent by his provisions for track-walkers, "highball" signals, and similar expediting phenomena to keep the streamliner on time. In spite of the General Manager's precautions the track is washed out. The track, bound to the hills, is subject to meteorological forces. The General Manager finds that boars stuffing culverts is just one more unanticipated problem that he must plan for before the next storm. In contrast to earthbound tracks and trains, Stewart describes the clipper on the "Twelfth Day" flying a course calculated by the plane crew to work *with* meteorological forces.[74]

Flexibility tends to be a matter of degree. Stewart delineates a scale of flexibility through his characters. The Road Superintendent, for example, is able to make adjustments as emergencies come up on Donner Pass. But to the extent that the Road Superintendent feels that machines are superior to men, he tends (like the personnel on the streamliner) to have a closed system of thought, a somewhat inflexible approach to situations. Ironically, it is the men who make the machines perform their tasks, and it is the men who in the end prove superior to the machines in rescuing themselves from an engulfing snowslide. Similarly, Max, driving from Reno to San Francisco, "knows the road like the back of his hand." Is Max's perception of his driving route also a description of inflexibility? To the extent that Max's confidence rules out chance and irrational elements, his fate is almost foreordained. Rick the lineman seems to have the same problem. Rick has climbed "hundreds" of poles; his ascending and descending actions are almost automatic. Diverted by his thoughts about his girl, Rick tends to overlook the chance element in most natural phenomena. Rick's experience seems to suggest that things will go well simply because they have gone well in the past. He lets his mind stray to other things and has an accident that costs him his life. Stewart's examples perhaps make the reader aware of a paraphrase of a famous truism: Eternal vigilance is the price of life.

On the graduated flexibility scale, the Road Superintendent, Max, and Rick seem to tend to the inflexible pole. Toward the flexible pole, Stewart presents Big Al and the Chief of the Weather Bureau. Both men recognize constantly the risks involved in their work, prepare for these risks as best they can, and leave themselves alternatives wherever possible. The Chief, for example, holds off on predicting rain for drought-ridden California in the "Fifth Day" because he knows the effects such a prediction can have. While the Chief tacitly agrees with the J.M., who confidently predicts "rain in forty-eight hours" on the "Fourth Day," the Chief cautions the J.M. on the unpredictability of weather. The Chief suspends his judgment, recognizing that slight wind-shifts can change the whole character of a given air mass. Relativity and flexibility characterize the Chief's behavior in carrying out his professional duties in the Weather Bureau. The Chief's reluctance to make flat statements, his hedging, is sometimes regarded as indecision. Yet the Chief's reluctance is based on the irrational nature of meteorological events and the far-reaching effects a flat statement such as "rain" can have on the public. Section "4" of the "Fifth Day" dramatically illustrates the effects of the Chief's predictions: Literally millions of dollars and thousands of lives are involved in a seemingly innocuous prediction of "rain."

Johnny Martley, chief of the French Bar Powerhouse, also demonstrates the kind of flexibility that Stewart suggests is necessary for man in the modern world. Martley's flexible nature is described in section "3" of the "Eleventh Day."[75] After opening the sluice gates to relieve some of the pressure on the French Bar Dam, Martley emerges from the dam to find himself cut off from the shore by a wall of water spilling over the top of the dam. Of the many alternatives open to him—to stay there and wait for rescue, to rage and curse helplessly about his fate, to try to send some signal to the shore—Martley chooses to try to rescue himself. He looks around and finds a piece of rusted cable that will, he judges, support the weight of a man. Knowing from memory and prior observation the details of the shore around the dam, Martley decides his best bet is to make a loop on the cable and cast it toward some rocks that ought to be at a certain position on shore. The spilling water makes sight contact with the rocks impossible. Casting again and again through the water toward the rocks, Martley finally snags the loop in such a way that he is willing to trust his full weight to the support of the cable. Then calculating the risks, he launches himself through the falling water to safety. Martley's chances of surviving the risk were fairly good, but even if he had failed and been killed, his death would still have been within the probability of irrational elements and a function of cosmic patterns. Courage and a sense of responsibility aided Martley in his escape from the dam. Both personality characteristics might have easily led to his death, but Stewart implies that men do things in accordance with their beliefs and values; they cannot do otherwise and be the individuals they are.

"Who," Stewart implicitly asks, "is responsible for making these crucial decisions, for behaving in accordance with an internal value system?" Stewart might have the reader answer, "Each individual." Stewart makes responsibility another interwoven theme in *Storm*. Again, teasing evidence for this theme out of the context in which it occurs does violence to the totality. Responsibility is woven into the natures of the "Everyman" characters. The leaders—the J.M., Big Al, the General, Johnny Martley, and others—all reflect responsibility as a trait on a graduated scale of behavior. Adding to these individual characters and their exemplification of responsible behavior, Stewart also considers the role of responsibility in mankind's historical past. The first section of each of the twelve days of the storm takes up man and his relationship to cosmic forces, to evolution, or to his fellowman. Always in these sections some man or some group of men take responsibility for questioning, for doubting, for demanding evidence for what is accepted and revered. Direct examples of the responsibility theme can be found in the opening sections of each day of *Storm*. Indirect evidence can be found in the first section of the "First Day," where Stewart's perceptions of man's relationship to the cosmos are viewed in terms of *entropy*. The opening section of the "Fourth Day" has already been described, but another opening section dealing with the mankind-responsibility nexus appears in the "Eleventh Day."[76] Stewart relates a fable: A primitive tribe living by a river near the ocean cannot figure out the tides. In their ignorance the tribe invents gods to explain the capricious nature of the river, and in times of famine human sacrifices are offered to the river-god. The pattern of sacrifice and suffering becomes fixed until a wise man points out that the river-god is stupid or at least subordinate to the sun-god, for if the people will observe the position of the sun at high tide, then observe the river on the following day when the sun is in the same position, they will find the tide high again. The wise man paid the price wise men pay in many societies when they disturb closed systems: "The priests were horrified, and had the man stoned to death for impiety, but the people found his ideas useful."[77]

Stewart applies this fable to man's problems with weather and speculates on what may happen when weather control becomes a reality:

> If the final success is attained, what will be the effect upon man? Will he at last have to stop talking and speculating about the weather? Will the foreknowledge that he must prepare against a tornado upon a given day be more strain than grasshopper-like ignorance and sudden disaster? Will the removal of the daily mystery only serve perhaps to make life at once safer and more boring?[78]

Stewart's questions seem rhetorical, especially when compared with other examples of mankind's responsibility. Using a balancing technique *(homeostasis)* again, Stewart laconically reports in section "2" of the "Fourth Day" that a two-by-four placed somewhat carelessly in a truck is bounced out onto the road when the truck hits a bump. By section "4" on the "Sixth Day" a succession of motorists dodge the two-by-four by swerving their cars to avoid hitting it. These motorists are anonymous—perhaps "Everyman" again—but suggest a somewhat characteristic "let George do it" attitude toward the obstacle in the road. Finally, in the same section, a loaded manure truck hits the two-by-four and spills part of its load next to the piece of wood in the road. The rain spreads the manure in a film across the surface of the road, and in section "11" of the "Sixth Day" Peter Goslin, the flour salesman, taking the shortcut recommended by Jim, the flour-buyer in San Francisco, also swerves to avoid hitting the two-by-four. But the film of manure causes the car to skid and Pete Goslin dies. Stewart emphasizes the importance of "if" in mankind's pattern of responsibility. "If" it had not been raining, Goslin might have lived; "if" the truck-driver had been more careful to secure the two-by-four in his truck, it might not have fallen out; "if" one motorist had taken the time to remove the two-by-four from the road, Goslin might have lived; "if" the manure-truck-driver had been more careful to secure his load or to avoid the two-by-four, Goslin might have lived; "if" Goslin himself had not been going at the maximum allowable speed but had slowed down for the rain, he might have saved himself. But all of these "ifs," Stewart implies, are within man's control, provided responsibility is one of man's values.

Stewart's answer to the inquiry "Am I my brother's keeper?" seems to be in the affirmative, if responsibility for each of his acts is part of each man's value system. Stewart describes a negative example of responsibility in Dirty Ed's firing of a .22 bullet through a switch box in the same section "2" of the "Fourth Day." Implicit in Dirty Ed's action is the question: Who is responsible for this boy's possession of a .22 rifle, and who is responsible for supervising his use of such a weapon? Unsupervised children from six to sixty are probably in the cosmic scheme of things, though as Stewart suggests the lack of supervision is not necessarily beyond man's control. Dirty Ed's irresponsible act is concluded in section "4" of the "Ninth Day" when some eighteen people are affected by Dirty Ed's bullet. The bullet left an opening in a switch box, allowing it to be filled by Maria's rain. Because the switch box controlled a sump pump that emptied water from an underpass, eighteen people were involved in a flooded-underpass situation. A potentially disasterous situation becomes in this instance ludicrous. Man's ingenuity at extricating himself from it extends Stewart's contrast of perceptions on the theme of responsibility versus irresponsibility. Two policemen viewing the traffic bottleneck caused by the flooded underpass agree (with the Road Superintendent's commitment to machines) that only a tow truck can unsnarl the mess. But by the time the tow truck arrives the underpass is clear; a truck-driver and some college students involved in the traffic tie-up have cleared the jam with their ingenuity and imagination. Through the specialized and stereotyped policemen, Stewart suggests that specialization sometimes leads to partial people—people who delegate to others (tow trucks, etc.) what they "could" do themselves.

On the positive side of the responsibility theme, Stewart describes the leaders' reactions to problem situations. The Road Superintendent, the Load Dispatcher, the Chief of the Weather Bureau, the General, Big Al, and Johnny Martley all recognize their responsibilities to their fellowmen. Most of the leaders also recognize man's fallibility and irrationality. The Road Superintendent, for example, recognizes that there are always motorists who fail to heed the warning to put on chains for the trip over Donner Pass. The Load Dispatcher recognizes that his crews cannot spot all of the defects in power lines—defects caused, for example, by the owl's electrocution that weakened a wire but that could not be spotted with the naked eye in regular checks of the wires. Stewart gives a graphic illustration of these leaders' recognition of their responsibilities in the Chief's nightmare:

> Standing on some miraculous point of lookout, possessing more than human vision, the Chief saw clearly the far reach of the Bay. Blue and quiet it lay in the sunshine. On its surface, with breeze just enough to fill their sails, moved hundreds of pleasure craft—yawls and ketches, starboats, and snipe-boats, little home-made pumpkinseeds. Then suddenly a great black cloud arose, covering all the southeastern sky, and the little boats turned for shore. But the storm struck, and they were overwhelmed. The bodies washed ashore where women stood screaming. Then upon the Chief fell a sense of unutterable shame and guilt, for he remembered that he had seen that great storm dominating all the map, and yet in some moment of incredible blindness he had forecast fair weather and on his word all those pretty craft had sailed out upon the Bay. And always, he knew—as he felt himself sinking into the pit of madness—that he would carry with him the horror of that sight and of the screaming.[79]

Comparable to the Chief's nightmare is the General's reality, where a decision must be made about the disposition of the flood waters brought about by the storm. Businessmen of the city urge one decision; asparagus farmers in the valley urge another. The General's decision, different from either, is based on the greatest good for the greatest number of people.[80] No matter what course the General takes some people will suffer. Responsibility for his decision rests with him and no one else; he gives the order to flood the valley. The General consoles himself with the conviction that he did the best he could under the circumstances. But the General feels old after his decision because he recognizes that other storms will come, and he remembers a saying that reflects a truism about *entropic* forces abroad in the universe: "Then he found the quotation somewhere back in his mind: 'All the rivers run into the sea; yet the sea is not full; unto the place from whence the rivers come, thither they also return again.'"[81]

"TWELFTH DAY"

It is significant that Stewart has the General make his decision on the "Twelfth Day," the final day of the storm and the book. Of the twelve sections that comprise the "Twelfth Day," the first eleven deal with readiness. Section "12" of the "Twelfth Day" is like section "1" of the "First Day" in that an omniscent perspective of the earth's planetary position in space is noted. But in this last section of his book Stewart states that a watcher from Venus might note that "It [earth] gave no signs that storms or men disturbed its tranquil round."[82] Geologically considered, man is "new" to the planet earth. Like the dinosaur, his days may be numbered. Considering the kinds of hydrogen storms modern man may have to weather, the reader may realize that the readiness factor coupled with the cooperation factor can lead to a mutually responsible human race or to extinction.

Readiness, like the other themes in *Storm,* is presented on the "Twelfth Day" as a graduated scale. Section "1" of the "Twelfth Day" takes up the philosophic question of weather and relativity in terms of "good" and "bad" and makes the point that both these judgment-words are human *perceptions* and have little to do with natural phenomena such as storms. Section "2" deals with the effects of Little Maria on the East Coast—suggesting a *microcosm* of Maria's effect on California. More important perhaps Stewart makes the reader aware that all parts of a country and the world are affected by events usually myopically perceived by man as "local." Furthering this point, section "3" gives a *simultaneous* picture of weather systems around the world that are directly related to Maria's and Little Maria's "local" influence on the weather. Section "4" deals with the General's battle with the river, with human pressure-blocks, and with himself. Stewart shows the General as a man who tends to exemplify the kinds of readiness and *perspective* needed to survive against cosmic forces, natural and manmade. Section "5" reemphasizes the likenesses between storms and men, stressing the *individuality* factor, the *relativity* factor in terms of *flexibility,* and the need for readiness for new storms. Section "6" deals with readiness at the individual level. The bodies of Max and Jen are found. Blinded by a snow flurry, Max drove their car over a cliff. Readiness for storm driving conditions Stewart implies, might have postponed this "conclusion." In section "7," Stewart uses the "clipper" to show how man can utilize the forces of the universe in helpful ways. Using a tail wind to speed its flight across the ocean, the clipper can, if necessary, avoid bad weather; it is flexible in its course. Section "8" presents road crews, railroad crews, and telephone and power crews all working not only to clean up the damage caused by Maria but to make ready for new storms. Stewart summarizes the readiness theme by quoting Hamlet's "readiness is all" speech in section "9." Section "10" describes the city's *homeostatic* return to "normal" conditions, with flags of the companies flying in the breeze. But in the same section the leaders in these companies—the L.D., the DTS, and the CSO—are all busy preparing for the next storm. Section "11" is a biblical quotation emphasizing that the wind "returneth again according to his circuits." Stewart is again suggesting that until weather control becomes a reality, readiness for relentless cosmic forces is the best preparation. Section "12" is the omniscent view of the planet earth in galactic space.

Themes, structures, and viewpoints other than those described in the early chapters of this book may be perceived in *Storm.* The "rightness" or "wrongness" of these other perspectives on *Storm* tend, in terms of some of Stewart's Introduction, to be a function of the reader's *frame of reference.* The individual nature of storms and men tends to make different perceptions of phenomena a function of the reader's *total* experience, which is of course different for each. Yet there are seemingly common *perceptions* of structure and process in *Storm.* The *structure* of the novel most readers would agree has a definite purpose. Starting with scattered isolated incidents—short and atomistic—the book, through a planned articulation of incidents, moves to form larger and larger patterns until the reader's perceptions reveal a mosaic. Bits and pieces of events, characters, and situations are placed one upon the other until in section "3" of the "Eleventh Day" a *total* picture is formed. That such a mosaic should emerge on the "Eleventh Day" without careful design on Stewart's part is questionable.

The gradual but marked *change* evident in the J.M.'s character from the "First Day" through the "Twelfth Day" seems to be another instance of definite planning and design by Stewart. Shifts in the J.M.'s perceptions seem plausible and consistent in terms of his experience in "creating" Maria and in his relationships with the staff of the Weather Bureau and the public.

Themes of *flexibility* and responsibility in each day of the storm's twelve days occur with a consistency indicating that something other than chance is involved. Stewart's use of language, one key to thematic enigmas, tends in many ways to support the themes identified. Stewart's life-in-death and death-in-life metaphor perhaps impels the reader to paraphrase the metaphor in *total* perspective when he observes that the end of the book is the beginning, and that the beginning is the end. The identical nature of section "1" of the "First Day" and section "12" of the last day makes credible such a conclusion. Stewart's quotations from the Bible and from Shakespeare also suggest the likeness of beginning and ending in this way: Each time the Bible or Shakespeare is read, new perceptions, new insights can be gained. McLuhan's identification of the twentieth-century's "do-it-yourself" literature coupled with Frost's, Eliot's, and Daiches' suggestions that literary criticism is not "autotelic" imply that constant new horizons exist in the study of literature because literature, in a field theory approach, is in a *constant state of becoming.*

THE FIELD THEORY APPROACH AND OTHER WORKS OF LITERATURE

Storm mirrors the cultural values of the society in which it was written, as do other works of art in other times and places. At times the works of the past speak more immediately to contemporary society than do current books that superficially seem more clearly related to current problems. The French, for example, turned to *Antigone* during World War II as an expression of reaction against their German masters. In this sense certain aspects of field theory as a technique of literary criticism merge with other historical, scholarly, and time-tested techniques. When, for example, an author attempts to present a vast, accurate panorama of society, the critic, in varying degrees, explores the culture that gave rise to the society, examines the characters representative of the society, notices the structure and technique by which the narrative unfolds, classifies the work according to some system, and evaluates the worth of the writing according to any of several acceptable criteria. At the surface level a field theory technique follows this pattern, and with the surface technique *Tom Jones, The Red and the Black, Vanity Fair,* or any literary work can be studied.

But below the surface, field theory as a critical technique is specialized for application to twentieth-century literature. The reason for this specialization lies in the existence of the so-called do-it-yourself literature. Beyond the fact that the reader must often supply his own conclusions to contemporary literary works, there is a growing tendency on the part of authors to make the reader provide the plot. The internal world of what Leon Edel refers to as the "plotless" novel[83] is exemplified in the works of Marcel Proust, James Joyce, and others where the "action" exists primarily in thought processes rather than in an ordered series of external events. The direct application of field theory principles in such recent works as *The Alexandria Quartet* (relativity) and *Teresa* (complementarity) demand a field-oriented approach.

Looking back on the field theory exploration of *Storm,* what unique qualities can be identified as generic to the technique?

A background in the concepts and theories discussed in the early chapters of this book is prerequisite for any use of field theory in a classroom. Most teachers and prospective teachers will have to gain this background now, but their students already have it by the time they reach senior (and sometimes even junior) high school English classes. They have learned these concepts and theories in their revised mathematics and science programs: The School Mathematics Study Group (SMSG) courses and the Biological Sciences Curriculum Study (BSCS) courses contain concepts such as "sets," "groups," "symbolic logic," "DNA," "ecology," "homeostasis," and "entropy." In addition to such concepts, students bring to English classes attitudes—acceptance of change, suspended judgments, relativity of position, indeterminacy—and techniques—detailed observation, scientific method, testing of hypotheses—that help them to identify similar concepts, attitudes, and techniques in contemporary literature.

The proper scientific background then is necessary for a field theory approach to the teaching of literature. This background dictates the teacher's selection of *Storm* over *Silas Marner* and other works from which he could have chosen; only in contemporary works of literature can some of these scientific concepts be found.

In the preceding exploration of *Storm* the reader was asked to consider the wholeness principle, to examine the book from flyleaf to index noting the arresting structure and getting an "overview." Then, from the point of view of a "teacher" rather than a "reader," a "field" was identified that immediately influenced the boundaries of perception. The focus on "teaching" narrowed and deepened the range of material and in so doing cut the breadth of perception. This narrowing of focus is one example of the all-pervasive entropy. A teacher can gain depth by specialization but loses breadth; his students (with perceptions different from teaching) may restore part of the breadth later on. But the time lost between the two occurrences is irreplaceable. Entropy is a universal and reflected, in some degree, in all literature; it is the grim paradox of existence.

From these first impressions a pattern—dim, flexible, and spare—took shape, with the reader to amend and add to the pattern as key points came up in interaction with the ordered waves of words that are *Storm*.

The reader was then asked to move into *Storm* with the recognition that he and *Storm* would be changed by the experience. His observer viewpoint changed; the field from the inside has marked differences from the field outside. Depending upon how well he understood the scientific principles laid down in the early chapters of this book, *he*, not *Storm*, set limits to the perceptions he obtained. As concepts (or descriptions that seemed to fit concepts) were discovered in the book, their structural position was noted, and perhaps they added to or modified the plan formed from "outside" perceptions. Here and there in the interaction with the inner field of *Storm*, microcosms were examined to see to what extent the miniature, inside sample matched the wholeness and totality of the book. Sometimes the reader's background may have set up temporary irrational eddies within the field, but these are part of all fields, and they became part of the reader's total perception when placed in perspective.

Dynamism was part of the interaction with *Storm*, and the reader became aware of many field theory concepts in this process. Simultaneity, through feedback, marked his progress: As ideas were communicated from *Storm*, they interacted with his individual background, were modified and put into a pattern, and then as he moved on were reduced to a dynamic symbol capable of regenerating the totality of the experience—all performed quickly and simultaneously with little comprehension of the complexity involved.

Individually, the symbol chosen for storing incidents perhaps differed. Some readers may recall "the airplane incident," others may recall "Big Al" or simply "Al" as the microcosm that spins out the association that puts the incident of section "3" of the "Eleventh Day" into pattern. The simultaneous contact, decoding, recording, abbreviating, and storing of such incidents provides a kind of efficiency that allows the reader to move on to other perceptions. Depending upon the amount and efficiency of this storage factor, an English teacher, for example, might simultaneously be reacting to his unique "programming" as a teacher and noting such things as linguistic variations, sentence patterns, literary allusions, and communication techniques along with his "environmentally programmed" eye to spelling, vocabulary, and punctuation. The circuit or set of his program—teaching—adds still other simultaneous perceptions: possible topics for composition, needed library work, research topics, interdisciplinary resources, passages for checking reading comprehension, and myriad other forms of feedback.

When the reader has finished his interaction with *Storm's* "Twelfth Day," relativity and homeostasis principles should come through clearly because of Stewart's structure and design: The reader is back to the perceptions with which the book opened —in a sense both a finite and infinite universe. But now a process of incubation and reflection sets in; a kind of gestation of ideas takes place that theoretically will continue as long as contact is renewed with *Storm.* New insights supplied to a teacher by new classes of students and new perceptions gained from the relegating of formerly difficult material to routine processes allow him to see relationships that his previous contacts with *Storm* had obscured because of the density of initially communicated ideas or because of inhibiting feedback barriers. And the storage factor, the symbolization of his contact with *Storm,* remains forever a part of his literary background—adding, modifying, and enriching his perceptions of other literary experiences.

Storm is not alone in its compass of contemporary fields. Other novels, plays, and collections of verse published since 1941 might as easily illustrate that the problems, values, and patterns of a culture are broadcast in its literature. This is not new: Shakespeare exemplified it in his so-called historical plays, in which he used remote historical figures when he was forbidden to present contemporary Elizabethan characters on his stage. But was it coincidence that *The Crucible* and the McCarthy hearings—both witch-hunts—appeared on the American scene at almost the same time? What accounts for the recent popularity of *Teahouse of the August Moon, Flower Drum Song,* and *The World of Suzie Wong* on Broadway as compared to *Madame Butterfly* of another, earlier time and perhaps of a society where the "East-West Twain" could never meet?

Certainly the values of any given society at an arrested point in time are reflected in its authors' works. But there are authors in each of these time blocks whose themes, techniques, and structures strike "timeless" cores of human behavior—perhaps "fields" of values common to all mankind. The authors and works discussed below have been arbitrarily chosen to suggest a progression of books from *Storm* to *The Alexandria Quartet* that are comprehensive enough to demand a field theory approach to enhance their patterns of values.

A Bell for Adano, by John Hersey has been translated into forty-six languages and is a cover-to-cover interrelated, structure-process whole that deals with the American army of occupation in Italy. But certain of the principles, truisms, and insights Hersey "renders" in his book could apply equally to Alexander the Great, Caesar Augustus, Napoleon, and other modern or future "armies of occupation." On the other hand, Hersey's concern for the unique metaphorical aspects of modern language marks the novel as contemporary and anticipates *The Ugly American.* Simultaneity, complementarity, relativity, observer viewpoint, and other field theory characteristics are tacitly explored throughout Hersey's book.

Remembrance Rock gives Carl Sandburg occasion to ask, rhetorically, "What did World War II mean to Americans?" Sandburg incloses three novels under his one title with the transitional device of a diary whose contents span time from the American Revolution to the days after World War II. Again language, symbol, metaphor, and relativity render the commonality of human aspirations in the time-space field. More important, Sandburg shows the values of the old: that man cannot "forget what brought us along," that he needs this heritage as a basis for shaping the new day. But this "new," in its proposed rapprochement of arts and sciences, is different in kind from either of the separate entities, "the old" and "the new," that went into making it.

In *The Old Man and the Sea* Ernest Hemingway explores the ecological role of the mythical "average" man in the cosmos. Each man in his lifetime, Hemingway seems to say, perceives the world subjectively: There is—as far as individuals are concerned—no history, no past, no future except as each individual, depending upon his field of life, affects and is affected by his fields of experience. The cultural impact of one old fisherman is a matter for world consideration because as a symbol of "Everyman" he reveals the influence of "each" on "all."

A Fable, William Faulkner's novel, reflects his characteristically involved symbolism and his constant broadcast of meanings in deepening waves. Using France in World War I as a setting (the author's personal background of experience), *A Fable,* published after World War II, explores a growing theme in world literature: world brotherhood and the commonality of mankind. Utilizing a Christ-like figure and "disciples" from many countries, Faulkner appears to contrast the desire of man the individual for peace with officialdom's (or perhaps governments') desire for war. Man's most mismanaged tool, language, in Faulkner's novel, again leads to "Christ's" execution. Field theory approaches to *A Fable* tend to reveal structures and processes, principles and concepts, noted in the early chapters of this book, particularly those dealing with communication as defined by Lennox Grey.

Lord of the Flies, William Golding's enlightening nightmare of the contemporary world, uses a band of children on an adult-free island as a microcosm of many of the new scientific principles and concepts. E. L. Epstein's notes on the book show that field theory ideas are appearing in literary criticism:

> What is unique about the work of Golding is the way he has combined and synthesized all of the characteristically twentieth-century methods of analysis of the human being and human society and used this unified knowledge to comment on a "test situation." In this book, as in few others of the present time, are findings of psychoanalysts of all schools, anthropologists, social psychologists and philosophical historians mobilized into an attack upon the central problem of modern thought: the nature of human personality and the reflection of personality on society.
>
> Another feature of Golding's work is the superb use of symbolism, a symbolism that "works." The central symbol itself, "the lord of the flies," is, like any true symbol, much more than the sum of its parts.[84]

It might be added to Epstein's penetrating statement that Golding was enrolled in a science curriculum until his sophomore year at Oxford, when he switched to English literature. Like

Huxley, the science is in his writing, and such principles as homeostasis, complementarity, microcosm, indeterminacy, irrationality, and relativity can easily be identified in it. With specific reference to English, it is interesting to ask in considering this book what happens to language (the vehicle of social control) when entropic forces work on it. How does this book differ from books with similar settings and structures *(The Admirable Crichton, Robinson Crusoe, Swiss Family Robinson)* from other times and cultures? As in *Storm,* the ending of Golding's *Lord of the Flies* implies a larger beginning—an adult macrocosm of the children's microcosm.

George Orwell's novel *1984,* with its "nuspeak," "black is white," and other dictums, also involves communication. Distortion of language, symbol manipulation, brainwashing, and other modern concerns of the "free" world are explored in a structure-process field that reveals field theory's "control of input, feedback, entropy" concepts. Unless individuals exercise control over groups that control communication (Orwell warns) the world of 1984 will be no fiction.

Alan Paton's *Too Late the Phalarope,* published early in the 1950's, is an oracle for the present crisis in Africa. The phalarope, a coastal bird, appears far inland, contrary to all ecological and migratory patterns. If a reader muses that "the time is out of joint," or "something is rotten in Denmark [Africa]," perhaps this is intended. Again, Paton reveals how environment shapes perceptions and how time changes values, but always these events take place in life-space fields where balances are foreordained by nature.

On the Beach, by Nevil Shute, takes its title from T. S. Eliot's "I'd rather be a pair of ragged claws. . . ." Shute's novel is a "communication" device that develops both the interpersonal and intrapersonal communications that structure the "field" of the personality. Irrational man through misunderstood communications sets off the ultimate destruction; it was all a mistake. The visual images of hemispheres, the structure of the book, its metaphor, theme, characterization—all lend themselves well to a field theory approach.

Fahrenheit 451, by Ray Bradbury, has an ironic title, for it happens to be the temperature at which books burn. Firemen, in Bradbury's fictional country, start fires whenever someone turns in an alarm that books are being read; it is their job to destroy all reading matter. Bradbury's people survive on government-controlled television. Again language, mass media, and symbol distortion are the means through which the individual has surrendered his rights to power controls. Digests, and digests of digests, made people more and more dependent on "interpreters" of events until finally they could no longer think for themselves. A few who did think for themselves by going to firsthand sources were executed or exiled. Atomic war caused by planned image distortions wipes out Bradbury's fictional society except for an underground group off in the woods who have specilized in memorizing passages from great books and who plan to write them down as a heritage for the survivors of the war.

The Fall, by Albert Camus, deals with the relations between man's inner and outer worlds. Man's responsibility to man, the individual's direct involvement in the state of society—no matter what that society may be—seems to be Camus' ecological theme. Blame not the words, the customs, the laws, the morals for man's miserable existences; rather blame your perceptions, your interpretations of words, and your cowardice for not, as an individual, revealing your feelings about injustice. A voice out of Algeria restating that no man is an island or that each man is a part of everything he meets and must show it seems to be Camus' "field of communication."

The Roots of Heaven, by Romain Gary, takes its title from the Islamic description of freedom. The title is significant and symbolic for reader-understanding of the protagonist's efforts to preserve the African elephant from extinction by "commercial" interests. The elephant to the protagonist (as wild horses to the characters in Arthur Miller's *Misfits*) symbolizes freedom. The implications of this novel with its African settings and its late 1950's publication date are all too obvious in the headlines of the 1960's. Characters in the novel are drawn from all nations with interests in Africa and represent a range of ecologically oriented people. A field theory approach to this novel reveals Gary's rendering of things to come accomplished again by skillful structure and insights into the ways levels of language affect human behavior.

Catch-22, Joseph Heller's reaction to World War II, is out of place in this chronology of successors to *Storm*. Published in 1961, it lacks the immediate postwar currency of Irwin Shaw's *The Young Lions* or Norman Mailer's *The Naked and the Dead*, though both of these books have field theory elements, e.g., Mailer's use of what he called "The Time Machine" to structure a four-part examination of the ecological impacts of war. *Catch-22* makes clear the emotional effect of war, but does it in a way that caused one reviewer to call the book a "new style of writing"[85] and another to compare it to *The Catcher in the Rye*. Perception, irrationality, semantics, psycholinguistics, entropy—these and more are used to illustrate, with telling effect, the interrelationships of language, behavior, rationality, and society. Microcosm seems to be the structural technique for Heller's plot, though some readers claim the book is too confusing to have a plot. As a model for the use of a field theory approach to literature, *Catch-22* exemplifies most of principles described in the early chapters of this book.

The Alexandria Quartet makes explicit the field theory ideas implicit in most of the foregoing novels. Admittedly, some of their authors might deny that they consciously used field theory principles or that they were even symbolically concerned about the word choices, settings, or characters they used. And at the conscious level their denials are relevant, but subconsciously, as studies in communications, psycholinguistics, and other fields have shown, authors are the product of their language and culture. Each word, each idea an author uses is selected from a storehouse of personal experience, and this selection is not haphazard but to a pattern as individually different as a fingerprint. It is reassuring then to find Lawrence Durrell explaining his pattern with reference to a field theory principle as follows: "*The Quartet* is a four-decker novel whose form is based on the relativity proposition. Three sides of space and one of time constitute the soup-mix recipe."[86]

Into *The Quartet* has gone "everything," and as Nigel Dennis, British novelist and critic, has noted:

> The problem that arises with this sort of writing is one of form, i.e., how to make one strong parcel out of so many differently shaped commodities, how to impose method on what would otherwise be madness. Durrell's solution—which many regard as the most revolutionary innovation in modern fiction—was not only to throw all his thoughts and characters into an invented city but to hitch space and time together under the yoke of Albert Einstein.[87]

Durrell did much more than "throw" his ideas and characters into his *Quartet,* as a careful reading shows, and the worldwide popularity of his work is one indication of the extent to which it speaks to its time-space-conscious audience. But one mathematician called Durrell's relativity format "poppycock," claiming that relativity could be applied only in mathematics and that to apply relativity to literature was "rubbish."[88] Gibbs, Bohr, Wiener, and Heisenberg might take issue with this criticism of Durrell's work.

Durrell's work is a masterpiece of perception. Essentially, *The Quartet* is the same story told from four different perceptions in which the total life space of each narrator completely changes the "factual" or "concrete" environment. Which perception is correct is a matter of physics' "indeterminacy" or the critics' "do-it-yourself search for meaning."

Instances of concern for field ideas can be found in almost any list of currently published books. Nigel Dennis, who so forcefully supported Durrell's attempts at a new novel form, is less impressed by Frank Baker's recent novel, which in microcosm comes close to Durrell's method. After indicating that the plot of Baker's book *Teresa* is that of a woman in search of self, Dennis comments on the author's technique as follows:

> He [the author] divides his book in thirty-five little chapters, with each chapter showing a stage in Teresa's unhappy life. Instead of starting with the stage of her infancy and ending with the stage of her death, he deliberately confounds the natural order. His first chapter does not contain Teresa at all; she has just been buried. Four pages farther on she appears, aged 65; and six pages after that she is only 20.
>
> He has chosen this technique because "at any point in Teresa's life, as in any other, the full yet unrevealed personality must exist." But does this method help to clear it?[89]

Whether Baker's method is successful or not, Dennis' review suggests that ideas of life-space field, perception, structure, and relativity (e.g., "natural" order is changed) are implicit in Baker's novel.

Having observed how a scholarly-critical method based on field theory principles tends to bring out values in *Storm*, it is possible to see the need for the teacher to set the stage, i.e., to manage the communication in the classroom, in such a way that students also become involved in field theory procedures. Principles from field theory contributing to the philosophical structure in the teacher's organizational field might include an approach to the work of art as a whole rather than piecemeal *(totality)*, assessing student viewpoints in search for significant patterns *(feedback)*, allowing students to explore simultaneous aspects of design in current culture *(simultaneity, ecology)*, providing opportunities for wide perspectives and conflicting opinions *(observer viewpoint, relativity, complementarity)*, focusing attention on the symbolic yet relative aspects of communication *(positioning, time and space)*, and evaluating students' growth in awareness and behavior change through careful attention to total perspectives *(life space, constant state of becoming)*.

Teachers, experienced in designing structures for student involvement in literary works of art, might organize the above ideas into a "plan" in which the interrelatedness of critical method and teaching method is revealed. This plan might be expected to consist of "key" ideas and "procedures" for implementing them. Inasmuch as the idea tends to structure the procedure, it is necessary to explore first a configuration of ideas *Storm* might inspire and then illustrate one of the ideas as it might structure and be structured by classroom procedures. The following is a list of some of the key ideas field-oriented teachers might use in a critical-teaching approach to *Storm:*

> A work of art grows from and reflects the culture in which the author lives and writes.
>
> A novel is a consciously structured work of art where design itself communicates both within and beyond the meanings of the words.
>
> Man's participation in his culture is through symbols, which

afford him an opportunity to sample wide-ranging forms of behavior and to evaluate them, without exposing himself in actuality.

Each man's understanding of his ephemeral state in the cosmos can increase his readiness to understand that his time-bound participation in his cultural milieu can affect and is affected by his perceptions of life space.

Man seeks to pattern all experiences so that a balance between himself and his environment is imminent.

Man's skill in interpreting symbolic communication depends on his unique perceptions of the frequency, intensity, priority, and breadth of his participation in his environmental and time-bound ethos.

Man's understanding of the principles of ecology increases his potential to offset the forces of entropy constantly at work in the cosmos.

Man's acceptance of flux, change, and dynamism as "natural" in the cosmic processes increases his readiness to adapt to amorphous perimeters in his life-space field.

Although these are not all of the "key" ideas experienced teachers might identify in their perusal of *Storm* with a "teaching *Storm*" frame of reference, they nevertheless represent a sample of the key ideas many teachers might phrase subconsciously for their "structural" design. The language of these ideas might exceed vocabulary limits of students for whom the design is intended, but the key ideas are those of the teacher and, depending on the grade level of the students involved, may or may not enter the students' perceptual field.

Putting into operational form one of these "key ideas," as it represents the rapprochement between critical method and teaching method through the application of field theory principles, might take the form of Table D.

This plan for making operational one of the many key ideas possible for increasing students' awareness of "fields" and their interrelationships has flexibility as part of its structure. Academic calendars circumscribe teachers' time and space, but the simultaneous aspects of this plan allow a teacher to work with students in identifying particular aspects of the space-time continuum that

TABLE D

KEY IDEA	PROCEDURES	LANGUAGE ARTS SKILLS
A work of art grows from and reflects the culture in which the artist lives.	Display and discuss paintings representing the key idea, e.g., Van Gogh's *Starry Night,* Picasso's *Guernica,* Dali's *Persistence of Memory.*	Speaking and listening as students and teacher discuss symbolic relationships of themes along lines of organizational patterns, color, choice of illustration, etc.
	Compare paintings with musical selections, e.g., Tchaikovsky's *1812 Festival Overture,* Gershwin's *An American in Paris,* Grofé's *Grand Canyon Suite.*	
	Have students glance through the ML edition of *Storm* with a readiness to comment on the copyright date, the Introduction, and the observable structure of the book.	Reading for a particular purpose—developing techniques of scanning and perusal for later skill-building.
	List social institutions, e.g., family, government, etc., and discuss ways of gathering information about values society gave to these institutions in 1940.	Reading, writing, and speaking. Library skills are reviewed in this discussion, which gives students a chance for speaking and listening as well as advancing note-taking skills.
	Assign library work on cultural backgrounds of the world of 1940 on topics volunteered by students under teacher-student suggested headings.	Speaking, listening, and reading. Application of library skills and review discussion of world culture *circa* 1940.

will in turn structure the field for studying *Storm.* A series of plans such as this one might be regarded as the microcosm-in-macrocosm aspect of field theory that the field-oriented teacher could use to manage the communication in the classroom. The outcome of students' experiences implied by the illustrative plan might be their development of a structural framework for viewing *Storm* similar to the one explored in the opening sections of the *Storm* analysis in this chapter.

Field theory approaches to the teaching of literature tacitly urge a rapprochement between the critical method and teaching method described, as seen in the early chapters of this book, by spokesmen from the sciences, the social sciences, and the humanities. To discover the extent of structures and processes for achieving this recommended rapprochement in programs for preservice teachers of English, it is necessary to explore programs that aspire to educate teachers of English within prescribed structures. Examples of prescribed structures for this purpose are undergraduate education programs and state-mandated requirements for certification as "teacher of English." In the next chapter it will be seen that field theory concepts have definite implications for programs of preservice teachers of English.

SIX

FIELD CONCEPTS AND THE TRAINING OF ENGLISH TEACHERS

In considering the wealth of concepts essentially new to the English teacher that have emerged in the preceding discussions of field theory, it is impossible to avoid the professional question of what they mean for programs for preservice teachers of English. Answers to this question of meaning might begin with the implications of the simultaneity principle for such programs. All disciplines are simultaneously experiencing fundamental changes in structures and processes. Prospective teachers of English need to increase their awareness of this phenomenon and at the same time discover ways of ordering these constellations of knowledge into a pattern for classroom communication. One of the ways English teachers' programs might provide experiences with methods for ordering simultaneous phenomena would be through courses in cultural anthropology. The anthropologist's method of merging himself (totally experiencing) all aspects of a culture simultaneously and then evolving constellations of related phenomena in an ordered way suggests a method urgently needed by preservice teachers of English in today's world of merging cultures.

The widespread concern in many disciplines for integrating knowledge suggests the need to provide prospective teachers of English with experiences in perimeter ideas in wide fields of human inquiry—beyond the broadfield courses in the sciences, social sciences, and humanities. Programs for prospective teachers of English must provide students with some disciplined method for exploring the new perimeters of knowledge. One of the ways this disciplined approach might be provided is through courses such as "Communication and the Communication Arts in the Modern Community"[1] offered at Teachers College, Columbia University. In this course specialists in psychology, sociology, mathematics, philosophy, language, the arts, and other disciplines discuss modern concepts and processes from their respective fields.[2] Students enrolled in the course perceive not only the perimeters of new knowledge in each discipline but also the simultaneity of these concepts as they influence the process common to all disciplines, communication. Courses similar in structure and purpose might be patterned around the kind of interdisciplinary experiences recorded in Lynn White's *Frontiers of Knowledge in the Study of Man,* Oliver Reiser's *The Integration of Human Knowledge,* or Roy Grinker's *Toward a Unified Theory of Human Behavior,* all of which use the integrative, interdisciplinary approach apparent in the Teachers College "Communication" course.

Design is fundamental to field theory in all disciplines. Awareness of design is particularly important for prospective teachers of English. It is the design of words in English that causes one pattern of words to be classified as prose, another pattern as poetry, and, depending on a host of relative perceptions and frameworks, still other patterns as conversation, dialogue, lecture, discussion, *ad infinitum.* In the potential universe of English words, which might be envisioned as chaos or, more familiarly, as an entropic force, it is the order, the form consciously imposed by the artist that produces the work of art. Programs for preservice English teachers must include opportunities for prospective teachers to discover this fundamental process of patterning as basic to exploring a work of art within the temporal limits of a given culture. The artist as innovator tends to design forms for the future. Stewart's design for *Storm* and Durrell's design for *The Alexandria Quartet* support design as center to the understanding of art forms. Educators are also wrestling with new information to shape designs for learning experiences for future students. (Simultaneity exists here—all disciplines are currently faced with the problem of design.) Preservice teachers of English must learn of this common struggle for design through programmed exploration of the perimeters of new knowledge so that they can come to discover that artists such as Stewart and Durrell are illustrating and extending man's constant struggle to order his life-space experiences. It is only as teachers of English can communicate their own program experiences with design that the "average" citizen will begin to comprehend the simultaneous goals of art and science.

Understanding of the creative process should be consciously prescribed as part of programs for preservice English teachers. Through courses in general education, the humanities, the communication arts, or other areas that deal with art forms, each teacher should become familiar with the distinct functions of each art form, not only in the culture but also in the personal development of human beings. It is this understanding of the creative process alone that will permit prospective English teachers to acknowledge the artist as a participant in the evolution of a culture.

No matter how worthwhile programs for preservice teachers of English appear from structural perspectives, without the constant interrelated and supportive processes recognized as characteristic of field theory the programs will not fulfill their field theory implications. Processes throughout such programs should provide prospective teachers with chances to experience the values of exploration in such a way that their students will have similar classroom experiences. As part of these processes, preservice teachers should be afforded opportunities to test the validity and integrity of class designs against their own personal integrity. Educational experiences of preservice teachers of English do not end automatically when they leave the classroom. Processes for making them aware of the valuable and contributing role of total life-space experiences to their educational programs will increase the chances that they will provide similar processes for their students.

The symbolic process is man's unique invention. As a unifying tool for all phases of the preservice teacher's program, the symbolic process should undergird and support structures and scholarly-critical methods that allow prospective English teachers to explore it as key to mankind's cultural heritage. Participation in experiences based on explorations of the symbolic process should encompass a prospective English teacher's total program. Each class in such a program should be an experience that makes the prospective teacher aware of teaching as an art. All classes in his program, taken together, should provide him with a paradigm consisting of articulated structures and critical-teaching methods, not as a final model but as an infinitely adaptable plan for artistic application with his students.

SAMPLE PROGRAMS FOR PRESERVICE TEACHERS

The New York State Education Department a short time ago initiated a Teacher Education and Certification Study. One phase of this study involved the examination of college programs for preservice teachers of academic subjects. The results of the study were reported in three monographs: *Characteristics of Effective Teachers, Analysis of Teacher Education Programs in New York State,* and *Studies of the Professional Content in Education Needed by Teachers of Academic Subjects.*[3]

An analysis of these reports focused on the field of English reveals that "variety" is the characteristic common to preservice programs for English teachers. Colleges selected by the Department's Bureau of Certification as representative of the patterns of teacher education in New York State were Cornell, Elmira, Fordham, Houghton, New York University, Queens, the State University of New York's College of Education at Albany, St. Lawrence, Syracuse, Union, and the University of Buffalo (now the State University of New York at Buffalo).

Reports on the findings of the Education Department's Teacher Education and Certification Study coupled with more recent recommendations made by committees of the Department's Academic Teacher Certification Project have prescribed programs having field-like structures. One result of the Department's recommendations has been a revision of programs for preservice

English teachers in some of the colleges surveyed in the Teacher Education and Certification Study. As might be expected, the Department's prescriptions would not materially alter the "variety" characteristic noted in the survey. In a field theory reference frame the tendency for each college to retain its unique "image," to put students through experiences that identify them as "Columbia," "Cornell," or "Albany" graduates, fits the "life-space" identification of "self" as a field principle.

Keeping in mind the unique aspects of each college, common patterns in programs for prospective English teachers can still be identified. Though broad, the "common" aspect exists in the fact that preservice English teachers come from:

1. Liberal arts programs *without* professional education courses;
2. Liberal arts programs *with* professional education courses;
3. Liberal arts or liberal arts with professional education *with* "general education" broadfield courses.

The University of Buffalo and Cornell offer unique but representative programs for preservice teachers of English along the general lines suggested above that can serve as "typical" program patterns for prospective English teachers.

From a field theory perspective, Buffalo's "unique" offerings to the liberal arts student who may aspire to teach English are characterized by the "tutorial"[4] plan and the "American Studies Program."[5] Seniors in the tutorial plan have the advantage of "individualized instruction" along with the "opportunity for increasing their understanding of the relationships between different areas of learning." The American Studies Program "provides an interdepartmental major in American civilization." The program offers the "sort of preparation which can serve as background for public school teaching." The English major seeking a bachelor of arts degree must take required courses on a graduated scale of complexity provided through a prerequisite system (a survey course in eighteenth-century literature must precede a course in eighteenth-century novelists). All course work is brought together in a required "comprehensive examination" that:

... will test the student's knowledge, his judgment, his intel-

> lectual development, and his literary taste. It is expected that he will display some knowledge of English history, an awareness of literary genres, some comprehension of English metrics, and certain factual knowledge of the principal verse forms used by the great English poets.[6]

Courses listed as possible background for the "comprehensive" examination include "Great Books," "Great English Poets," "Narrative Literature," "Types of Literature: the Epic," "Types of Literature: Tragedy,"[7] and similar courses. The tutorial plan and the comprehensive examination tacitly supply the articulation for courses taken by the English major in his program at Buffalo.

Students at Buffalo who take professional education courses as part of their degree programs are offered a field-like experience described as the "Professional Unit":

> [The] Professional Unit . . . meeting the minimal requirements for certification to teach in New York State, is offered juniors and seniors in the College of Arts and Sciences who wish to teach academic subjects in secondary schools, or who wish to teach art or music in elementary or secondary schools.[8]

All students at Buffalo, no matter what their degree programs, must take what is known as "The Common Curriculum."[9] In this required freshman-sophomore experience, areas of "English, Mathematics, Social Sciences, Natural Sciences, Humanities"[10] are mandated, with some election within the categories. "The Common Curriculum" appears to be a conscious attempt to have students explore and articulate their experiences in specialized areas of knowledge. Prospective English teachers who make this articulation are those who presumably would find a field theory approach to literature useful in their classrooms.

Students seeking a bachelor of arts degree at Cornell must also take a "program of common studies." This program provides students with what Cornell defines as a "liberal education," further defined as "a special knowledge of some field of human understanding, erected upon a fundamental training in the humanities, the natural sciences and the social studies."[11] These common studies plus specialization and election provide "the means whereby man has come to understand himself and the world in which he lives."[12] Recognizable in Cornell's common studies program is the interrelated structure characteristic of field theory as a concept. But the apparent absence of the necessary and equally important *process* for implementing structure, so prevalent in field theory, suggests that colleges still have a long way to go in achieving the program objective of the student coming to "understand himself and the world in which he lives."

Programs for preservice teachers of English at Cornell require students to make early identification with teaching as a career:

> Prospective teachers of English in secondary schools must elect a special sequence of related courses and should consult the Chairman of the Department, preferably during the second term of their freshman year, before making out their programs for the sophomore year.[13]

The almost tutorial relationship that exists between the chairman of the English Department and a prospective teacher might be the means for a student's articulation of his required courses in English. Examination of the offerings of the English Department reveals under the heading "Intermediate Courses" such course titles as "Expository Writing: Organization," "The Twentieth Century," and "The American Literary Heritage."[14] Under the heading "Courses for Upperclassmen" are listed "The Eighteenth Century," "The Victorian Period," "Shorter Forms of Fiction," "The English Language," and similar courses.[15] Articulation of the contents of these courses other than that provided by the departmental chairman is implicit in the prerequisite technique.

The School of Education at Cornell appears to perceive its function within the university as a service to graduate students. Statements about professional education for undergraduates imply such a focus on graduate programs:

> Undergraduate students must be registered in one of the undergraduate colleges rather than in the School of Education, and may work toward teaching certification while meeting the degree requirements of their college.[16]

The programs at Buffalo and Cornell reflect the nature of most preservice programs for training teachers of English. From a structural perspective both universities, and others like them, show explicit concerns for relationships and structural wholes.

But there are not in any of these programs conscious attempts to achieve relatedness among required courses. More important from the perspective of the teacher preparing to teach in a secondary classroom, no attempt is apparently made to teach students the methods of relational thinking that characterize field theory as a concept.

REQUIREMENTS FOR CERTIFICATION

The need for interrelated programs and their implicit relational thinking is being recognized by state departments of education. New York State, for example, recently listed English certification requirements that call for studies in such potentially broad fields as linguistics, world literature, and communication. The state's Bureau of Certification anticipates that five years will be necessary for teachers to fulfill the requirements for permanent certification listed below:

> (a) To teach English
> (i) Permanent certificate. At least 51 semester hours in English, 15 of which shall be in approved advanced courses
> (ii) Provisional certificate. At least 36 semester hours in English
>
> The total preparation for teaching English shall include work (although not necessarily separate courses) in the following areas:
>
> Advanced writing
> Concepts, processes and media of communication
> Development, structure and function of the English language
> Improvement of reading
> Literary materials for adolescents
> Literature: American, English, and world
> Oral composition (public speaking, argument or discussion)
> Oral interpretation (of prose, poetic, or dramatic literature)[17]

Examination of the basis for the recommended work of the preservice teacher of English reveals that the state's Bureau of Certification recognizes that "*all* the areas listed will not necessarily be offered in a college English department . . . [but that] the prospective teacher will need preparation in these areas regardless of the department within which they may be offered."[18]

Following the above statement are detailed descriptions of background "fields" for prospective teachers of English:

A. Literature continues to be the major vehicle through which the English instructor can teach a perception of human problems, can elevate the taste and critical faculties of the student and can transmit and preserve part of the heritage of our civilization. A high school teacher of English should, therefore, be thoroughly grounded in British, American and world literature, classic and contemporary, their genres and leading authors.

B. The teacher of English should know the nature and expressive potentialities of the English language. He should know enough about linguistics and the development of the English language to explain its structure and its effective use and to help students understand the literature of different eras.

C. The teacher of English should be able to write clear, organized prose; to read with comprehension, speed and accuracy; to read aloud in such a way as to make meanings clear; and to speak correctly and forcefully. A high level of personal performance in writing, speaking and reading must be demanded of him. He must also have the insight to discover the values of the literature he is teaching and the imagination to devise various ways of presenting this material to his classes.

D. The teacher of English must be able to exercise judgment as to the kind of critical appraisal required by the material, and he must be able to adapt the instruction with a regard for the pupil.

E. The teacher of English should be well acquainted with the communication skills of observing, reading, writing, listening and speaking in varied situations in connection with various media—print, radio, television, film, drama, graphic arts, etc.

F. The improvement of reading for the high school teacher of English includes teaching the methods of efficient reading to those who have not acquired the skill and helping students read to discover significant direct

> meaning. It further includes teaching the art of apprehending significant implicative meanings and their relationship to human experience. It includes the cultivation of a desire to read as well as the skills, enlarging the pupil's awareness of the rewards and challenges of that variety of literature available to a competent and appreciative reader.[19]

Elsewhere in the regulations of the New York Bureau of Certification the interrelatedness concept of field theory is structurally present in the recommendation that the prospective teacher of English take courses in "general-liberal"[20] education and that the "total program in teacher education be balanced."[21] In terms of external frameworks, the new certification requirements, effective September 1, 1963, contain many of the principles characteristic of field theory.

But the difference between an external framework and a critical-teaching method is strategically important, as the examination of field theory in this book has revealed. It is the skillful and constant combination of framework and method and their flexible, reciprocal interplay that suggests that any teacher-to-be work in the perimeters of new knowledge in the broadfields of science, social science, and humanities. No matter what the prospective teacher's particular course, his total program should always relate to education, focusing on the way method in each course is pertinent to pattern thinking.

With a continuous focus on reciprocal relationships in his program, a prospective English teacher's methods courses, student-teaching courses, or seminars become opportunities for his personal structuring of all the new information about the subject matters of English and education. From these personal perceptions, each prospective teacher creates an individually arrived at design for each of his classes and patterns his experiences for the work of art each of his classes should be.

As has been seen in earlier descriptions of field theory, it is the relationships of matter, organic and inorganic, that define a "field." Putting these relationships into a viable order from which patterns may be evolved on an individually perceived basis leads to the new experience, the dynamism, that characterizes the art of teaching.

THE INFINITE FIELD OF ENGLISH-TEACHING

In light of George Stewart's *Storm* or Lawrence Durrell's *Clea,* it is obvious that field theory implications for the study of literature and for programs of prospective English teachers can not be "complete" or "final" in the usual sense of the words. Durrell expresses the idea:

> Among the weakpoints at the end of this volume [or this book] I have sketched a number of possible ways of continuing to deploy these characters and situations in further instalments—but this is only to suggest that even if the series [or the implications for preservice programs for teachers of English] were extended indefinitely the result would never become a roman fleuve (an expansion of the matter in serial form) but would remain strictly part of the present word-continuum. If the axis has been well and truly laid down . . . it should be possible to radiate in any direction without losing the strictness and congruity of the continuum.[22]

Durrell's statement seems apt, for it also is based on concepts of field theory. The simultaneity principle is apparent in it, and educators so inclined could find almost point-for-point correspondence between the implications of field theory principles for the study of literature as they apply to programs for preservice teachers of English and field theory principles for man's understanding of self-in-life-space as described in Durrell's *Clea.* But Durrell's statement also has direct bearing on programs for preservice teachers of English. From the principle he expresses, an inference can be drawn that programs for preservice teachers of English should provide concepts and principles simultaneously present in all aspects of prospective teachers' total study. Where such simultaneity exists, where common principles are a basis for a structure-process program, each student, no matter what his "speciality" (science, social science, humanities), comes to discover that all specialities have common roots, that there is *an art to science* and *a science to art.*

Durrell's statement also implies the field theory principle of indeterminacy, which can be "translated" into program implications for preservice teachers of English. Programs for preservice teachers should make students aware of the need for habitual questioning, research, exploration, and experimentation not only in their educational program but as an integral part of their future teaching duties. To the extent that programs for preservice teachers incorporate structure-process approaches to knowledge, to that extent will the teachers tend to discover the dynamism and indeterminacy of "fields" in the classroom.

Exploring new horizons, according to the field theory principle of indeterminacy, may lead to "failures." But such failures are sometimes the price of exploration, and prospective teachers of English should be ready to acknowledge this "irrational" element in their broad application of content from their total preservice programs.

Programs for preservice teachers of English that are based on field theory principles should make prospective teachers aware that the end of their program is but the beginning of a lifetime of continuous search for new principles, of readiness to adapt to new information, and of the desire to contribute new scholarly-critical designs for the study of literature. Programs for prospective English teachers based upon field theory principles should develop teachers not only aware of the exciting areas that comprise contemporary English scholarship but also ready to explore, through scholarly-critical methods, interpersonal values of English, whether in the local community or on the international horizons of the contemporary world.

APPENDIX

CONTENT SUMMARY OF *STORM*

FIRST DAY

SECTION 1
Thermal balances and cosmic simultaneity perceived in macrocosm and microcosm. Atmosphere described as agency of transport from setting to rising sun.

SECTION 2
Californians' dependence on weather and its effect on California and others. Balance of effect stressed by comparing farmers and stockmen in drought to "city folk" profiting from tourist trade.

SECTION 3
Cold air mass and its movement from Siberia to the Desert of Gobi to the China Sea described. Effect of air movement on man described: "wincing nomads, cursing foreigners, stoic coolies and the dying poor" mark its passage.

SECTION 4
Genesis of storms described. Points made relative to birth: birth a function of all other weather conditions on earth at that time; birth a function of the presence of a single mountain on a small island; birth followed "complex but orderly" pattern around single point. Analogy to human gestation is drawn.

SECTION 5
Radio operator on ship in transit gives first report of the storm as routine ship-to-shore communication used by weather stations around the world.

SECTION 6
Junior Meterologist introduced. His background, training, method of operation, and imagination are described in detail. Maria, the storm, discovered and named.

END OF FIRST DAY.

SECOND DAY

SECTION 1
Man is a creature of air not land; biological and historical data introduced to show man's relationship to air.

SECTION 2
Chief of Weather Bureau introduced and described *in re* layman's perceptions of "weatherman," international aspects of meteorology, the "know-how" required for the responsibilities of the job with reference to communication and forecasting.

SECTION 3
Characteristics, composition, and magnitude of the storm described. Cold fronts, warm fronts, movements and effects of air masses involved are all described.

SECTION 4
Navigator introduced as one who is aware of distortions in personal perceptions. He uses instead instruments to "confidently" predict weather. Effects of weather on his personal life explored.

SECTION 5
History of Donner Pass described *in re* the sacrifice, courage, and "whim" that went into the choice of a main route for world communication.

SECTION 6
Road Superintendent introduced as a man aware of the need for readiness to keep Donner Pass open in winter storms. Feels machines superior to men in keeping road open.

SECTION 7
Maria's further progress plotted. J.M. continues analogy of Maria to human being, noting storm is "half grown." J.M. shown as growing in enthusiasm for his work. World picture of weather again emphasized.

SECTION 8
San Francisco described historically, symbolically, and with focus on various businesses and their geographically dominant position on the hills of the city. Effects of drought on businesses and merchants contrasted: merchants profiting from fair weather, businesses expending monies to use auxiliary power to compensate for loss of water power.

END OF SECOND DAY.

THIRD DAY

SECTION 1
Man's cyclical description of weather in terms of war between the forces of light and darkness noted. Balance and system to nature's "war" stressed.

SECTION 2
An owl electrocutes itself by accidently touching a power line somewhere in the forests of California. A wildcat makes a meal of the owl's carcass.

SECTION 3
The old man, former chief of the Weather Bureau, is introduced. Contrast of W.B. facilities and techniques from old man's day to facilities and techniques of modern W.B. made. Respect for old man's contribution to meteorology by W.B. personnel noted.

SECTION 4
Load Dispatcher introduced. The L.D.'s image to his men, his method of operation, his duties, and his background for the job *in re* weather problems described. L.D.'s philosophy: Experience and good men can cope intelligently with weather. Johnny Martley introduced—Chief of French Bar Power House.

SECTION 5
General Manager of the Railroad, Chief Service Officer at Bay Airport, and the District Traffic Supervisor of the telephone company introduced. Background, training, and preparation for winter storms for each man described.

SECTION 6
Pete Goslin introduced. Flour salesman who asks Jim, S.F. client, for a shortcut from Colusa to San Francisco, plans to arrive "Sunday."

SECTION 7
"Public Service" performed by J.M. in describing services of Weather Bureau to visiting students. J.M. learning to adapt to "public" by "simplifying" esoteric meteorological concepts. Analogy of Maria continued, now in "girlhood stage." Intellectual snobbery and intolerance displayed by J.M. toward fellow workers and the old man; one of the J.M.'s colleagues regards the old man as "The Old Master."

SECTION 8
Water-vapor mass one thousand miles long and five hundred miles wide over an ocean region near the Hawaiian Islands is described. Effect of this air on ocean-liner passengers described.

SECTION 9
Jen, the waitress, introduced. Jen in Reno calls sister Dot in S.F. to tell her she is coming to S.F. with her boyfriend, Max Arnim, to spend the weekend.

SECTION 10
Polar air compared to crowd being held in check by police. Police in this case defined as storm belts and mountains surrounding the polar air. Pressure of the air mass seeking some weak spot to break through. Fur-trader introduced. Living on Victoria Island, he experiences polar air and decides to stay inside knowing that even for that region an unusual cold is upon the land. Constant build-up of polar air described with the prediction that the hour of the break "drew closer."

END OF THIRD DAY.

FOURTH DAY

SECTION 1
Man's concern with weather described from historical perspective. Instinct, superstition, augury, and science as they were applied by men to weather summarized. Language viewed as hindrance and help in weather-forecasting. Common endeavor of man—international—contributed to scientific weather study.

SECTION 2
A two-by-four falls on a California road and comes to rest by the roadside but on the pavement. A tree sprouting in 1579 and toppled by a windstorm in 1789 left a twenty-by-two-foot bole that is being consumed by the "slow fire of decay." Dirty Ed and his friend fire a .22 caliber shell through a switch box. Tony Airolo's boar, Blue Boy introduced as "sure-footed," a necessity for boars living on hills above railroad tracks.

SECTION 3
Storm described as reaching "maturity." Human analogy continued and extent of its coverage compared to land masses in the U.S. and France.

SECTION 4
Effect of California drought described in suicide of farmer Oscar Carlson. Other side of drought picture presented in Secretary of Trade Association's report that the market for meal and prepared feeds is good.

SECTION 5
Maria's effect on *Byzantion* described in two ways: impersonally, as a ship at a position on the earth's surface experiencing a storm front; personally, as a crew trapped in a storm with families living in the Bay area. Mutual respect for competence in their work of meteorology described as bringing the Chief and J.M. closer together.

SECTION 6
Pete Goslin's preparation for trip described. Has car checked to make ready for his trip.

SECTION 7
Byzantion's encounter with the full fury of the storm described. First Officer lost, washed overboard, Johnny the Greek suffers a dislocated shoulder. *Eureka* coming full-steam to stand by, but *Byzantion* and crew helpless before the storm.

SECTION 8
Max Arnim's preparations for trip from Reno to S.F. described. Max boasts, "I know old U.S. 40 like a book."

SECTION 9
Contrast between the plight of men on *Byzantion* and the lives of people in "sunny San Francisco" made. Unbridled sensationalism of press reported. Extent of storm described.

SECTION 10
Rick the lineman is introduced. He is enchanted by a girl he meets at a dance and falls in love with her.

SECTION 11
The River and its historical implications for civilizations are described. Man's selfishness to his fellowman is described as being offset by government—other men trained to regard the whole as more than a simple sum of the parts.

END OF FOURTH DAY.

FIFTH DAY

SECTION 1
Byzantion crew's encounter with storm concluded. Human analogy with storm extended to include total life process. Storm also compared to nation and to ethos of nation that exists even when there may be no nation as such.

SECTION 2
Release of the polar air described. Down through Canada into Montana and other western states with winds of fifty miles an hour and blinding snow the air mass sped. Life and property destroyed—man "cowered" against the fury of the polar air.

SECTION 3
The storm's imminent arrival on the West Coast described. J.M. reveals more tolerant attitude toward the old man. Chief describes responsibilities of weather-forecasting. Role of private vs. public meteorology defined with reference to training and responsibility.

SECTION 4
Effect of predicted rain on Californians described. Topic of headlines, radio, bar conversations, and parent-child admonitions, the predicted rain dominates the plans of San Franciscans.

SECTION 5
Effect of storm prediction on L.D., Chief Service Officer, General Manager of the Railroad, and DTS of the telephone company described. Though nervous, all leaders feel ready for the impending storm.

SECTION 6
Rick the lineman assigned as extra help on the "Pass" in view of impending storm. Rick likes his work but is a little careless because he is in love.

SECTION 7
The General introduced—his job, flood control. Expert on reading gauges and spotting danger spots in the levees, the General inspects the river and keeps himself ready for the forecast of rain.

SECTION 8
Effects of the rain forecast further described from viewpoints of: dept. store manager, director of an observatory, amusement park operator, owner of lumber yard, advertising manager of a newspaper. Depending on weather effects on their businesses, these decision-makers ordered or canceled quantities of goods.

SECTION 9
Change in company banners described. New forces in the elements listed as cause. Banners limp position described as symbolic of "interregnum and change."

SECTION 10
Progress of polar air mass continued. Described as "raider" more fierce than Indians who raided the plainsmen. People are described as freezing to death, and cities such as Duluth, Pierre, Casper, St. Paul, Sioux City, and North Platte feel the blizzard.

END OF FIFTH DAY.

SIXTH DAY

SECTION 1
Man's dependence on water described from viewpoints of evolution, Bible, myth, religion, physiology. Direct application of California's need for water hinted.

SECTION 2
Arrival of Jen and Max from Reno at Dot's home in San Francisco described.

SECTION 3
Nightmare of the Chief described. Implications of life and death in weather-forecasting explored. Visible evidence of correct forecast for rain observed by Chief in cloud cover moving in over Bay area.

SECTION 4
Incident of the two-by-four extended through descriptions of motorists' reactions to it: some swerve, others go over it. Truck-driver with load of manure goes over it, and a few pounds of manure are added to the road next to the two-by-four.

SECTION 5
"Pain wave" described. Nerve endings of war wounds, arthritic joints, overworked mothers all felt the pain wave immediately preceding the arrival of the rain.

SECTION 6
A rural preacher praying for rain described. Invocation recalls man's historic prayer for rain—a necessity for growing. Biblical examples of prayers for rain given.

SECTION 7
Progress of the polar air mass continued. Down through Cincinnati and Louisville, down to Little Rock and Shreveport, straight through Texas the polar air rolled. Warned by radio, men made ready for it with smudge pots and extra mooring lines.

SECTION 8
Visible effects of the storm and its magnitude described. Comparison made between storm and microcosm of wave in rocky cave. Both eventually engulf obstacles in their way. Maria goes over the San Francisco hills.

SECTION 9
Airport's CSO's dependence on communications described. Radio and telephone keys to his dispatching or canceling flights.

SECTION 10
Max Arnim and Jen, the waitress, start back toward Reno from Dot's home in San Francisco in a rainstorm.

SECTION 11
Pete Goslin's use of the shortcut described. Incident of the lost two-by-four and the displaced manure completed. Pete swerves to avoid the two-by-four, skids on the manure made slippery by the rain, and "rolls over twice" in a "terrific" crash and is presumed dead.

SECTION 12
The Road Superintendent's preliminary battle with the snow on U.S. 40 caused by the storm's arrival in California described. The skill and danger in plowing snow described.

SECTION 13
The CSO's concern with the storm in terms of a transcontinental flight described. Telephoned news that the "Transcontinental" was all right allowed him to sleep.

SECTION 14
Historical role of the California lighthouses described. Description implies their antiquity by time comparison to *Hamlet* as a new play at the Globe when the lighthouse points were being discovered by Viscaíno.

END OF SIXTH DAY.

SEVENTH DAY

SECTION 1
Man's historic homage to the powers within the air described. Zeus, Thor, Indra, Pulugu, Tlaloc of Mexico named, also Jehovah and Moses, his servant.

SECTION 2
Man's ingenuity in maintaining power lines in storm belt described. Reasons for small iced lines described. Wires ordinarily hold ice and survive. Exception: The electrocution of an owl weakened one of the wires in the French Bar Power House area.

SECTION 3
Further effects of polar air mass described and traced. Across Texas, the Rio Grande, the Gulf, and into Mexico until stopped by the mountains the polar air flowed. Then through the pass at Tehuantepec to end up at Costa Rica by joining the Westerlies.

SECTION 4
J.M.'s perspective on two subjects changed. First, textbook storms with everything balanced are not working out with real storm: highly complex and irrational elements change the J.M.'s "perfect" to "imperfect." Second, human analogy of storm makes him think of Maria as "middle-aged," as "too individualized to fit any rules."

SECTION 5
Incident of the wire weakened by owl's electrocution completed. Wire collapses and a series of relays—machines and men—have power restored almost as the wire hits the ground. L.D. gives credit to men as professionals.

SECTION 6
Parched land's reaction to initial rains described. Growth and decay both aided by rainfall. Process of rain joining with groundwater through habits of insects, etc., described.

SECTION 7
Rotary plowing as a function of perception and skill described. Swenson, Peters, and the Road "Super" described—perceptual field of vision and ground. Plow brought to halt by discarded tire chain that fouls augurs.

SECTION 8
"Press" perceptions of storm described. Weather described as news in America, Canada, Mexico, and Central America all related to same system. Individual man grumbled because "he did not realize that the wind on his cheek was part of a planetary system."

SECTION 9
Radio report of rain and its "good" effect described through KTEY "newsy." Death of Pete Goslin, flour salesman, confirmed.

SECTION 10
Rick the lineman's repair of broken wire described. Rick completes job and thinks about girl's radio voice going over wire, which brings to mind his girl's image.

SECTION 11
Max's and Jen's disappearance described from perspective of Max's fellow worker talking to Bob, gas station attendant who filled Max's car with gas before S.F. trip.

SECTION 12
Progress of railroad's flanger in keeping tracks open described. Programming use of flanger described as function of Ass't Div. Engineer and Chief Trainmaster.

SECTION 13
Effect of storm on planes described. Some icing conditions but planes could avoid ice area or fly through before icing got serious.

SECTION 14
Readiness for flood control described through the eyes of the General. Knowledge, preplanning, ability to make decisions, but above all readiness for the rains described as key to flood control.

SECTION 15
Effect of storm on the City described and contrasted with earlier description of the City in dry weather. Man's uncomfortable struggle with the powers of dampness noted.

END OF SEVENTH DAY.

EIGHTH DAY

SECTION 1
Man's survival in geologic battles with weather examined. Man's survival described as result of wisdom not racial aptitude. Civilization as a function of temperate climate examined.

SECTION 2
Status of world weather viewed as function of relativity and perception. "Cause and effect" described as convenient words but "not meaning much." North and South America, Antarctica, and Western Australia seen as equally influential on weather in southern United States.

SECTION 3
Comparisons among various trees of the Sierras made with reference to how they rid themselves of heavy snow. Most trees that retain flexibility in getting rid of snow survive; those that are rigid break and die.

SECTION 4
Max's and Jen's disappearance described from point of view of bosses, friends, and the curious. Rumor vs. action leads to telephone check with Jen's sister, Dot, in S.F. Dot confirms couple left for Reno Sunday night. Police alerted to be on lookout for couple.

SECTION 5
Coyote's reaction to storm described. It uses man's resources for locomotion—railroad tracks, highway. At the approach of a car, the coyote hides. Later as it moves from its hiding place, it notices a strange smell as of meat and eating and records the place of the smell for future reference.

SECTION 6
Rick the lineman's "accident" described. Rick, thinking of his girl, forgets or overlooks safety measures. He fails to check pole before descending, hooks into a leaning tree, and falls on mutually supporting ski poles. Tries to get to truck on highway but tangles himself in bushes. Overhead, world traffic and complaint go through wires.

SECTION 7
Bole of decaying cedar tree, Blue Boy's wandering on hills above trains, and switch box penetrated by Dirty Ed's bullet all described *in re* storm's effect or foreshadowed effect on man's destinies.

SECTION 8
Police radio and Reno newspaper reports of Max's and Jen's disappearance noted. Full names given and effect of reports on the "public" recorded.

SECTION 9
The reaction of the Chief Service Officer to weather (fog) described. Using science and alternate routes CSO satisfied that he is ready for weather situations.

SECTION 10
Rotary plowing, railroad style, described. Danger of crew in this work described, technique of cross-checking signals for accuracy in moving ahead demonstrated.

SECTION 11
General's assessment of storm's effect on rivers described. Based on accurate information received General predicts slow rise of river but suggests readiness for California cities affected.

SECTION 12
Road Superintendent's handling of a road block described from two perspectives: those who help their fellowmen in emergencies and those who by selfishness, carelessness, and indifference cause the emergencies. "Super's" ability to analyze and to prescribe solutions to blocks described as a function of experience and training.

SECTION 13
The District Traffic Superintendent's assessment of storm's effect described. DTS, informed of Rick's disappearance, feels men "don't work well when that sort of thing's in the air." Noted that DTS's job during storm was a twenty-four-hour one.

SECTION 14
Mountains affected by the rains of the storm described. Names (and sometimes origins of names), locations, and relative heights in terms of effect on storm listed.

END OF EIGHTH DAY.

NINTH DAY

SECTION 1
Man's geologic destiny described. Natural entropic forces overcome by man's learning from the animals, but this learning tends to be "planless."

SECTION 2
Natural forces of erosion described. Rain washing down gully caused tall rock to move "a quarter of an inch," causing the rock to fall and triggering four million tons of earth toward its ultimate end, the sea.

SECTION 3
Rick's telephone truck discovered in snow drift by crew of rotary plow. Crew requests instructions about whether to search for man. They are told not to because they lack equipment and a man buried for that long in snow is presumed dead.

SECTION 4
Incident of .22 caliber bullet in switch box concluded. Eight vehicles and assorted passengers and drivers are affected by the flood caused when rain seeping through the .22 caliber hole caused by Dirty Ed shorts out a sump pump for an underpass.

SECTION 5
Adjustments of DTS to continuing storm described. DTS arranges for telephone relays through L.A., Okla. City, and St. Louis. These precautions taken, the DTS sleeps soundly.

SECTION 6
Parallel flow of other "river" of polar air described. Instead of land, second mass went over water to affect humid air mass over Hawaii. Slight shift in the world's winds started Hawaiian mass in northeasterly direction toward California, followed by old polar air of second mass.

SECTION 7
J.M.'s decision to remain with Weather Bureau described. J.M. discovers he and the Chief can communicate; bond develops on human not scientific basis. Maria has a "baby."

SECTION 8
Mr. Reynoldhurst introduced. He and others like him are used to illustrate what happened when the cedar bole crashed into the Central Transcontinental Lead. Effects on human destiny and the tortuous relays needed described. Rick the lineman's death confirmed.

SECTION 9
Newspapers' attempt to make a "story" out of Max's and Jen's disappearance described. Professional work of highway patrol in following up leads described; findings: no clues.

SECTION 10
Reason for sea gulls on University campus described as result of fury of storm on gulls' natural habitat of reefs and ledges. Perspective for description, professor of literature, paraphrasing Stein: "sea gulls on the grass, alas."

SECTION 11
The Road Superintendent's battle to keep the "Pass" open described. Intelligent use of men, machines, leadership, and adaptations successful in maintaining open road.

SECTION 12
Effect of rain on California rivers described. The General, faced with rising rivers and prediction of more rain, is subjected to pressure from asparagus farmers and the Chamber of Commerce. To protect City, farms must be destroyed; to save farms, City will be flooded. General indicates he will make the necessary decision when time comes.

SECTION 13
L.D.'s estimate of the storm noted as "pretty easy time of it so far." The CSO noted that tropical air was moving in but felt that conditions for flying would be "pretty quiet."

SECTION 14
Route of the Transcontinental Streamliner described. Crack train, it was given priority and the highball so that it remained on schedule: Chicago to San Francisco in forty hours.

SECTION 15
Effect of rain on the cultivated products and the various soil types of California described. Five hundred miles of land receive the storm's rain.

END OF NINTH DAY.

TENTH DAY

SECTION 1
Man's historical battle against the elements described with a new perspective: the cliff dwellers of Mesa Verde. Cliff dwellers withdrew from weather elements. Modern man cannot withdraw. Withdrawn or not, man's fate is the same: he is a creature of the air and subject to the entropic forces of the universe.

SECTION 2
The coyote's return to the spot below the cliff where he had first encountered the strange smell described. The smell still made him drool, but the snow was deeper than he anticipated, so he left for a still later return.

SECTION 3
Layman's perception of weather as a "crazy-quilt" is contrasted with J.M.'s perception of its following a "precise pattern." J.M.'s tolerance and respect for the old man complete. J.M. and Chief work together as "equals." The old man seized by chill and doctor sent for.

SECTION 4
Streamliner's progress described from passenger's perspective. Bored with the precision and uneventfulness of trip and weather. Contrast with work crews making the tracks safe for schedule-keeping trains described. Blue Boy, the boar, from his lofty perch described as looking down incuriously at the trains passing below.

SECTION 5
Progress of tropical air mass described. Laden with moisture, pushed by polar air masses, the tropical air rises over the California mountains and discharges its heavy water burden in poetically named creeks.

SECTION 6
The Road Superintendent's battle with snow in the "Pass" described. Belief in the superiority of machines over men shaken when Peters and Swenson succeed in digging themselves out of snowslide before machines can get to them.

SECTION 7
The General's battle with the rivers and with vested interests described. Information and readiness to cope with emergency situations described as keys to control of flooding rivers. Man's inhumanity to man for money's sake disgusts the General, and his treatment of a committee from the businessmen of the City reflects this pessimism.

SECTION 8
The Chief Service Officer's uneasiness about strange cloud formation behind tropical air mass described. Experience and readiness suggested as base for the CSO's feeling. CSO feels he should warn his night relief but recognizes that assistant would only understand nervousness of his boss, not the experience-based causes.

SECTION 9
Battle to clear snowslide and open the "Pass" described. Machines and men battle the blocked road and make halting progress. Peters and Swenson dig themselves out of slide and return to work. Crew's morale described as low because they had lost the "Pass" to the storm.

SECTION 10
Supremacy of snow in the mountains of the Sierras described. Warm tropic air hurled to the top of mountain peaks turned cold, formed snow that spread for five hundred miles over the mountain tops of central California.

END OF TENTH DAY.

ELEVENTH DAY

SECTION 1
Prediction of tides is compared to prediction of weather. Both phenomena described as function of physical forces. Future weather predictions can be as accurate as tide predictions, but man has to overcome "quarrelsomeness" before this can take place.

SECTION 2
Restoration of thermal balance on plains described. Odyssey of the Chinook as a physical process of the cold air flow described. Cosmic balances again emphasized.

SECTION 3
The effect of the "minor detail" of the storm, the old polar air described. Effect of this detail on the General Manager, Jen's sister, the Chief Service Officer, the L.D., the District Traffic Superintendent, and the Chief described. Separate description of effect of the "detail" on the General described. Big Al Bruntton, the pilot, introduced. Progress of plane and train contrasted. Streamliner comes into Reno, Chief finishes forecast. Blue Boy, the boar, heads for a dry shed. Johnny Martley predicts cloudburst and Rick the lineman lies in his coffin. All of these separate but interrelated incidents completed. Blue Boy plugs a drain and stops the train. Johnny Martley performs his job of opening the sluice gates with courage and daring, and Big Al fights his plane through a violent turbulence to safety as the J.M. and the Chief predict the end of the storm while the old man lays dying in a hospital.

SECTION 4
Storm metaphorically compared to Ozymandius and biblical sayings: "to everything there is a season" and "this too shall pass away." The "strong warrior, Time," is described as accounting cosmically for the "death" of the storm.

END OF THE ELEVENTH DAY.

TWELFTH DAY

SECTION 1
General effects of storm described from meteorologist's viewpoint and as a function of relativity to "good" and "bad."

SECTION 2
Effect of Little Maria, Maria's baby, on the East Coast and particularly New York City and State described. Balances of "good" and "bad" effects described. In essence New York's battle with Little Maria a microcosm of California's battle with Maria herself. Power lines, telephone lines, ships, snows, etc., all described as miniature repetitions of West Coast's problems.

SECTION 3
Effect of the line of linked storms in North America described *in re* Great Britain and Europe. The weather in any given country is a direct result of the weather in other countries around the world. And all weather is based on basic physical patterns which have systematic nexi in the cosmos.

SECTION 4
The General's battle with the flooding rivers described. Based on his decisions, the City was saved but highways and farmland were flooded. The inevitability of Nature's triumph over man and his works makes him feel old.

SECTION 5
"The Old Master's" death reported. The J.M. and the Chief pay respects to his professional competence in the light of the information the old man had to work with for forecasting. Chief "poetically" comments on the likenesses between men and storms. Even with the best knowledge and information the elements of chance and change are always implicit in storms and men. The J.M. begins to look for other "football"-shaped isobars.

SECTION 6
Captain of the Highway Patrol introduced. With the help of the Road Superintendent, the Captain finds the bodies of Max and Jen by digging in the snow under the coyote tracks.

SECTION 7
Resumption of clipper flights described. Clipper's course charted so that weather serves as an ally to men instead of a hindrance.

SECTION 8
Aftermath of the storm described. Road crews, railroad crews, telephone and power crews clean up Maria's aftermath but make ready for the inevitable next storm. Above the crews, planes in clear air pick up the beam for the Bay Airport.

SECTION 9
Hamlet's speech on "readiness is all" quoted.

SECTION 10
The City's return to good weather described. Readiness for next storm by the General Manager, the L.D., the DTS, and the CSO described. Again the banners of commerce—blue, blue and white, maroon, crimson and black—stood out stiffly in the northwest wind.

SECTION 11
Biblical quotation of "the son of David" noted. Winds go south and return north and whirl continually, and the wind "returneth again according to his circuits."

SECTION 12
Earth's planetary position described from viewpoint of a "watcher in the skies." Such a watcher sees a planet that gives no sign that "storms or men disturb its tranquil round."

END OF BOOK.

NOTES

INTRODUCTION

1. Francis Shoemaker, "Self-Realization, Communication, and Aesthetic Experience," *Communication in General Education,* Earl J. McGrath, ed. (Dubuque, Ia.: William C. Brown Co., 1949), pp. 240-243.
2. Milton Eisenhower, president of Johns Hopkins University, in an address to the Schenectady, N. Y., Alumni of Johns Hopkins University, May, 1960.
3. Cf. Arthur E. Bestor, *Educational Wastelands* (Urbana, Ill.: University of Illinois Press, 1953). Mortimer Smith, *The Diminished Mind: A Study of Planned Mediocrity in Our Public Schools* (Chicago: Henry Regnery Co., 1954).
4. Cf. James B. Conant, *The American High School Today* (New York: McGraw-Hill Book Co., 1959), p. 50. Commission on English of the College Entrance Examination Board, *Preparation in English for College-bound Students* (Boston: College Entrance Examination Board, 1960), p. 6. Council for Basic Education, *The Decline of English* (Washington, D. C.: Council for Basic Education, 1960).
5. Cf. Roy R. Grinker, ed., *Toward a Unified Theory of Human Behavior* (New York: Basic Books, 1956). Lynn White, Jr., ed., *Frontiers of Knowledge in the Study of Man* (New York: Harper & Bros., 1956). Oliver L. Reiser, *The Integration of Human Knowledge* (Boston: Porter Sargent, 1958).
6. Jerome S. Bruner, *The Process of Education* (Cambridge, Mass.: Harvard University Press, 1960), p. 18.
7. Cf. Francis Shoemaker, *Aesthetic Experience and the Humanities* (New York: Columbia University Press, 1943), pp. 228-233. Lennox Grey, *What Communication Means Today,* NCTE Pamphlets on Communication (Chicago: National Council of Teachers of English, 1944), pp. 73-74.
8. Cf. Benjamin Bloom, ed., *Taxonomy of Educational Objectives* (New York: Longmans, Green & Co., 1956), p. 31. Howard Lee Nostrand, "Toward Agreement on Cultural Essentials," *Journal of General Education,* XI (January, 1958), p. 11.
9. Freeman J. Dyson, "Innovation in Physics," *Scientific American,* CIC (September, 1958), p. 74.

10. Allen H. Benton and William Werner, Jr., *Principles of Field Biology and Ecology* (New York: McGraw-Hill Book Co., 1958), pp. i-vii.
11. Cf. Ralph Buchsbaum and Mildred Buchsbaum, *Basic Ecology* (Pittsburgh, Pa.: Boxwood Press, 1957). Ernest Neal, *Woodland Ecology* (Cambridge, Mass.: Harvard University Press, 1958).
12. Anatol Rapoport, "Homeostasis Reconsidered," *Toward a Unified Theory of Human Behavior*, p. 228.
13. *Ibid.*, p. 234. "Homeostasis," *Handbook of Experimental Psychology*, S. S. Stevens, ed. (New York: John Wiley & Sons, 1955), *passim.*
14. Lennox Grey, "Literary Audience," *Contemporary Literary Scholarship*, Lewis Leary, ed. (New York: Appleton-Century-Crofts, 1958), p. 455.
15. *Ibid.*, pp. 403-461.

ONE

1. Carter V. Good and Douglas E. Scates, *Methods of Research* (New York: Appleton-Century-Crofts, 1954), p. 482.
2. *Ibid.*, pp. 482, 483.
3. Freeman J. Dyson, "Innovation in Physics," *Scientific American*, CIC (September, 1958), p. 76.
4. James Clerk Maxwell, *The Scientific Papers of James Clerk Maxwell*, Sir William Davidson Niven, ed. (New York: Dover Publications, 1890), I, p. 527.
5. *Ibid.*, pp. 532-533.
6. *Ibid.*, p. 533.
7. *Ibid.*, p. 534.
8. Albert Einstein, *The World As I See It* (New York: Crown Publishers, 1934), cited by Saxe Commins and Robert N. Linscott in *Man and the Universe: The Philosophers of Science* (New York: Random House, 1947), pp. 475-476.
9. *Ibid.*, p. 480.
10. Albert Einstein and Leopold Infeld, *The Evolution of Physics* (New York: Simon and Schuster, 1951), pp. 166 ff., 186 ff., 259.
11. Lincoln Barnett, *The Universe and Dr. Einstein* (New York: Mentor Books, 1952), chap. 12.
12. "Atoms and Human Knowledge," *Bulletin of the American Academy of Arts and Sciences*, XI (December, 1957), p. 2.
13. Dyson, *Scientific American*, CIC (September, 1958), p. 74.
14. *Bulletin of the American Academy of Arts and Sciences*, XI (December, 1957), p. 2.
15. *Ibid.*
16. Dyson, *Scientific American*, CIC (September, 1958), p. 76.
17. *Ibid.*, p. 78.
18. Cf. criminologist-educator Nathaniel Cantor, *The Teaching-Learning Process;* philosopher-educator John S. Brubacher, *Eclectic Philosophy*

of Education; chemist-biologist J. Needham, *Biochemistry and Morphogenesis;* economist-philosopher Kenneth Boulding, *The Image;* anthropologist-psychologist Clyde Kluckhohn, *Personality: In Nature, Society and Culture.*

19. Norbert Wiener, *The Human Use of Human Beings, Cybernetics and Society* (Garden City, N. Y.: Doubleday Anchor Books, 1954), p. 12.
20. *Ibid.*
21. *Ibid.*, p. 24.
22. *Ibid.*
23. *Ibid.*, p. 16.
24. Howard L. Kingsley, *The Nature and Conditions of Learning* (New York: Prentice-Hall, 1946), pp. 243, 494-511.
25. Kurt Lewin, "Field Theory and Learning," *The Psychology of Learning,* Forty-first Yearbook of the National Society for the Study of Education (Chicago: University of Chicago Press, 1942), II, pp. 215-231.
26. Kurt Koffka, *Principles of Gestalt Psychology* (New York: Harcourt, Brace & Co., 1935).
27. Wolfgang Köhler, *Gestalt Psychology* (New York: Liveright Publishing Corp., 1929).
28. Asahel D. Woodruff, *The Psychology of Teaching* (New York: Longmans, Green & Co., 1948), p. 140.
29. Howard S. Bartley, *Principles of Perception* (New York: Harper & Bros., 1958), p. 22.
30. Lewin, "Field Theory and Learning," *The Psychology of Learning,* II, p. 238.
31. Bartley, *Principles of Perception,* pp. 22, 45.
32. Lewin, "Field Theory and Learning," *The Psychology of Learning,* II, p. 239.
33. Cf. Donald B. Lindsley, "Emotion," and Ernest R. Nilgood, "Methods and Procedures in the Study of Learning," *Handbook of Experimental Psychology,* S. S. Stevens, ed. (New York: John Wiley & Sons, 1958), pp. 473, 517.
34. Hubert Bonner, *Group Dynamics* (New York: Ronald Press Co., 1959), pp. 3, 13, 18, 19.
35. Cf. M. A. Wenger, F. Howell Jones, and Margaret H. Jones, *Physiological Psychology* (New York: Henry Holt & Co., 1956). Donald Olding Hebb, *A Textbook of Psychology* (Philadelphia: W. B. Saunders Co., 1958).
36. Donald Olding Hebb, "Drives and C.N.S.," *Psychological Review,* LXII (July, 1955), p. 244.
37. Louis Kaplan, *Mental Health and Human Relations in Education* (New York: Harper & Bros., 1959), pp. 234-235.
38. Hebb, *Psychological Review,* LXII (July, 1955), p. 249.
39. Hebb, *A Textbook of Psychology,* p. 213.
40. Jean Piaget, *Logic and Psychology* (New York: Basic Books, 1957), p. xv.
41. *Ibid.*, p. 24.

42. *Ibid.*, pp. 47-48.
43. *Ibid.*, p. 48.
44. Robert W. Leeper, *Lewin's Topological and Vector Psychology*, (Eugene, Ore.: University of Oregon, 1943), p. 165.
45. Martin Scheerer, "Cognitive Theory," *Handbook of Social Psychology, Theory and Method*, Gardner Lindzey, ed. (Cambridge, Mass.: Addison-Wesley Publishing Co., 1954), II, p. 92.
46. Gardner Murphy, "Human Potentialities," *Journal of Social Issues*, VII (Fall, 1953), p. 5.
47. Gardner Murphy, *Personality: A Biosocial Approach to Origins and Structure* (New York: Harper & Bros., 1947), p. 5.
48. Murphy, *Journal of Social Issues*, VII (Fall, 1953), p. 4.
49. *Ibid.*, p. 7.
50. *Ibid.*, pp. 8-10.
51. *Ibid.*, p. 12.
52. *Ibid.*
53. Claude Bernard, *An Introduction to the Study of Experimental Medicine*, Henry C. Green, trans. (New York: Dover Publications, 1957), Foreword.
54. Anatol Rapoport, "Homeostasis Reconsidered," *Toward a Unified Theory of Human Behavior*, Roy R. Grinker, ed. (New York: Basic Books, 1956), p. 225.
55. *Ibid.* Kenneth Boulding, *The Image* (Ann Arbor, Mich.: University of Michigan Press, 1956), p. 21.
56. Walter B. Cannon, *The Wisdom of the Body* (New York: W. W. Norton & Co., 1939), pp. 24, 59.
57. William L. Laurence, "Science in Review," *New York Times*, September 7, 1958, p. E11.
58. *Toward a Unified Theory of Human Behavior*, p. 162.
59. Edward S. Dempsey, "Homeostasis," *Handbook of Experimental Psychology*, p. 233.
60. Rapoport, "Homeostasis Reconsidered," *Toward A Unified Theory of Human Behavior*, p. 234.
61. Bernard, *An Introduction to the Study of Experimental Medicine*, p. 93.
62. George Wald, "Innovation in Biology," *Scientific American*, CIC (September, 1958), p. 110.
63. Edmund W. Sinnott and L. C. Dunn, *Principles of Genetics* (New York: McGraw-Hill Book Co., 1925).
64. Edmund W. Sinnott, *Botany Principles and Problems*, (New York: McGraw-Hill Book Co., 1929).
65. Edmund W. Sinnott, L. C. Dunn, and Thomas Dobzhansky, *Principles of Genetics* (New York: McGraw-Hill Book Co., 1950), p. 449.
66. *Ibid.*
67. *Ibid.*, p. 461.
68. Laurence, *New York Times*, September 7, 1958, p. E11. "The Secret of Life," *Time*, LXXII (July 14, 1958), pp. 50-54.

69. Laurence, *New York Times,* September 7, 1958, p. E11.
70. *Time,* LXXII (July 14, 1958), p. 53.
71. Boulding, *The Image,* pp. 172-175.
72. *Ibid.,* p. 175.
73. W. E. Agar, *A Contribution to the Theory of the Living Organism* (Second edition; Melbourne, Australia: 1951), p. 95. Cited by Boulding, *The Image,* p. 42.
74. Boulding, *The Image,* p. 115.
75. *Ibid.,* p. 162.

TWO

1. Anatol Rapoport, "Mathematics: The 'Empty' Science," *Frontiers of Knowledge in the Study of Man,* Lynn White, Jr., ed. (New York: Harper & Bros., 1956), p. 252. Paul R. Halmos, "Innovation in Mathematics," *Scientific American,* CIC (September, 1958), p. 71.
2. T. C. McCormack, *Elementary Social Statistics* (New York: McGraw-Hill Book Co., 1941), pp. 156-165. Anatol Rapoport, "Statistical Boundaries," *Toward a Unified Field of Human Behavior,* Roy R. Grinker, ed. (New York: Basic Books, 1956), p. 324.
3. Dorwin Cartwright, ed., *Field Theory in Social Science: Selected Theoretical Papers* (New York: Harper & Bros., 1951). Clyde Kluckhohn, *Mirror for Man* (New York: McGraw-Hill Book Co., 1949), p. 280.
4. Clyde Kluckhohn, "Cultural Anthropology: New Uses for Barbarians," *Frontiers of Knowledge in the Study of Man,* p. 36.
5. Vernor C. Finch and Glenn T. Trewartha, *Physical Elements of Geography* (New York: McGraw-Hill Book Co., 1942), pp. 45, 115-122.
6. George W. Hartmann, "The Field Theory of Learning and Its Educational Consequences," *The Psychology of Learning,* Forty-first Yearbook of the National Society for the Study of Education (Chicago: University of Chicago Press, 1942), II, p. 165.
7. "Stresses Need for Integration," *State University Newsletter,* State University of New York, September, 1959, p. 2.
8. Cf. Donald P. Cottrell, ed., *Teacher Education for a Free People* (Oneonta, N. Y.: American Association of Colleges of Teacher Education, 1956). Commission on Teacher Education, *The Improvement of Teacher Education* (Washington, D. C.: American Council on Education, 1946).
9. "An Emerging Concern," *Time,* LXXIV (December 14, 1959), p. 59.
10. Ashley Montagu, "Behavior as Viewed in the Behavioral Sciences and by American Education," *Teachers College Record,* LX (May, 1959), p. 447.
11. Arthur T. Jersild, *When Teachers Face Themselves* (New York: Bureau of Publications, Teachers College, Columbia University, 1955), p. 84.
12. Gardner Murphy, "Human Potentialities," *Journal of Social Issues,* VII (Fall, 1953), p. 13.

13. Francis Shoemaker, "Communication Arts in the Curriculum," *Teachers College Record,* LXVII (November, 1955), p. 119.
14. Kenneth E. Boulding, *The Image* (Ann Arbor, Mich.: University of Michigan Press, 1956), p. 18.
15. Florence Stratemeyer, "Relating the Several Parts of the Teacher-Education Program," *Teacher Education for a Free People,* p. 231.
16. Cottrell, *Teacher Education for a Free People,* pp. 18, 56, 84, 145, 183.
17. *Ibid.,* pp. 260-261.
18. Freeman J. Dyson, "Innovation in Physics," *Scientific American,* CIC (September, 1958), p. 80.

THREE

1. Walter V. Kaulfers and Holland D. Roberts, *A Cultural Basis for the Language Arts: An Approach to a Unified Program in the English and Foreign Language Curriculum* (Stanford University, Calif.: Stanford University Press, 1937), p. 60.
2. *Ibid.,* pp. 51-52.
3. *Ibid.,* p. 53.
4. Francis Shoemaker, *Aesthetic Experience and the Humanities* (New York: Columbia University Press, 1943), p. 75.
5. Oscar J. Campbell, ed., *The Teaching of College English* (Chicago: National Council of Teachers of English, 1934).
6. W. Wilbur Hatfield, ed., *An Experience Curriculum in English* (Chicago: National Council of Teachers of English, 1935).
7. Ruth M. Weeks, ed., *A Correlated Curriculum* (New York: Appleton-Century, 1936).
8. Dora V. Smith, ed., *The English Language Arts* (Vol. I of "The English Language Arts Series," Dora V. Smith, ed. 5 vols. New York: Appleton-Century-Crofts, 1952-1960). See pages 441-480 for citations of articles from journals dealing with "core," "unit," and "integrated" approaches to English.
9. *Ibid.,* p. vii.
10. *Ibid.,* pp. 389-391. See also pp. 42-44, 53-54, 184-185, 377-381.
11. Cf. National Council of Teachers of English, *Language Arts for Today's Children* (New York: Appleton-Century-Crofts, 1954), II, pp. 302-312, and *The English Language Arts in the Secondary School* (New York: Appleton-Century-Crofts, 1956), pp. 70 ff., 405 ff.
12. Smith, *The English Language Arts,* 153-155, 165-166, 388-389.
13. *Ibid.,* p. 167.
14. "Basic Issues in the Teaching of English," Supplement to *Elementary English,* XLVIII (October, 1959), pp. 1-16.
15. Ingrid M. Strom, "Summary of Investigations Relating to the English Language Arts in Secondary Education," *English Journal,* XLIX (February, 1960), p. 126.
16. Shoemaker, *Aesthetic Experience and the Humanities,* pp. 3-4.
17. *Ibid.,* p. 7.

18. *Ibid.*, p. 72.
19. *Ibid.*, p. 6.
20. *Ibid.*, p. 230.
21. Ingrid Strom, "Summary of Investigations Relating to the Language Arts in Secondary Education: 1961-1962," *English Journal,* LII (February, 1963), p. 131.
22. Kaulfers and Roberts, *A Cultural Basis for the Language Arts,* p. 9.
23. *Ibid.*, p. 14.
24. H. Sweet, *The Practical Study of Language* (New York: Henry Holt, 1899).
25. Peter Hagbolt, "The Teaching of Language from the Middle Ages to the Present: A Historical Sketch," *Twentieth Century Modern Language Teaching,* Maxim Newmark, ed. (New York: Philosophical Library, 1948), pp. 1-21.
26. Roger Brown, *Words and Things* (Glencoe, Ill.: Free Press of Glencoe, 1958), pp. 258-259.
27. Harry Hoijer, ed., *Language in Culture* (Chicago: University of Chicago Press, 1954), p. 252.
28. Leonard Bloomfield, *Language* (New York: Henry Holt & Co., 1933), p. 3.
29. Charles E. Osgood, ed., "Psycholinguistics," *Supplement to The Journal of Abnormal and Social Psychology* (Baltimore, Md.: Waverly Press, 1954), p. 50.
30. George Winchester Stone, Jr., ed., *Issues, Problems and Approaches in the Teaching of English* (New York: Holt, Rinehart & Winston, 1961).
31. Robert Anderson and Thurston Womack, *Processes in Writing* (Rev. ed. San Francisco: Wadsworth Publishing Co., 1961), pp. 25-43.
32. Joseph H. Greenberg, 'The Linguistic Approach," *Supplement to The Journal of Abnormal and Social Psychology,* p. 8.
33. Rene Wellek and Austin Warren, *Theory of Literature* (New York: Harcourt, Brace & Co., 1949), pp. 88, 220. William Rose Benét, ed., *The Reader's Encyclopedia* (New York: Thomas Y. Crowell Co., 1948), p. 910.
34. John Gardner, "Foreword," *Supplement to The Journal of Abnormal and Social Psychology,* p. iii.
35. Hobart Mowrer, "The Psychologist Looks at Language," *American Psychologist,* IX (November, 1954), p. 664-668.
36. Gardner, *Supplement to The Journal of Abnormal and Social Psychology,* p. iv.
37. *Ibid.*, p. i.
38. Joseph H. Greenberg, "Problem of Meaning in Linguistics," *Supplement to The Journal of Abnormal and Social Psychology,* p. 15.
39. Bess Sondel, *The Humanity of Words: A Primer of Semantics* (New York: World Publishing Co., 1958), p. 19.
40. Literature as the focus of this chapter is influenced, tacitly, by the foregoing statements in this way: Any lengthy piece of literature tends to contain most of the concepts related to the language arts approach to English and the concepts associated with psycholinguistics. Bohr's physical theory of "complementarity" applies here, in that any single

piece of literature tends to contain most of the elements associated with a field of literature as a whole. Bohr makes an analogical statement with reference to physics. Applying Bohr's theory to literature, one should find by analyzing the piece of literature most of the "rules" of grammar, some of the structures associated with linguistics, and a "style" associated with current approaches to literary criticism. In terms of the language arts concept, a given piece of literature would tend to show the author's demonstration of skills associated with writing, dialogue associated with speaking, descriptions associated with listening, and style associated with the "appreciation" aspect of reading.

41. Thomas A. Sebeok and Frances J. Ingemann, "Structural Analysis and Content Analysis in Folklore Research," *Studies in Cheremis* (New York: Wenner-Gren Foundation for Anthropological Research, 1956), II.
42. Sondel, *The Humanity of Words,* p. 19.
43. Robert H. Moore, *General Semantics in the High School English Program* (Columbus, Ohio: Ohio State University Press, 1945), p. 35.
44. Margaret Bryant, *Modern English and Its Heritage* (New York: Macmillan Co., 1948), p. 353.
45. Moore, *General Semantics in the High School English Program,* p. 43.
46. Solon T. Kimball, "Anthropology and Communication," *Teachers College Record,* LVII (November, 1955), p. 64.
47. Edward Sapir, "Language," *Encyclopaedia of the Social Sciences,* cited by Clyde Kluckhohn, *Mirror for Man* (New York: McGraw-Hill Book Co., 1949), p. 167.
48. Clyde Kluckhohn, "Cultural Anthropology: New Uses for 'Barbarians,'" *Frontiers of Knowledge in the Study of Man,* Lynn White, Jr., ed. (New York: Harper & Bros., 1956), p. 44.
49. Shoemaker, *Aesthetic Experience and the Humanities,* pp. 61-63.
50. Robert Redfield and Milton Singer, "Foreword," *Language in Culture,* Harry Hoijer, ed. (Chicago: University of Chicago Press, 1954).
51. Hoijer, *Language in Culture,* p. vii.
52. Stuart Chase, *The Power of Words* (New York: Harcourt, Brace & Co., 1954), pp. 101-102.
53. John B. Carroll, Paul M. Kjeldergaard, and Aaron S. Carton, "Number of Opposites vs. Number of Primaries as a Response Measure in Free Association Tests," *Journal of Verbal Language and Verbal Behavior,* I (July, 1962), p. 29.
54. Francis Shoemaker, "Canons of Culture," *Communication Lines,* August, 1957, p. 4.
55. Susanne K. Langer, *Philosophy in a New Key* (Cambridge, Mass.: Harvard University Press, 1942), pp. 277-278.
56. Lennox Grey and Consultants, *What Communication Means Today* (Chicago: National Council of Teachers of English, 1944), p. 28.
57. Lennox Grey, "No Signs, No Symbols! Uses A-B-C's: A Problem of Practical Definition," *Communication in General Education,* Earl J. McGrath, ed. (Dubuque, Ia.: William C. Brown Co., 1949), p. 15.
58. *Ibid.*
59. Marshall McLuhan, "A Historical Approach to the Media," *Teachers College Record,* LVII (November, 1955), p. 106.

60. *Ibid.*, p. 107.
61. *Ibid.*, p. 110.
62. Susanne K. Langer, *Feeling and Form* (New York: Charles Scribner's Sons, 1953), p. 378.
63. Francis Shoemaker, "Communication Arts in the Curriculum," *Teachers College Record,* LVII (November, 1955), p. 112.
64. Langer, *Feeling and Form,* p. 332.
65. Shoemaker, *Teachers College Record,* LVII (November, 1955), p. 114.
66. Marshall McLuhan, *The Gutenberg Galaxy* (Toronto: University of Toronto Press, 1962), p. iii.
67. *Ibid.*, p. 1.
68. *Ibid.*, p. 258.
69. *Ibid.*, p. 259.
70. Lennox Grey and Francis Shoemaker, *General Education in Relation to Vocational-Technical Education in the New York State Institutes of Applied Arts and Sciences,* (Albany, N. Y.: State Education Department, 1946), p. 5.
71. *Ibid.*, pp. 20-21.
72. *Ibid.*, pp. 44-53.
73. Francis Shoemaker, "Self-Realization, Communication, and Aesthetic Experience," *Communication in General Education,* p. 243.
74. Francis E. Bowman, ed., *College Composition and Communication,* VIII (October, 1957), p. 129.
75. Lennox Grey, "Test Case," *Teachers College Record,* LVII (November, 1955), p. 138.
76. *Ibid.*
77. Francis Shoemaker and Louis Forsdale, eds., *Communication in General Education* (Dubuque, Ia.: William C. Brown Co., 1960), pp. xvi-xvii.
78. Kenneth S. Lynn, *Huck Finn: Texts, Sources and Criticism* (New York: Harcourt, Brace & World, 1961). Cf. William Van O'Connor and Edward Stone, *A Casebook on Ezra Pound* and Gerald Willen, ed., *A Casebook of Henry James' "Turn of the Screw,"* (New York: Thomas Y. Crowell, 1960).
79. Lynn, *Huck Finn,* p. 217.

FOUR

1. Lennox Grey, "No Signs, No Symbols! Uses A-B-C's: A Problem of Practical Definition," *Communication in General Education,* Earl J. McGrath, ed. (Dubuque, Ia.: William C. Brown Co., 1949), pp. 1-2.
2. Lennox Grey, ed., *What Communication Means Today* (Chicago: National Council of Teachers of English, 1944), p. 41.

3. Francis Shoemaker, "Self-Realization, Communication, and Aesthetic Experience," *Communication in General Education,* p. 237.
4. Alfred Schutz, "Symbol, Reality and Society," *Symbols and Society,* Lyman Bryson and others, eds. (New York: Harper & Bros., 1955), p. 138. The reference to Cassirer's work is Ernst Cassirer, *An Essay on Man* (New Haven, Conn.: Yale University Press, 1944), pp. 32-35.
5. Robert S. Hartman, "Philosophy of Symbolic Forms," *The Philosophy of Ernst Cassirer,* Paul Arthur Schlipp, ed. (Evanston, Ill.: Library of Living Philosophers, 1949), pp. 302-303. The reference to Cassirer's work is to Ernst Cassirer, *Philosphie Der Symbolischen in Formen* (Berlin: Bruno Cassirer, 1929), III, p. 117.
6. Francis Shoemaker, "Communication through Symbols in Literature," *English Journal,* XXXVII (May, 1948), p. 239.
7. *Ibid.,* p. 240.
8. Cf. William Rose Benét, ed., *The Reader's Encyclopedia* (New York: Thomas Y. Crowell Co., 1948), p. 1091. Bradford A. Booth, "The Novel," *Contemporary Literary Scholarship,* Lewis Leary, ed. (New York: Appleton-Century-Crofts, 1958), pp. 270-271.
9. Booth, "The Novel," *Contemporary Literary Scholarship,* p. 271.
10. *Ibid.,* pp. 271-272.
11. John Ciardi, *How Does a Poem Mean* (Boston: Houghton Mifflin Co., 1959), p. 709.
12. Dante Alighieri, *Divine Comedy,* Dorothy L. Sayers, trans. (Baltimore, Md.: Penguin Books, 1954), I, pp. 12-13.
13. Kenneth Burke, *The Philosophy of Literary Form* (Baton Rouge, La.: Louisiana State University Press, 1941), p. 396.
14. Rene Wellek and Austin Warren, *Theory of Literature* (New York: Harcourt, Brace & Co., 1948), p. 193.
15. Robert Ulich, "Symbolism and the Education of Man," *Symbols and Society,* p. 205.
16. Northrop Frye, *Anatomy of Criticism* (Princeton, N. J.: Princeton University Press, 1957), p. 341.
17. *Ibid.*
18. *Ibid.,* pp. 71-128.
19. *Ibid.,* p. 346.
20. Thomas De Quincey, "The Literature of Knowledge and the Literature of Power," *Criticism: The Foundations of Modern Literary Judgment,* Mark Schorer, Josephine Miles, and Gordon McKenzie, eds. (New York: Harcourt, Brace & Co., 1948), p. 473.
21. *Ibid.*
22. *Ibid.,* p. 474.
23. Wellek and Warren, *Theory of Literature,* p. 3.
24. *Ibid.*
25. *Ibid.*
26. *Ibid.,* p. 17.
27. *Ibid.,* pp. 19-28.
28. *Ibid.,* pp. ix-x, 19-28.

29. *Ibid.*, pp. 30-31, 4.
30. *Ibid.*, pp. 140-141.
31. *Ibid.*, p. 298.
32. Howard Mumford Jones, "Literature: Truth, Fiction and Reality," *Frontiers of Knowledge in the Study of Man*, Lynn White, Jr., ed. (New York: Harper & Bros., 1956), p. 195.
33. *Ibid.*, p. 206.
34. Francis Shoemaker, *Aesthetic Experience and the Humanities* (New York: Columbia University Press, 1943), p. 14.
35. L. A. Strong, *The Sacred River* (London: Methuen & Co., 1949), p. 85.
36. William Barrett, ed., *Zen Buddhism: Selected Writings of D. T. Suzuki* (New York: Doubleday Anchor Books, 1956), p. 121.
37. Aldous Huxley, *Do What You Will* (London: Chatto & Windus, 1931), pp. 48-51.
38. Strong, *The Sacred River*, p. 85.
39. William York Tindall, *James Joyce* (New York: Charles Scribner's Sons, 1950), p. 81.
40. Jacques Barzun, "The Scholar-Critic," *Contemporary Literary Scholarship*, Lewis Leary, ed. (New York: Appleton-Century-Crofts, 1958), p. 7.
41. I. A. Richards, *Coleridge on Imagination* (New York: W. W. Norton Co., 1950), p. 54.
42. Samuel T. Coleridge, *Biographia Literaria* (Oxford: Clarendon Press, 1907), p. 172.
43. Schorer, Miles, and McKenzie, *Criticism: The Foundations of Modern Literary Judgment*, p. 254.
44. Marshall McLuhan, "Speed of Cultural Change," *College Composition and Communication*, IX (February, 1958), pp. 17-18.
45. *Ibid.*, p. 17.
46. *Ibid.*, p. 17.
47. Wallace Stegner, "One Way to Spell Man," *Saturday Review*, LI (May 24, 1958), p. 9.
48. *Ibid.*, pp. 9-10.
49. Lewis Leary, "Literary Scholarship and the Teaching of English," *Contemporary Literary Scholarship*, p. 9.
50. *Ibid.*, p. 21.
51. Q. D. Leavis, *Fiction and the Reading Public* (London: Chatto & Windus, 1932), pp. xiii-xv.
52. David Daiches, *Critical Approaches to Literature* (Englewood Cliffs, N. J.: Prentice-Hall, 1956), pp. 391-392.
53. Paul B. Sears, *This Is Our World* (Norman, Okla.: University of Oklahoma Press, 1937), p. 8.
54. John Steinbeck and Edward F. Ricketts, *Sea of Cortez* (New York: Viking Press, 1941), p. 4.
55. Lennox Grey, "Literary Audience," *Contemporary Literary Scholarship*, p. 455.
56. *Ibid.*, p. 453.

57. *Ibid.*, pp. 453-454.
58. *Ibid.*, p. 453.
59. *Ibid.*, p. 455.
60. Louise M. Rosenblatt, *Literature as Exploration* (New York: D. Appleton-Century Co., 1938), p. v.
61. *Ibid.*, p. 54.

FIVE

1. Lewis Leary, "Literary Scholarship and the Teaching of English," *Contemporary Literary Scholarship,* Lewis Leary, ed. (New York: Appleton-Century-Crofts, 1958), pp. 10-11.
2. Marjorie Nicolson, *Science and Imagination* (Ithaca, N. Y.: Cornell University Press, 1956), pp. 80, 110.
3. These editions were published by Random House (1941), Sun Dial Press (1943), and the Modern Library (1947). The Modern Library (ML) edition is the basis for the references in this chapter. It is the only edition that has the author's Introduction, in which Stewart describes reasons for writing *Storm* that contribute to an understanding of a field theory approach to the novel.
4. George R. Stewart, *Storm* (New York: Modern Library, 1947), p. v.
5. *Ibid.*, p. i.
6. *Ibid.*, p. vii.
7. *Ibid.*, p. viii.
8. *Ibid.*, p. viii.
9. *Ibid.*
10. *Ibid.*, pp. 348-349.
11. *Ibid.*, pp. v-ix.
12. *Ibid.*, p. vii.
13. *Ibid.*, p. 145.
14. *Ibid.*, pp. 3-4.
15. *Ibid.*, p. 5.
16. *Ibid.*, pp. 9-10.
17. *Ibid.*, p. 21.
18. *Ibid.*, p. 51.
19. *Ibid.*, p. 55.
20. *Ibid.*, p. 15.
21. *Ibid.*, p. 13-14.
22. *Ibid.*, p. 16.
23. *Ibid.*, pp. 16-17.
24. *Ibid.*, p. 17.
25. *Ibid.*, p. 20.
26. *Ibid.*, pp. 20-21.

27. The Appendix of this book attempts to show the pattern of these appearances.
28. Stewart, *Storm*, p. 21.
29. *Ibid.*
30. *Ibid.*, p. 27.
31. *Ibid.*, p. 31.
32. *Ibid.*, p. 37.
33. *Ibid.*, p. 42.
34. *Ibid.*, pp. 274-275.
35. *Ibid.*, p. 285.
36. United Nations Scientific and Cultural Organization, *United States National Commission for the United Nations Scientific and Cultural Organization,* (Washington, D. C.: Government Printing Office, 1946), p. 11.
37. Stewart, *Storm*, p. 44.
38. *Ibid.*, p. 45.
39. *Ibid.*, p. 46.
40. *Ibid.*
41. *Ibid.*, p. 101. Other instances of governmental support for individuals caught in the impersonality of organizations will be found in the Appendix.
42. *Ibid.*, p. 50.
43. *Ibid.*
44. *Ibid.*, pp. 50-51.
45. *Ibid.*, p. 66.
46. *Ibid.*, p. 76
47. *Ibid.*, pp. 78-79.
48. "Seemingly" is used because, as the Appendix indicates, there is a planned pattern of appearance of the owl, Pete the flour salesman, Jen and Max, and the weather that bedeviled the fur-trader.
49. Stewart, *Storm*, p. 56.
50. *Ibid.*, p. 58.
51. *Ibid.*, pp. 62-63.
52. *Ibid.*
53. *Ibid.*
54. *Ibid.*, p. 73.
55. *Ibid.*, p. 74.
56. *Ibid.*
57. *Ibid.*, p. 73.
58. *Ibid.*, p. 74.
59. *Ibid.*, p. 80.
60. *Ibid.*, pp. 80-81.
61. *Ibid.*, p. 82.
62. *Ibid.*

63. *Ibid.*, p. 87.
64. *Ibid.*, p. 88.
65. *Ibid.*, pp. 88-89.
66. *Ibid.*, pp. 116-117.
67. *Ibid.*, p. 297.
68. *Ibid.*, p. 236.
69. *Ibid.*, p. 310.
70. George W. Hartmann, "The Field Theory of Learning and Its Educational Consequences," *The Psychology of Learning,* Forty-first Yearbook of the National Society for the Study of Education (Chicago: University of Chicago Press, 1942), II, p. 165.
71. Readers tracing any of the leaders, e.g., the DTS, through the twelve days of the storm, section by section as listed in the Appendix, can observe the pattern of alternatives and the uses made of them by the leaders.
72. See Appendix.
73. Stewart, *Storm,* p. 303.
74. *Ibid.*, p. 345.
75. *Ibid.*, p. 318.
76. *Ibid.*, p. 288.
77. *Ibid.*, p. 289.
78. *Ibid.*, p. 290.
79. *Ibid.*, p. 123.
80. *Ibid.*, p. 339.
81. *Ibid.*, p. 340.
82. *Ibid.*, p. 349.
83. Leon Edel, *The Modern Psychological Novel* (New York: Grove Press, 1959), p. 15.
84. E. L. Epstein, "Notes on Lord of the Flies," in William Golding, *Lord of the Flies* (New York: G. P. Putnam's Sons, 1959), p. 251.
85. Cf. *New York Times Book Review,* April 29, 1962, pp. 16-17.
86. Lawrence Durrell, quoted by Nigel Dennis, "New Four-Star King of Novelists," *Life,* XLIX (November 21, 1960), p. 98.
87. *Ibid.*
88. *Ibid.*
89. Nigel Dennis, "Eighty-five Years in Search of Self," *New York Times Book Review,* January 29, 1961, p. 34.

SIX

1. Teachers College, Columbia University, *Teachers College Bulletin, 1962-1963,* p. 108.
2. *Ibid.*

3. Cf. Frank M. Calabria, *Characteristics of Effective Teachers* (Albany, N. Y.: State Education Department, 1959) and *Analysis of Teacher Education Programs in New York State* (Albany, N. Y.: State Education Department, 1959). Philip Cowen and others, *Studies of the Professional Content in Education Needed by Teachers of Academic Subjects* (Albany, N. Y.: State Education Department, 1960).
4. The University of Buffalo, *Bulletin, 1960-1961*, p. 14.
5. The University of Buffalo, *College of Arts and Sciences, 1960-1962*, p. 21-22.
6. *Ibid.*, p. 63.
7. *Ibid.*, p. 64.
8. The University of Buffalo, *Bulletin, 1960-1961*, p. 16.
9. *Ibid.*, p. 38.
10. *Ibid.*
11. Cornell University, *General Information, 1960-1961*, p. 8.
12. *Ibid.*
13. Cornell University, *Arts and Sciences, 1961-1962*, p. 42.
14. *Ibid.*, pp. 42-43.
15. *Ibid.*, pp. 43-44.
16. Cornell University, *General Information, 1960-1961*, p. 19.
17. *Amendment to Regulations of the Commissioner of Education* (Albany, N. Y.: Bureau of Teacher Education and Certification, 1961), pp. 2-3.
18. *Ibid.*, p. 15.
19. *Ibid.*, pp. 15-16.
20. *Ibid.*, p. 13.
21. *Ibid.*, p. 14.
22. Lawrence Durrell, *Clea* (New York: Pocket Books, 1961), Author's Note.

SELECTED BIBLIOGRAPHY

ASTRONOMY

Bizony, M. Y., and Giffin, R., eds. *The Space Encyclopedia: A Guide to Astronomy and Space Research.* New York: E. P. Dutton & Co., 1957.

Clason, Clyde B. *Exploring the Distant Stars.* New York: G. P. Putnam's Sons, 1958.

Kahn, Fritz. *Design of the Universe.* New York: Crown Publishers, 1954.

Moore, Patrick. *The Story of Man and the Stars.* New York: W. W. Norton & Co., 1955.

Pfeiffer, John. *The Changing Universe.* New York: Random House, 1956.

Velikovsky, Immanuel. *Worlds in Collision.* New York: Doubleday & Co., 1950.

BIOLOGY

Ashby, W. R. *The Human Brain.* New York: John Wiley & Sons, 1952.

Bonner, John Tyler. *Cells and Societies.* Princeton, N. J.: Princeton University Press, 1955.

Brazier, Mary A. B. *The Electrical Activity of the Nervous System.* New York: Macmillan Co., 1951.

Cannon, Walter B. *The Wisdom of the Body.* New York: W. W. Norton & Co., 1939.

Carlson, Anton J., and Johnson, Victor. *The Machinery of the Body.* Chicago: University of Chicago Press, 1953.

Gerard, R. W. "Biological Roots of Psychiatry," *Science,* CXXII (August, 1955), pp. 225-230.

Grant, Madeline Parker. *Microbiology and Human Progress.* New York: Rinehart & Co., 1953.

Herrick, C. J. *Brains of Rats and Men.* Chicago: University of Chicago Press, 1926.

Hurd, Paul. *Biological Education in American Secondary Schools, 1890-1960.* Washington, D. C.: American Institute for Biological Studies, 1961.

LaBarre, Weston. *The Human Animal.* Chicago: University of Chicago Press, 1954.

Schrodinger, E. *What is Life?* New York: Cambridge University Press, 1948.

Scott, John Paul. *Animal Behavior.* Chicago: University of Chicago Press, 1957.

Scott, W. C. M. "Some Embryological, Neurological, Psychiatric and Psychoanalytic Implications of the Body Scheme," *International Journal of Psycho-Analysis,* XXIX (May, 1948), pp. 141-155.

Sinnott, Edmund W. *Matter, Mind and Man.* New York: Harper & Bros., 1957.

Von Frisch, K. *Bees: Their Vision, Chemical Senses, and Language.* Ithaca, N. Y.: Cornell University Press, 1950.

Zipf, G. K. *The Psycho-Biology of Language.* Boston: Houghton Mifflin Co., 1935.

Zubek, John P. *Human Development.* New York: McGraw-Hill Book Co., 1954.

CHEMISTRY

Asimov, Isaac. *The Chemicals of Life.* New York: Abelard-Schuman, 1954.

Borek, Ernest. *Man, the Chemical Machine.* New York: Columbia University Press, 1952.

Needham, J. *Biochemistry and Morphogenesis.* New York: Cambridge University Press, 1942.

COMMUNICATION

Bateson, Gregory, and Ruesch, Jurgen. *Communication: The Social Matrix of Psychiatry.* New York: W. W. Norton & Co., 1951.

Berelson, Bernard. "Communication and Public Opinion," *Communication and Modern Society,* Wilbur Schramm, ed. Urbana, Ill.: University of Illinois Press, 1948.

———. *Content Analysis.* Glencoe, Ill.: Free Press of Glencoe, 1952.

Berkeley, Edmund C., and Wainwright, Lawrence. *Computers: Their Operation and Applications.* New York: Reinhold Publishing Corp., 1956.

Birdwhistell, R. L. *Introduction to Kinesics: An Annotation System for Analysis of Body Motion and Gesture.* Washington, D. C.: Foreign Service Institute, Department of State, 1952.

Black, Max. *Language and Philosophy.* Ithaca, N. Y.: Cornell University Press, 1949.

Bryson, Lyman, ed. *The Communication of Ideas.* New York: Harper & Bros., 1948.

Cherry, Colin. *On Human Communication.* Cambridge, Mass.: Technology Press of M.I.T., 1957.

Deutsch, Karl W. "Communication Theory and Social Science," *Selected Papers on Psychotherapy, Purpose and Communication.* New York: American Orthopsychiatric Association, 1952.

McLuhan, Marshall. *The Gutenberg Galaxy.* Toronto: University of Toronto Press, 1962.

Rusinoff, S. E. *Automation in Practice.* Chicago: American Technical Society, 1957.

Shannon, Claude, and Weaver, Warren. *The Mathematical Theory of Communication.* Urbana, Ill.: University of Illinois Press, 1949.

Sinnott, Edmund W. "The Biology of Purpose," *Selected Papers on Psychotherapy, Purpose and Communication.* New York: American Orthopsychiatric Association, 1952.

Von Foerster, Heinz. *Cybernetics.* New York: Josiah Macy, Jr., Foundation, 1952.

Wiener, Norbert. *Cybernetics: Or Control and Communication in the Animal and the Machine.* New York: John Wiley & Sons, 1948.

———. *The Human Use of Human Beings.* Boston: Houghton Mifflin Co., 1950.

CULTURAL ANTHROPOLOGY

Benedict, Ruth F. *The Chrysanthemum and the Sword: Patterns of Japanese Culture.* Boston: Houghton Mifflin Co., 1946.

———. *Patterns of Culture.* Baltimore: Pelican Books, 1946.

Kluckhohn, Clyde, and Kelley, William H. "The Concept of Culture," *The Science of Man in the World Crisis,* Ralph Linton, ed. New York: Columbia University Press, 1945.

Mead, Margaret, ed. *Cultural Patterns and Technical Change.* New York: New American Library, 1955.

ECOLOGY

Benton, Allen H., and Werner, William E., Jr. *Principles of Field Biology and Ecology.* New York: McGraw-Hill Book Co., 1958.

Buchsbaum, Ralph, and Buchsbaum, Mildred. *Basic Ecology.* Pittsburgh, Pa.: Boxwood Press, 1957.

Collins, Stephen. *The Biotic Communicites of Greenbrook Sanctuary.* Englewood, N. J.: Palisades Nature Association, 1956.

Elton, Charles. *The Ecology of Animals.* New York: John Wiley & Sons, 1950.

Hylander, Clarence J. *World of Plant Life.* New York: Macmillan Co., 1956.

Leach, William. *Plant Ecology.* New York: John Wiley & Sons, 1956.

Lemon, Paul C. *An Ecologist Looks at Natural Areas.* New York: State University of New York, 1959.

Leopold, Luna B., and Maddock, Thomas, Jr. *The Flood Control Controversy.* New York: Ronald Press Co., 1954.

Neal, Ernest. *Woodland Ecology.* Cambridge, Mass.: Harvard University Press, 1958.

Schultz, Ida Beth. "A Way of Developing Children's Understanding of Ecology," *Dissertation Abstracts 15,* No. 12, p. 243.

Sears, Paul B. *Deserts on the March.* Norman, Okla.: University of Oklahoma Press, 1947.

Storer, John H. *The Web of Life: A First Book of Ecology.* New York: Devin-Adair Co., 1956.

EDUCATION

Barzun, Jacques. *Teacher in America.* New York: Doubleday & Co., 1954.

Bloom, Benjamin S., ed. *Taxonomy of Educational Objectives.* New York: Longmans, Green & Co., 1956.

———. "Thought-Processes in Lectures and Discussions," *Journal of General Education,* VII (April, 1953), pp. 160-169.

Brown, Stanley B. "A Consideration of the Learning Process in Science Teaching," *Science Education,* XLII (February, 1958), pp. 79-86.

Butts, R. Freeman, and Cremin, Lawrence. *A History of Education in American Culture.* New York: Henry Holt & Co., 1953.

Cantor, Nathaniel. *The Teaching-Learning Process.* New York: Dryden Press, 1953.

Fallico, A. B. "Existentialism and Education," *Educational Theory,* IV (April, 1954), pp. 166-172.

Gardner, John W. *Excellence.* New York: Harper & Bros., 1961.

Good, Carter V., and Scates, Douglas E. *Methods of Research.* New York: Appleton-Century-Crofts, 1954.

Habein, Margaret L., ed. *Spotlight on the College Student.* Washington, D. C.: American Council on Education, 1959.

Mayer, Martin. *The Schools.* New York: Harper & Bros., 1961.

Kelley, Earl, and Rasey, Marie. *Education and the Nature of Man.* New York: Harper & Bros., 1952.

Montagu, Ashley. *Education and Human Relations.* New York: Grove Press, 1958.

Nostrand, Howard Lee. "The Agenda for a New Generation," *Journal of General Education,* X (October, 1957), pp. 190-204.

———. "Toward Agreement on Cultural Essentials," *Journal of General Education,* XI (January, 1958), pp. 7-27.

Reid, Robert H. "American Degree Mills: The Problem and an Analysis of the Danger," *Educational Record,* XL (October, 1959), pp. 294-300.

Waggoner, George R. "The Development of Programs for the Superior Student in Large Universities," *Educational Record,* XL (October, 1959), pp. 319-325.

Whitehead, Alfred North. *The Aims of Education.* New York: New American Library, 1949.

Wirth, A. G. "On Existentialism, the Emperor's New Clothes and Education," *Educational Theory,* V (July, 1955), pp. 152-157.

ENGLISH-EDUCATION

Bailey, Matilda. "Therapeutic Reading," *ABC Language Arts Bulletin.* New York: American Book Co., 1948.

———. "The Magic Mirror of Books," *ABC Language Arts Bulletin.* New York: American Book Co., 1953.

Baker, Franklin T. "Preparation of High School Teachers of English," *English Journal,* IV (May, 1915), pp. 322-332.

Baker, Harold S. *The High School English Teacher: Concept of Professional Responsibility and Role.* Toronto: Ryerson Press, 1949.

Bryant, M. *Modern English and Its Heritage.* Rev. ed. New York: Macmillan Co., 1962.

Finocchiaro, Mary. *Teaching English as a Second Language.* New York: Harper & Bros., 1958.

Kitzhaber, Albert. *Themes, Theories and Therapy: The Teaching of Writing in College.* Champaign, Ill.: National Council of Teachers of English, 1963.

Loban, Walter. *Literature and Social Sensitivity.* Champaign, Ill.: National Council of Teachers of English, 1954.

Postman, Neil. *Television and the Teaching of English.* New York: Appleton-Century-Crofts, 1961.

Roberts, Holland D., Kaulfers, Walter V., and Kefauver, Grayson N. *English for Social Living.* New York: McGraw-Hill Book Co., 1943.

Roberts, Paul. *English Sentences.* New York: Harcourt, Brace & World, 1962.

Roberts, Paul. *Patterns of English.* New York: Harcourt, Brace & Co., 1956.

Strom, Ingrid M. "Summary of Investigations Relating to the English Language Arts in Secondary Education," *English Journal,* XLIX (February, 1960) and LII (February, 1963).

Weiss, M. Jerry. *An English Teacher's Reader.* New York: Odyssey Press, 1962.

GENERAL SCIENCE

Adams, J. "Expressive Aspects of Scientific Language," *On Expressive Language,* H. Werner, ed. Worcester, Mass.: Clark University Press, 1955.

Asimov, Isaac. *Only a Trillion: Specialization and Explorations on the Marvels of Science.* New York: Abelard-Schuman, 1957.

Blanchet, Waldo W. E. "Principles of Science: A Look Ahead," *Science Education,* XLI (February, 1957), pp. 1-9.

Braithwaite, Richard Bevan. *Scientific Explanation: A Study of the Function of Theory, Probability and Law in Science.* Cambridge: Cambridge University Press, 1955.

Deason, Hilary J., ed. *The Traveling High School Science Library.* Washington, D. C.: American Association for the Advancement of Science, 1958.

Henry, Nelson B. *Rethinking Science Education.* Chicago: University of Chicago Press, 1960.

Lewin, Kurt. *Field Theory in Social Science: Selected Theoretical Papers.* New York: Harper & Bros., 1951.

Plotz, Helen, ed. *Imagination's Other Place: Poems of Science and Mathematics.* New York: Thomas Y. Crowell Co., 1955.

Quattlebaum, Charles. *Development of Scientific, Engineering, and Other Professional Manpower.* Washington, D. C.: Government Printing Office, 1957.

Rapoport, Anatol. *Science and the Goals of Man.* New York: Harper & Bros., 1950.

Russell, Bertrand. *Impact of Science on Society.* New York: Simon & Schuster, 1953.

Savory, T. H. *The Language of Science.* London: Deutsch, 1953.

Smith, Herbert A. *The Emergence and Development of Educational Research Related to Science Instruction for the Elementary and Junior High School.* University Park, Pa.: Department of Secondary Education, Pennsylvania State University, 1963.

Snow, C. P. *The Two Cultures and the Scientific Revolution.* New York: Cambridge University Press, 1962.

Wightman, P. D. William. *The Growth of Scientific Ideas.* New Haven, Conn.: Yale University Press, 1953.

Young, J. Z. *Doubt and Certainty in Science.* Oxford: Oxford University Press, 1961.

GENETICS

Dobzhansky, Theodosius. *Evolution, Genetics and Man.* New York: John Wiley & Sons, 1955.

Sears, R. R., Whiting, J. W. M., Nowlis, V., and Sears, P. S. "Some Child-Rearing Antecedents of Aggression and Dependency in Young Children," *Genetic Psychology Monographs,* XLVII (1953), pp. 135-234.

Serb, Adrian M., and Owen, Ray. *General Genetics.* San Francisco, Calif.: W. H. Freeman & Co., 1958.

Simpson, G. G. *The Meaning of Evolution.* New Haven, Conn.: Yale University Press, 1950.

INTERDISCIPLINARY

Boulding, Kenneth E. *The Image.* Ann Arbor, Mich.: University of Michigan Press, 1956.

Dampier, Sir William. *A History of Science and Its Relations with Philosophy and Religion.* Cambridge: Cambridge University Press, 1952.

Grinker, Roy R., ed. *Toward a Unified Theory of Human Behavior.* New York: Basic Books, 1956.

Irving, John A. *Science and Values: Explorations in Philosophy and the Social Sciences.* Toronto: Ryerson Press, 1952.

National Society for the Study of Education. *The Integration of Educational Experiences.* Chicago: University of Chicago Press, 1958.

Nicholson, Marjorie. *Science and Imagination.* Ithaca, N. Y.: Cornell University Press, 1956.

Reiser, Oliver, ed. *The Integration of Human Knowledge.* Boston: Porter Sargent, 1958.

Shoemaker, Francis. *Aesthetic Experience and the Humanities.* New York: Columbia University Press, 1943.

Squire, James R. "Searching for Simplicity in Complexity," *California Journal for Instructional Improvement,* II (October, 1959), p. 2.

Toynbee, Arnold. *A Study of History,* 11 vols. London: Oxford University Press, 1934-1954.

White, Lynn, Jr., ed. *Frontiers of Knowledge in the Study of Man.* New York: Harper & Bros., 1956.

LINGUISTICS

Bloch, B., and Trager, G. L. *Outline of Linguistic Analysis.* Baltimore: Linguistic Society of America, 1942.

Bloomfield, Leonard. *An Introduction to the Study of Language.* New York: Henry Holt & Co., 1933.

Empson, W. *The Structure of Complex Words.* New York: New Directions, 1952.

Fries, C. C. *American English Grammar.* New York: Appleton-Century-Crofts, 1940.

———. *Teaching and Learning English as a Foreign Language.* Ann Arbor, Mich.: University of Michigan Press, 1945.

Goad, Harold. *Language in History.* Baltimore: Penguin Books, 1958.

Nida, E. A. *Morphology: The Descriptive Analysis of Words.* Ann Arbor, Mich.: University of Michigan Press, 1946.

Pike, K. L. *Phonemics: A Technique for Reducing Languages to Writing.* Ann Arbor, Mich.: University of Michigan Press, 1947.

Sturtevant, E. H. *Introduction to Linguistic Science.* New Haven, Conn.: Yale University Press, 1947.

LITERARY CRITICISM

Adams, Phoebe. "Reader's Choice," *Atlantic*, CCV (March, 1960), pp. 114-115.

Bateson, F. W. *English Poetry: A Critical Introduction*. London: Longmans, Green & Co., 1950.

Booth, Wayne C. *The Rhetoric of Fiction*. Chicago: University of Chicago Press, 1961.

Burke, Kenneth. *A Grammar of Motives*. New York: Prentice-Hall, 1945.

———. *The Philosophy of Literary Form*. Baton Rouge, La.: Louisiana State University Press, 1941.

Cornell, Kenneth. *The Post-Symbolist Period*. New Haven, Conn.: Yale University Press, 1958.

Cowley, Malcolm. "The Miserly Millionaire of Words," *Reporter*, XVI (February, 1957), pp. 38-40.

Craig, Hardin, ed. *A History of English Literature*. New York: Oxford University Press, 1950.

Daiches, David. *Critical Approaches to Literature*. Englewood Cliffs, N. J.: Prentice-Hall, 1956.

Fay, Eliot. *Lorenzo in Search of the Sun*. New York: Bookman Associates, 1953.

Frye, Northrop. *Anatomy of Criticism*. Princeton, N. J.: Princeton University Press, 1957.

Givens, Seon, ed. *James Joyce: Two Decades of Criticism*. New York: Vanguard Press, 1948.

Harvey, Sir Paul, and Heseltine, Janet E. *The Oxford Companion to French Literature*. London: Oxford University Press, 1959.

Hopkins, Vivian C. "Emerson and Bacon." *American Literature*, XXIX (January, 1958), pp. 408-430.

Jones, William Powell. *James Joyce and the Common Reader*. Norman, Okla.: University of Oklahoma Press, 1955.

Kaufmann, Walter. "Franz Kafka," *Existentialism From Dostoyevsky to Sartre*. New York: Meridian Books, 1957.

Leary, Lewis, ed. *Contemporary Literary Scholarship*. New York: Appleton-Century-Crofts, 1958.

Lowenthal, Leo. *Literature and the Image of Man*. Boston: Beacon Press, 1957.

Lynn, Kenneth S. *Huck Finn: Texts, Sources and Criticism*. New York: Harcourt, Brace & World, 1961.

O'Connor, William, and Stone, Edward. *A Casebook on Ezra Pound*. New York: Thomas Y. Crowell, 1960.

Pearce, Roy Harvey. *The Continuity of American Poetry*. Princeton, N. J.: Princeton University Press, 1961.

Preston, John H. "A Conversation with Gertrude Stein," *The Creative Process*. New York: The American Library, 1952.

Richards, Ivor Armstrong. *Coleridge on Imagination*. New York: W. W. Norton & Co., 1950.

Shayon, Robert Lewis. "Discovering the Whole Man," *Saturday Review*, (September, 1958), pp. 15-17, 53.

Stegner, Wallace. "One Way to Spell Man," *Saturday Review*, (May, 1958), pp. 8-10, 43-44.

Tindall, William York. *James Joyce.* New York: Twentieth Century Press, 1950.

Trilling, Lionel. "George Orwell and the Politics of Truth: Portrait of the Intellectual as a Man of Virtue," *Commentary*, XIII (March, 1952), pp. 218-227.

Willen, Gerald, ed. *A Casebook of Henry James' "Turn of the Screw."* New York: Thomas Y. Crowell Co., 1960.

MATHEMATICS

Alexandroff, P. S. *Introduction to the Theory of Groups.* Toronto: Ryerson Press, 1959.

Allendoerfer, C. B., and Oakley, C. O. *Principles of Mathematics.* New York: McGraw-Hill Book Co., 1955.

Altwerger, Samuel I. *Modern Mathematics: An Introduction.* New York: Macmillan Co., 1960.

Christian, Robert R. *Introduction to Logic and Sets.* Toronto: Ginn & Co., 1958.

Dantzig, Tobias. *Number, the Language of Science.* New York: Macmillan Co., 1954.

Mathematics Staff of the College. *Numbers, Statements and Connectives.* Chicago: University of Chicago Press, 1956.

Mathematics Staff of the College. *Sentences, Sets.* Chicago: University of Chicago Press, 1956.

Oettinger, Anthony G. *Automatic Language Translation.* Cambridge, Mass.: Harvard University Press, 1960.

Reid, Constance. *From Zero to Infinity.* New York: Thomas Y. Crowell Co., 1955.

METEOROLOGY

Laird, Charles, and Laird, Ruth. *Weathercasting.* Englewood Cliffs, N. J.: Prentice-Hall, 1955.

Longstreath, T. Morris. *Understanding the Weather.* New York: Macmillan Co., 1953.

Shapley, Harlow, ed. *Climatic Change: Evidence, Causes, and Effects.* Cambridge, Mass.: Harvard University Press, 1954.

PHILOSOPHY

Adler, Mortimer J., and Mayer, Milton. *The Revolution in Education.* Chicago: University of Chicago Press, 1958.

Barrett, William. *Irrational Man: A Study in Existential Philosophy.* New York: Doubleday & Co., 1958.

———, ed. *Zen Buddhism: Selected Writings of D. T. Suzuki.* New York: Doubleday & Co., 1956.

Buber, M. *Between Man and Man.* R. G. Smith, trans. Boston: Beacon Press, 1955.

Cassirer, Ernst. *An Essay on Man.* New Haven, Conn.: Yale University Press, 1944.

Conger, George P. "Integration," *Essays in East-West Philosophy,* Charles A. Moore, ed. Honolulu: University of Hawaii Press, 1951.

Dewey, John. *Problems of Men.* New York: Philosophical Library, 1946.

———. "Theory of Valuation," *International Encyclopedia of Unified Science.* Chicago: University of Chicago Press, 1947.

———, and Bentley, Arthur F. *Knowing and the Known.* Boston: Beacon Press, 1949.

Drucker, Peter F. "The New Philosophy Comes to Life," *Harper's,* CCXV (August, 1957), pp. 36-40.

Durant, Will. *The Story of Philosophy.* New York: Pocket Books, 1954.

Kadushin, Max. *The Rabbinic Mind.* New York: Jewish Theological Seminary of America, 1952.

Kierkegaard, S. *Fear and Trembling, the Sickness Unto Death.* New York: Doubleday & Co., 1954.

Michaleon, C., ed. *Christianity and Existentialists.* New York: Charles Scribner's Sons, 1956.

Pepper, S. C. *The Sources of Value.* Berkeley, Calif.: University of California Press, 1958.

Rapoport, Anatol. *Operational Philosophy.* New York: Harper & Bros., 1953.

Sartre, J. P. *Existentialism and Human Emotions.* New York: Philosophical Library, 1957.

Schilipp, Paul Arthur, ed. *The Philosophy of Ernst Cassirer.* 10 vols. Evanston, Ill.: Library of Living Philosophers, 1949.

Tillich, Paul. *The Courage to Be.* New Haven, Conn.: Yale University Press, 1952.

Unamuno, M. *The Tragic Sense of Life.* J. E. C. Flush, trans. New York: Dover Publications, 1954.

Von Mises, Richard. *Positivism.* Cambridge, Mass.: Harvard University Press, 1951.

Wilson, Colin. *The Outsider.* Boston: Houghton Mifflin Co., 1956.

———. *Religion and the Rebel.* Boston: Houghton Mifflin Co., 1957.

PHYSICS

Asimov, Isaac. *Inside the Atom.* New York: Abelard-Schuman, 1956.

Barnett, Lincoln. *The Universe and Dr. Einstein.* New York: New American Library, 1952.

Barton, A. W. *A Text Book on Light.* New York: Longmans, Green & Co., 1939.

Cousins, Norman. "Clean Bombs and Dirty Wars," *Saturday Review,* XL (July, 1957), p. 20.

Einstein, Albert. "Autobiographical Notes," *Albert Einstein: Philosopher-Scientist,* Paul Arthur Schilipp, trans. New York: Tudor Publishing Co., 1951.

———, and Infeld, Leopold. *The Evolution of Physics.* New York: Simon & Schuster, 1951.

Fermi, Laura. *Atoms in the Family: My Life with Enrico Fermi.* Chicago: University of Chicago Press, 1954.

Frank, Philipp. *Relativity: A Richer Truth.* Boston: Beacon Press, 1950.

Giedion, Sigfried. *Space, Time and Architecture.* Cambridge, Mass.: Harvard University Press, 1956.

Kaempffert, Waldemar. "The Many Uses of the Atom," *Headline Series 117.* New York: Foreign Policy Association, 1956.

Pierce, John R. *Electrons, Waves and Messages.* New York: Hanover House, 1956.

Starling, S. K. *Electricity and Magnetism for Advanced Students.* New York: Longmans, Green & Co., 1912.

Wilson, William. *A Hundred Years of Physics.* London: Gerald Duckworth & Co., 1950.

PSYCHOLINGUISTICS

Bryson, Lyman, *et al.*, eds. *Symbols and Values: An Initial Study.* New York: Harper & Bros., 1954.

Cassirer, Ernst. *Das Mythische Denken.* Vol. II of *Philosophie der Symbolischen Formen.* Berlin: Bruno Cassirer, 1925.

Hoijer, Harry. *Language in Culture.* Chicago: University of Chicago Press, 1954.

Lee, Irving J. *Customs and Crises in Communication.* New York: Harper & Bros., 1954.

Morris, Charles. *Signs, Language and Behavior.* New York: George Braziller, 1955.

Mowrer, O. Hobart. *Learning Theory and the Symbolic Processes.* New York: John Wiley & Sons, 1960.

Osgood, Charles E., ed. "Psycholinguistics," *Supplement to The Journal of Abnormal and Social Psychology.* Baltimore: Waverly Press, 1954.

Piaget, J. *Logic and Psychology.* New York: Basic Books, 1957.

Richards, I. A. "Communication Between Men: The Meaning of Language," *Cybernetics,* Heinz von Foerster, ed. New York: Josiah Macy, Jr., Foundation, 1952.

Rogers, Carl R. "A Process Conception of Psychotherapy," *American Psychologist,* XIII (April, 1958), pp. 142-149.

Ruesch, Jurgen. "Synopsis of the Theory of Human Communication," *Psychiatry: Journal for the Study of Interpersonal Processes,* XVI (August, 1953), pp. 215-243.

Sattler, William M. "Inference and Predition as Communication Barriers," *Personnel Journal,* XXXVI (September, 1957), pp. 140-142.

Suci, George J., Osgood, Charles E., and Tannenbaum, Percy H. *The Measurement of Meaning.* Urbana, Ill.: University of Illinois Press, 1957.

Whorf, B. L. *Language, Thought, and Reality.* Cambridge, Mass.: Technology Press of M.I.T., 1956.

PSYCHOLOGY

Allport, Gordon W. *Becoming: Basic Considerations for a Psychology of Personality.* New Haven, Conn.: Yale University Press, 1955.

Arnheim, Rudolph. "Perceptual Abstraction in Art," *Psychological Review,* LIV (June, 1947), pp. 66–82.

———. "The Priority of Expression," *Journal of Aesthetics,* VIII (December, 1949), pp. 106–109.

Bartlett, F. C. *Remembering.* London: Cambridge University Press, 1932.

Bartley, Howard S. *Principles of Perception.* New York: Harper & Bros., 1958.

Binet, A. *L'Etude expérimentale de l'Intelligence.* Paris: Schleicher, 1903.

Blackwood, Paul E. *How Children Learn to Think.* Washington, D.C.: U. S. Office of Education, 1951.

Bruner, Jerome. *Process of Education.* Cambridge, Mass.: Harvard University Press, 1960.

Brunier, J. S. "Personality Dynamics and the Process of Perceiving," *Perception: An Approach to Personality,* R. R. Blake and G. V. Ramsey, eds. New York: Ronald Press Co., 1951.

———, Goodnow, J. J., and Austin, G. A. *A Study of Thinking.* New York: John Wiley & Sons, 1956.

Brunswik, Egon. "The Conceptual Framework of Psychology," *International Encyclopedia of Unified Science,* Vol. I, No. 10. Chicago: University of Chicago Press, 1952.

Combs, Arthur W., and Snygg, Donald. *Individual Behavior.* New York: Harper & Bros., 1959.

Cronbach, L. J. *Educational Psychology.* New York: Harcourt, Brace & Co., 1954.

Dollard, J., and Miller, N. E. *Personality and Psychotherapy: An Analysis in Terms of Learning, Thinking, and Culture.* New York: McGraw-Hill Book Co., 1950.

Duffy, Elizabeth. "The Psychological Significance of the Concept of 'Arousal' or Activation," *Psychological Review,* LXIV (September, 1957), pp. 265–275.

Frandsen, Arden N. *How Children Learn.* New York: McGraw-Hill Book Co., 1957.

Gibson, J. J. *The Perception of the Visual World.* Boston: Houghton Mifflin Co., 1950.

Hartmann, G. W. *Gestalt Psychology.* New York: Ronald Press Co., 1935.

Havighurst, Robert. *Human Development and Education.* New York: Longmans, Green & Co., 1953.

Hebb, Donald Olding. *A Textbook of Psychology.* Philadelphia: W. B. Saunders Co., 1958.

———. "Drives and the C.N.S." *Psychological Review,* LXII (July, 1955), pp. 243–253.

Heller, Erich. "The World of Franz Kafka," *The Disinherited Mind.* New York: Meridian Books, 1959.

Henneman, Richard H. "Sensation and Perception Get Married," *Contemporary Psychology,* III (December, 1958), pp. 353–355.

Hull, Clark L. *A Behavior System.* New Haven, Conn.: Yale University Press, 1952.

Kadushin, Max. *Organic Thinking.* New York: Jewish Theological Seminary of America, 1938.

Lewin, Kurt. *A Dynamic Theory of Personality.* New York: McGraw-Hill Book Co., 1935.

———. *Field Theory in Social Science.* New York: Harper & Bros., 1951.

———. *Principles of Topological Psychology.* New York: McGraw-Hill Book Co., 1936.

———. *Resolving Social Conflicts.* New York: Harper & Bros., 1948.

Lorenz, Konrad Z. "The Comparative Method in Studying Innate Behavior Patterns," *Physiological Mechanisms in Animal Behavior.* Cambridge: Academic Press, 1950.

Mowrer, O. Hobart. *Learning Theory and Behavior.* New York: John Wiley & Sons, 1960.

———. *Learning Theory and Personality Dynamics.* New York: Ronald Press Co., 1950.

Murphy, Gardner. *Personality: A Biosocial Approach to Origins and Structure.* New York: Harper & Bros., 1947.

Russell, David H. *Children's Thinking.* New York: Ginn & Co., 1956.

Symonds, Percival M. "What Education Has to Learn from Psychology," *Teachers College Record,* LVI (February, 1955), LVII (October, 1955), LVII (April, 1956), LVIII (March, 1957), and LIX (November, 1957).

Witkin, H. A. *Personality Through Perception.* New York: Harper & Bros., 1953.

SEMANTICS

Bréal, Michel. *Essai de Sémantique.* 5th ed. Paris: Hachette, 1911.

———. *Semantics: Studies in the Science of Meaning.* London: Heinemann, 1900.

Brown, Roger. *Words and Things.* Glencoe, Ill.: Free Press of Glencoe, 1958.

Carnap, Rudolf. *Meaning and Necessity.* Chicago: University of Chicago Press, 1947.

Chase, Stuart. *The Proper Study of Mankind.* New York: Harper & Bros., 1948.

Hayakawa, S. I. *Language in Thought and Action.* New York: Harcourt, Brace & Co., 1941.

———. "Linguistic Science and the Teaching of Composition," *ETC,* VII (Winter, 1950), pp. 97–103.

Korzybski, Alfred. *Manhood of Humanity,* 2nd ed. Lakeville, Conn.: Institute of General Semantics, 1950.

———. *Science and Sanity: An Introduction to Non-Aristotelian Systems and General Semantics.* Lakeville, Conn.: Institute of General Semantics, 1933, 1941, 1948, 1958.

Lee, Irving J. *How to Understand Propaganda.* New York: Rinehart & Co., 1952.

Ogden, C. K., and Richards, I. A. *The Meaning of Meaning.* 5th ed. New York: Harcourt, Brace & Co., 1938.

Osgood, Charles, Suci, George J., and Tannenbaum, Percy H. *The Measurement of Meaning.* Urbana, Ill.: University of Illinois Press, 1957.

Pei, Mario. *One Language for the World.* New York: Devin-Adair Co., 1958.

Sondel, Bess. *The Humanity of Words.* New York: World Publishing Co., 1958.

———. "An Organismic Logic: Kadushin's *The Rabbinic Mind,*" *General Semantics Bulletin,* 12-13 (Spring-Summer, 1953), pp. 44-48.

SOCIOLOGY

Adorno, T. W., Frenkel-Brunswik, Elso, Levinson, D. J. and Sanford, R. N. *The Authoritarian Personality.* New York: Harper & Bros., 1950.

Black, Kurt. *Social Pressures in Informal Groups.* New York: Harper & Bros., 1950.

Coleman, James S., Menzel, Herbert, and Katz, Eluhu. "The Diffusion of an Innovation Among Physicians," *Sociometry,* XX (December, 1957), pp. 253–270.

Ichheiser, C. "Misunderstandings in Human Relations," *American Journal of Sociology,* LV (September, 1949), pp. 1–4.

Riesman, David. *Individualism Reconsidered.* Glencoe, Ill.: Free Press of Glencoe, 1954.

TEACHER EDUCATION

Armstrong, W. Earl, Kollis, Ernest, and Davis, Helen. *The College and Teacher Education.* Washington, D.C.: American Council on Education, 1954.

Beecher, Dwight E., and Bump, Janet W. *The Evaluation of Teaching in New York State.* Albany, N.Y.: University of the State of New York, 1950.

Conant, James B. *The Education of American Teachers.* New York: McGraw-Hill Book Co., 1963.

Evenden, E. S., ed. *National Survey of the Education of Teachers.* 6 vols. Washington: Government Printing Office, 1935.

Jersild, Arthur T. *When Teachers Face Themselves.* New York: Bureau of Publications, Teachers College, Columbia University, 1955.

Koerner, James D. *The Miseducation of American Teachers.* Boston: Houghton Mifflin Co., 1963.

McCune, Shannon, *et al. The New College Plan.* Amherst, Mass.: Amherst Press, 1958.

Maul, Ray C. "Will New College Teachers Be Adequately Prepared?" *Educational Record,* XL (October, 1959), pp. 326–329.

Medley, Donald M., and Mitzel, Harold E. "Measuring Classroom Behavior by Systematic Observation," *Handbook of Research on Teaching,* N. L. Gage, ed. Chicago: Rand McNally & Co., 1963.

Ryans, David G. *Characteristics of Teachers.* Washington, D.C.: American Council on Education, 1960.

Tyler, Ralph. "The Education of Teachers: A Major Responsibility of Colleges and Universities." *Educational Record,* XXXIX (July, 1958), pp. 253–261.

INDEX

Fagan.

Field.